Home Cooks
EASY RECIPES

EASY-TO-MAKE RECIPES FOR YOU AND YOUR FAMILY

OVER 600 EASY TO MAKE RECIPES

Paradise Press, Inc.

HOME COOKS' EASY RECIPES

Editorial Director
Vivian Rothe
Associate Editors
Ramona Lehrman
Judi K. Merkel
Peggy Moss
Production
Carol Dailey
Cathy Reef
Sandra Ridgway
Photography
Rhonda Davis
Nora Elsesser

Copyright © Magazine Printers, Inc.
Berne, Indiana 46711
All rights reserved.

ISBN #1-884907-53-9

Exclusive Distribution by Paradise Press, Inc.

Appetizers
TO SAVOR

Peanut Butter-Chocolate Bonbons

2 cups sifted confectioners' sugar
1 cup graham cracker crumbs
3/4 cup chopped pecans
1/2 cup flaked coconut
1/2 cup butter
1/2 cup peanut butter
1 1/2 cups semisweet chocolate pieces
3 tablespoons shortening

Combine confectioners' sugar, graham cracker crumbs, pecans and coconut. Melt butter and peanut butter; pour over coconut mixture. Blend until mixture is moistened. Shape mixture into 1-inch balls. Melt chocolate pieces with shortening over low heat. Spear balls on wood picks; dip into chocolate mixture to coat. Place on waxed paper; chill to set. Makes 4 dozen.

Winter's Eve Fondue

1 envelope onion soup mix
2 cups dry white wine
4 cups shredded Swiss cheese (about 1 pound)
2 tablespoons cornstarch
2 tablespoons kirsch (optional)
French bread, cut into bite-size cubes

In medium saucepan, heat onion soup mix blended with wine. When wine begins to simmer, gradually add cheese mixed with cornstarch, stirring after each addition, until completely melted. Stir in kirsch.
Pour into fondue pot or chafing dish. Serve by dipping speared bread cubes into fondue.

Variation: Use 2 1/4 cups apple juice for wine and kirsch.

Tortilla Appetizer Wedges

1 (8-ounce) package cream cheese, softened
1/2 cup sour cream
1 (4.25-ounce) diced green chilies
1/2 cup sliced green onions
1 tablespoon minced green jalapeño peppers
Salt and pepper
10 (6–8-inch) flour tortillas
Salsa

Mix together cream cheese and sour cream; mix well. Stir in chilies, onions and jalapeños. Season with salt and pepper. Spread 1 tortilla with 1/4 cup cream cheese mixture; top with another tortilla. Spread and stack tortillas until 4 tortillas high; top with plain tortilla. Make another stack with 5 remaining tortillas. Wrap tortilla stacks in plastic wrap; refrigerate 1 hour. Cut each stack into 18 wedges. Serve with salsa. Makes 36 servings.

Confetti Popcorn Balls

1 (3.5-ounce) bag microwave popcorn
1/2 cup candy-coated chocolate pieces
1/3 cup peanuts
2 1/2 cups mini marshmallows
1/4 cup margarine
1/2 cup raisins

In greased bowl, combine popcorn, candy, peanuts and raisins. Melt marshmallows and margarine in pan. Pour melted mix over popcorn mix. Toss until well coated. Form into balls. Wrap in colored or clear plastic and hang on Christmas tree.

Cheese Zucchini Crisps

1/3 cup cornflake crumbs
2 tablespoons grated Parmesan cheese
1/2 teaspoon seasoned salt
Dash garlic powder
4 small unpeeled zucchini, cut in 3 1/2-inch strips
1/4 cup butter, melted

Combine cornflake crumbs, cheese and seasonings. Dip zucchini strips in butter then coat with crumb mixture. Bake at 375 degrees for 10 minutes or until crisp. Makes 4 servings.

Holiday Toddy

3 cups boiling water
5 tea bags
2 whole cloves
1/8 teaspoon ground nutmeg
1/4 cup sugar
1 (12-ounce) can ginger ale

In teapot, pour boiling water over tea bags, cloves and nutmeg; cover and brew 5 minutes. Remove tea bags and cloves; stir in sugar.

Serve in cups or mugs and top with splash of ginger ale. If desired, stir in additional sugar. Serves 6.
A party favorite.

Pistachio Crescents

1¾ cups (9 ounces) shelled, unsalted pistachio nuts, blanched, divided*
¾ cup sugar, divided
1 cup (2 sticks) butter, softened**
1 egg
2 teaspoons vanilla extract
2 cups all-purpose flour
Dash salt
4–6 drops green food color, if desired

Place ¾ cup nuts and ¼ cup sugar in food processor or blender; cover. Process until nuts are finely chopped; set aside. Cream butter in large mixer bowl. Gradually add remaining ½ cup sugar; beat until light and fluffy. Mix in egg and vanilla. Gradually stir in flour, salt and nut mixture; mix well. Stir in food color. Wrap dough in plastic wrap and refrigerate 1–2 hours, or until firm.

Preheat oven to 375 degrees. Coarsely chop remaining nuts; spread on waxed paper. Work with half of the dough at a time; leave remaining dough wrapped and refrigerated. Roll tablespoonfuls of dough to form a 3-inch log. Roll in chopped nuts. Place on unbuttered cookie sheets, 1 inch apart. Shape into crescents.

Bake 10–12 minutes, or until golden. Cool on cookie sheets a few minutes. Remove from cookie sheets and cool completely on wire racks. Store in airtight metal containers in cool place up to 3 weeks. Freeze up to 6 months. Makes 4 dozen.

*Roasted, unsalted cashew nut pieces may be substituted for the pistachio nuts. Omit green food color.

**For ease in creaming butter taken directly from refrigerator, cut butter into 8–10 pieces and proceed as directed.

Cheese Spread

1 (2-pound) box soft cheese
1 can Milnot
1 cup milk
⅓ stick margarine

Melt together cheese, Milnot, milk and margarine in double boiler. When melted, beat thoroughly with egg beater.

Appetizer Tomato Cheese Bread

1 medium onion, minced
2 tablespoons butter
½ cup dairy sour cream
¼ cup mayonnaise
4 ounces grated cheddar cheese
¾ teaspoon salt
¼ teaspoon pepper
¼ teaspoon leaf oregano
Pinch leaf sage
⅔ cup milk
2 cups biscuit mix
3 medium tomatoes, peeled, seeded and sliced ¼-inch thick
Paprika

Sauté onion in butter until tender; blend with sour cream, mayonnaise, cheese, salt, pepper, oregano and sage; set aside. Stir milk into biscuit mix to make a soft dough. Lightly knead on floured board for 10–12 strokes.

Pat dough in buttered 13 x 9 x 2-inch baking pan, pushing dough up sides of dish to form a shallow rim. Arrange tomato slices over dough. Spoon onion mixture on dough; sprinkle with paprika. Bake at 400 degrees for 25 minutes. Let stand 10 minutes before cutting. Makes 12 servings.

Party Shrimp Pâté

1 envelope unflavored gelatin
¼ cup lemon juice
¼ cup water
2 cups (16 ounces) sour cream
¾ cup chili sauce
2 tablespoons horseradish
1½ cups chopped cooked shrimp (about ½ pound)
Assorted crackers and party-size bread

In medium saucepan, sprinkle unflavored gelatin over lemon juice and water; let stand 1 minute. Stir over low heat until gelatin is completely dissolved, about 5 minutes; cool. Blend in sour cream, chili sauce and horseradish; fold in shrimp. Turn into 3½-cup mold or bowl; chill until firm. Serve with crackers and party-size bread. Makes about 3½ cups pâté.

Chicken Salad Log

1 (8-ounce) package cream cheese, softened
¼ cup mayonnaise
2 tablespoons lemon juice
½ teaspoon salt
¼ teaspoon ground ginger
⅛ teaspoon pepper
4 drops red pepper sauce
2 cups finely cut-up cooked chicken
2 hard-boiled eggs, chopped
¼ cup sliced green onions
3 green pepper rings, cut into strips
4 tablespoon toasted sesame seed
3 tablespoons sliced pitted ripe olives

Mix together cream cheese, mayonnaise, lemon juice, salt, ginger, pepper and pepper sauce. Stir in chicken, eggs and ¼ cup green onions. Shape into 8 x 2-inch log. Refrigerate until firm, about 4 hours.

Place green pepper strips diagonally across log, dividing log into 4 sections. Sprinkle with sesame seeds. Decorate with olives Serve with crackers. Makes 4 cups.

Fruit Pizza

1 (20-ounce) package refrigerated sugar cookies
1 (8-ounce) package cream cheese, softened
⅓ cup sugar
½ teaspoon vanilla
Assorted fruit
½ cup orange marmalade
2 tablespoons water

Freeze cookie dough 1 hour; slice into ⅛-inch slices. Arrange slices on foil-lined 14-inch pizza pan; overlapping edges slightly. Bake at 375 degrees for 12 minutes or until golden brown. Cool. Invert on serving platter; remove foil; turn right side up.

Mix together cream cheese, sugar and vanilla until well blended. Spread over crust. Arrange fruit over cream cheese layer. Glaze with combined orange marmalade and water; chill. Cut into wedges. Makes 10–12 servings.

4

Turkey Pâté

½ cup finely chopped carrot
½ cup finely chopped celery
⅓ cup finely chopped onion
2 tablespoons cooking oil
⅓ cup dry white wine
1¼ teaspoons salt
2 teaspoons dried dill weed
1 teaspoon finely chopped drained capers
¼ teaspoon pepper
3 cups ground cooked turkey
½ cup finely chopped almonds
2 hard-boiled eggs, chopped
Leaf lettuce

Cook carrots, celery and onion in oil until tender but not brown; remove from heat. Stir in wine, salt, dill weed, capers and pepper. Add ground turkey, nuts and eggs. In blender, process about ¼ of mixture at a time until smooth. Turn mixture into an oiled 4-cup mold. Refrigerate several hours. Unmold onto lettuce-lined serving plate.

Christmas Dip

2 envelopes onion Cup-a-Soup
1 cup (8 ounces) sour cream
1 medium avocado, mashed
¼ cup diced green pepper
¼ cup finely chopped pimiento
1 teaspoon lemon juice
¼ teaspoon garlic powder

In medium bowl, blend all ingredients; chill. Makes about 2½ cups dip.

Crabmeat Spread

1 (6-ounce) can crabmeat, drained, cartilage removed
½ cup mayonnaise
2 tablespoons celery flakes
1 tablespoon lemon juice
2 teaspoons finely chopped onion
¼ teaspoon salt
Dash paprika

Mix together crabmeat, mayonnaise, celery flakes, lemon juice, onion, salt and paprika. Refrigerate until firm, about 2 hours.

Cottage Cheese Sticks

1 cup flour
1 teaspoon salt
½ teaspoon baking powder
⅓ cup butter, softened
½ cup creamed cottage cheese
Milk
Celery seed

Mix together flour, salt and baking powder; cut in butter until particles are fine. Stir in cottage cheese. Form into a ball. Roll out on floured board to 1 12-inch square. Brush with milk. Sprinkle with celery seed. Cut into 4 x 1-inch strips. Bake on greased cookie sheets at 425 degrees for 10–15 minutes until light golden brown.

Soft Pretzels

1 package dry yeast
1½ cups warm water
1 teaspoon salt
1 tablespoon sugar
4 cups flour
1 egg, beaten
Coarse salt

Mix yeast with water; stir until dissolved. Add salt, sugar and flour. Knead dough. Make small balls of dough into letters, numbers, snakes, etc. Place pretzels on greased cookie sheet and brush with beaten egg; sprinkle with salt. Bake at 425 degrees for 12–15 minutes.

Cheese Hooies

¼ pound butter
¼ pound grated strong American cheese
2 cups flour
1 teaspoon salt
Dash Cayenne
Confectioners' sugar

Cream together butter and cheese; add salt and cayenne. Work in flour until thoroughly blended. On floured board, knead dough until smooth. Roll into a long thin roll; refrigerate. When chilled, slice thinly and bake on a cookie sheet at 350 degrees for 8–10 minutes until brown. Dust with confectioners' sugar.

Cocktail Meatballs

1 pound ground beef
½ cup dry bread crumbs
⅓ cup finely chopped onion
¼ cup milk
1 egg
1 tablespoon snipped parsley
1 teaspoon salt
½ teaspoon Worcestershire sauce
⅛ teaspoon pepper
¼ cup shortening
1 (12-ounce) bottle chili sauce
1 (10-ounce) jar grape jelly

Mix together ground beef, bread crumbs, onion, milk, egg, parsley, salt, Worcestershire sauce and pepper; gently shape into 1-inch balls. Brown meatballs in shortening; remove from heat; drain fat. Heat chili sauce and jelly in skillet, stirring constantly, until jelly is melted. Add meatballs and stir until coated. Simmer uncovered for 30 minutes.

Cracker Jack

1 stick margarine
2 cups brown sugar
2 cups corn syrup
¼ cup water
1 teaspoon vinegar
1 teaspoon vanilla

Melt margarine in pan, stir in brown sugar, corn syrup, water, vinegar and vanilla. Bring to boil for 5 minutes. Do not scorch. Pour over popped popcorn. Bake in oven 15 minutes at 250 degrees.

Pepperoni Bread

½ pound pepperoni, thinly sliced
½ pound American cheese, thinly sliced
1 pound pizza dough *or* bread dough, room temperature

Stretch dough with hands to about the size of a cookie sheet. Place pepperoni slices on dough evenly covering whole sheet. Cover pepperoni with cheese. Roll up dough, pinching each end to seal so cheese will not come out sides. Bake at 350 degrees for 45 minutes or until brown. Slice.

Spinach Dip

2 (10-ounce) packages frozen chopped spinach, thawed, drained
1 (8-ounce) can water chestnuts, drained, finely chopped
1 cup dairy sour cream
1 cup plain yogurt
1 cup finely chopped green onions
1 teaspoon salt
½ teaspoon dried tarragon leaves, crushed
½ teaspoon dry mustard
¼ teaspoon pepper
1 clove garlic, crushed

Mix together spinach, water chestnuts, sour cream, yogurt, green onions, salt, tarragon leaves, mustard, pepper and garlic. Refrigerate 1 hour. Serve with crackers, if desired.

Avocado Dip

2 large ripe avocados, mashed
2 tomatoes, finely chopped
1 medium onion, chopped
2 jalepeño peppers, seeded, finely chopped
1 clove garlic, minced
2 tablespoons finely snipped cilantro
1 tablespoon oil
Juice of ½ lime
½ teaspoon salt
Dash pepper
Tortilla chips

Combine avocados, tomatoes, onion, peppers, garlic, cilantro, oil, lime, salt and pepper; refrigerate 1 hour. Serve with chips.

Microwave Caramel Apple Slices

1 bag caramels
1–2 tablespoons water
5–6 apples, sliced and cored

Melt caramels with water in microwave bowl, stirring occasionally. When ready, spoon over apples slices.

Apple Dip

4 large apples, cut into dipping pieces
8 ounces cream cheese
7 ounces marshmallow cream

Blend together cream cheese and marshmallow cream. Serve immediately with apple chunks.

Blue Cheese Dip

1 (4-ounce) package blue cheese, crumbled
1 cup sour cream
½ teaspoon freshly ground pepper
½ teaspoon Worcestershire sauce
1 small onion, finely chopped
Apples, sliced

Mix together cheese, sour cream, pepper, Worcestershire sauce and onion; refrigerate 1 hour. Serve with apples.

Apples With Caramel Dip

1 stick butter *or* margarine
1 package caramels
1 can sweetened condensed milk
Apples, sliced

Mix together butter, caramels and sweetened condensed milk in top of double boiler. Heat until all ingredients are blended. Dip apple slices into hot caramel mixture

Chocolate-Dipped Strawberries

8 large strawberries with leaves
1 (6-ounce) package semisweet chocolate chips, melted
½ cup chilled whipping cream
1 tablespoon cherry brandy

Dip strawberries ¾ of the way in chocolate; place on waxed paper. Refrigerate 30 minutes. Beat together cream and brandy. Divide whipped cream mixture among 4 dishes; top each with 2 chocolate-dipped strawberries. Makes 4 servings.

Caramel Apples

1 package caramels
1 cup nuts, crushed
10 apples
10 popsicle sticks

Melt caramels in double boiler. Put sticks in top of apples; dip in caramel. Sprinkle nuts on top; set on waxed paper. Cool.

Caramel Corn

2 cups brown sugar
1 cup margarine
½ cup corn syrup
1 teaspoon salt
1 teaspoon vanilla
½ teaspoon baking soda
8 quarts popped popcorn

Boil brown sugar, margarine, corn syrup and salt for 5 minutes. Remove from heat and add vanilla and baking soda. Mix, then pour over 8-quarts of popcorn. Put in oven and bake at 200 degrees for 1 hour. Stir every 15 minutes. (Will not stick to your teeth—excellent for folks who wear dentures.)

Kabobs

2 apples, cut in chunks
2 bananas, cut into chunks
1 can pineapple chunks, drained
Raisins
Miniature marshmallows

Skewer alternate pieces of fruit, raisins and marshmallows; serve.

Sugared Nuts

⅔ cup sugar
1 teaspoon ground cinnamon
¼ teaspoon ground allspice
¼ teaspoon salt
1 cup pecan halves
1 cup whole almonds

Mix together sugar, cinnamon, allspice, salt, pecan halves and almonds. Heat until sugar is melted and nuts are coated, about 20 minutes. Place on waxed paper; break apart.

Smoked Turkey Rolls

1 (8-ounce) package herbed cream cheese
4 (8-inch) flour tortillas
12 smoked turkey breast slices
2 green onions, sliced lengthwise into quarters

Spread tortillas with half of cream cheese; layer turkey slices. Spread turkey with remaining cheese. Lay green onion slice at edge and roll like a pinwheel. Wrap each tortilla in plastic and refrigerate overnight. Before serving slice into 1/2-inch slices. Makes 50–60 appetizers.

Cheese Squares

1 pound margarine
1 1/2 tablespoons Beau Monde
1 1/2 teaspoons Worcestershire sauce
Dash cayenne pepper
20 ounces process yellow cheese spread
2 teaspoons dill weed
1 teaspoon hot pepper sauce
2 loaves sliced sandwich bread

Remove crusts from bread. Blend together margarine, Beau Monde, Worcestershire sauce, cayenne pepper, cheese, dill weed and hot pepper sauce. Spread mixture on bread slices and layer 2 or 3 high. Cut into 4 squares and spread cheese mixture on top and sides.

Put on tray and freeze. When frozen, store in plastic bags until ready to use. To bake, take directly from freezer and bake at 350 degrees for 20 minutes. Makes 75–100 appetizers.

Sausage On Rye

Rye cocktail bread slices
Hot pepper sauce
Bulk pork sausage
American cheese

Fry sausage and drain grease. Add as much American cheese as desired. Flavor to taste with hot pepper sauce. We like ours real hot. Spread on cocktail bread slices and freeze individually, then layer between waxed paper in large container. When ready, take what is needed and broil until bubbly.

Spirit of the Season Punch

1 quart boiling water
8 tea bags
1 gallon apple cider
1 cup lemon juice
2 1/4 cups brown sugar
12 whole allspice
12 whole cloves
4 cinnamon sticks, broken
1 bottle (4/5-quart) burgundy wine
Apple slices

In large saucepan, pour boiling water over tea bags; cover and brew 5 minutes. Remove tea bags. Add cider, lemon juice, sugar and spices. Simmer 10 minutes, stirring occasionally. Remove spices; add wine and heat through. Garnish with apple slices. Makes about 35 (5-ounce) servings.

Barbecued Meatballs

2 pounds ground beef
1 pound ground pork
6 green onions, chopped
2 eggs
1/2 cup chopped celery
1 cup milk
1 1/2 cups rolled oats
Salt and pepper
Bottled barbecue sauce

Mix together ground beef, pork, onions, eggs, celery, milk, oats, salt and pepper; mix well. Form into balls. Bake at 325 degrees for 25–35 minutes. Freeze. When thawed, pour barbecue sauce over and stir to coat. Warm.

Sautéed Artichoke Hearts

2 slices bacon, cut up
1 (14-ounce) can artichoke hearts, drained, cut in half
1 teaspoon lemon juice

Fry bacon until partially cooked. Add artichokes; cook until hot, about 3 minutes. Stir in lemon juice and cook 10 seconds longer.

Italian Alpine Caps

24 mushrooms (about 1 pound)
1/4 cup Italian or Caesar dressing
1 cup soft bread crumbs
1/4 cup grated Parmesan cheese
1 tablespoon finely chopped parsley

Preheat oven to 350 degrees. Remove and finely chop mushroom stems.

In medium bowl, combine Italian dressing, bread crumbs, cheese, parsley and chopped stems. Fill caps with bread crumb mixture; place in shallow baking dish. Add water to barely cover bottom and bake 20 minutes. Makes 24 stuffed mushrooms.

Spinach Balls

1 (10-ounce) package frozen spinach
2 beaten eggs
1/2 cup shredded cheddar cheese
1/4 cup butter
1 (8.5-ounce) package corn muffin mix
1/2 cup chopped onion
1/2 cup Parmesan cheese
1/2 cup bleu cheese dressing
1/8 teaspoon garlic powder

Cook spinach and onion as directed on package. Drain and press out all liquid. Combine all ingredients and mix well. Cover and chill for 2 hours. Shape into 1-inch balls and freeze. When ready to bake, put directly into oven; bake at 350 degrees for 10–12 minutes.

Crab Butter

1/2 cup margarine
1 (8-ounce) package cream cheese, softened
1 tablespoon chopped onion
Dash garlic salt
1 teaspoon lemon juice
1/2 pound crab meat
Crackers

Whip margarine until light and fluffy; add cream cheese and whip until light. Add onion, salt and lemon juice. Mix well. Add crab meat. Before serving, let set out 1 hour. Serve with crackers.

Pecan Tassies

½ cup margarine
3 ounces cream cheese
1 cup flour
1 egg
¾ cup brown sugar
1 tablespoon margarine
1 teaspoon vanilla
    Dash salt
½ cup chopped pecans

Beat together margarine, cream cheese and flour; beat well; chill. Mix egg, brown sugar, margarine, vanilla and salt; fold in pecans. In greased mini muffin tins or tart tins, place dough in bottom and around sides. Fill with filling and bake at 325 degrees for 25 minutes. Makes 20–24.

Spicy Plums

2 pounds firm ripe plums
4 small diced red chilies
6 whole cloves
4 allspice berries
4 (1-inch) cinnamon sticks
4 blades of mace
3 cups distilled vinegar
3 cups sugar

Prick plums with toothpick. Place plums, chilies and cloves, allspice berries, cinnamon sticks and mace in 2 (1-quart) canning jars. Bring vinegar and sugar to boil; boil 5 minutes. Pour hot liquid into jars to cover completely. Attach lids to moist rims of jars. Process 20 minutes in a boiling water bath. Store 1 month before serving.

Caramel Corn

1 stick margarine
1 cup brown sugar
1 cup corn syrup
1 teaspoon baking soda
10 quarts popped popcorn

Stir together margarine, brown sugar and corn syrup to a rolling boil. Boil for 5 minutes. Remove from stove and add baking soda; stir until foaming. Pour over popcorn that's been sorted from kernels and in a greased pan; mix well. Put on cookie sheets and bake at 200 degrees, until golden.

Truffles

1 (12-ounce) package semisweet chocolate chips
1 cup ground walnuts
¾ cup sweetened condensed milk
1 teaspoon vanilla
    Dash of salt
    Chopped nuts, coconut or confectioners' sugar

In medium bowl, microwave chocolate chips at MEDIUM-HIGH (70 percent) power until melted, 2–4 minutes. Stir twice during the cooking time. Stir in ground walnuts, condensed milk, vanilla and salt. Cool 5 minutes.

Shape into 1-inch balls. Gently roll in coating (chopped nuts, coconut or confectioners' sugar). Place on waxed-paper–lined tray and refrigerate until set. Makes 50–60 candies.

Cheese Ball

2 (8-ounce) packages cream cheese
1 (4-ounce) package dried ham
1 small jar blue cheese spread
1 small jar old English cheese
½ teaspoon salt
½ teaspoon garlic powder
2 teaspoons Accent
2 teaspoons onion flakes
2 teaspoons parsley flakes

Mix together cream cheese, ham, blue cheese spread, old English cheese, salt, garlic powder, Accent, onion flakes and parsley flakes. Shape in ball.

Warmed Chipped Beef

1 (8-ounce) package cream cheese
2 tablespoons diced green pepper
2 tablespoons milk
⅛ teaspoon black pepper
¾ cup chipped beef
½ cup sour cream
2 tablespoons minced onion
¼ cup chopped nuts

Mix together cream cheese, green pepper, milk, black pepper, chipped beef, sour cream and onion. Bake at 350 degrees for 15 minutes. Sprinkle with nuts. Serve warm with crackers.

Salami Cornucopias

    Salami
    Herbed cream cheese

Roll salami into cones and pipe cheese in with a pastry bag, or you can spread a layer of cream cheese over salami with a knife and roll into a cone shape. You may or may not need to secure with toothpicks depending on the thickness of the salami.

Dena's Granola

7 cups oatmeal
2 cups coconut
1 teaspoon salt
1½ cups brown sugar
1 cup margarine
    Raisins, dates or nuts

Melt margarine and stir in oatmeal, coconut, salt and brown sugar. Add raisins, dates or nuts. Bake at 350 degrees until golden. Stir often to avoid burning.

Stuffed Tomatoes

    Cherry tomatoes
    Herbed cream cheese

Core tomatoes and, using a pastry bag, fill with cream cheese. These are beautiful and add a lot to any platter. Cover with plastic and chill until ready to use.

Stuffed Dates

1 pound dates
4 ounces roasted, salted almonds
1¼ pounds bacon

Stuff dates with almonds. Wrap with a piece of bacon. Bake at 400 degrees for 15 minutes or until bacon is done.

Roquefort Grapes

1 (8-ounce) package cream cheese
¼ pound Roquefort cheese
2 tablespoons cream
1 pound grapes
10 ounces chopped toasted pecans

Mix together cream cheese, cream and Roquefort cheese; drop grapes in cheese to coat. Roll in nuts. Chill until ready to serve.

Stuffed Mushrooms

18 large mushrooms
   Butter
¼ pound sausage
¼ cup diced onion
   Chopped stems
   Bread crumbs
   Parmesan cheese
   Garlic
   Cooking sherry

Cook mushrooms in butter for 3–4 minutes. Fry sausage, onion and chopped stems. Then add the rest of the ingredients to taste, with enough cheese to hold together. Stuff mushrooms and bake at 350 degrees for 10–15 minutes.

Artichoke Puffs

   Cocktail bread slices
2 cups mayonnaise
2 cups Parmesan cheese
   Artichoke hearts, diced

Blend together cheese, mayonnaise and artichoke hearts; mix well. Keep in refrigerator. On the morning of the party, spread on bread slices; keep refrigerated until ready to use. Broil at last minute until bubbly.

Ham & Cheese Crescents

   Crescent rolls
   Thin cheese slices
   Shaved ham
   Mustard

Spread crescent roll very lightly with mustard. Layer ham and cheese slice on each. Roll as usual and bake according to package directions. Can be made the day before, covered with plastic and refrigerated until ready to bake.

Eggnog & Liqueur

¾ cup coffee liqueur
1 quart eggnog
   Whipped cream
   Nutmeg

Mix together liqueur and eggnog; top with whipped cream and a dash of nutmeg.

Irish Coffee

1 cup chilled whipping cream
¼ cup confectioners' sugar
1 teaspoon vanilla
   Coffee
½ cup Irish whiskey
4–8 teaspoons sugar

Beat cream, sugar and vanilla until stiff; refrigerate. Place 2 tablespoons whiskey and 1–2 teaspoons sugar in mug; stir. Pour hot coffee into each mug. Top with whipped cream; serve immediately. Makes 4 servings

Hot Cinnamon Cider

3 quarts apple cider
⅓ cup red cinnamon candies
1 tablespoon whole allspice
3 tablespoons honey

Place allspice in cheesecloth bag. Heat cider, candies and allspice to boiling; reduce heat. Cover and simmer 5 minutes. Remove allspice; stir in honey. Makes 24 servings.

Spiced Cider

1 quart apple cider
1 teaspoon whole cloves
6 whole allspice
4 small sticks cinnamon

Bring cider to almost boiling. Tie spices into cheesecloth, tied loosely. Heat for 10 minutes, do not boil. Remove spice bag and serve cider in mugs.

Mississippi Punch

1 cup fresh strawberries
1 cup fresh peaches
⅓ cup sugar
3 (⅘ quart) bottles chilled champagne
   Fresh strawberries

Puree strawberries and peaches; mix in sugar. Refrigerate 30 minutes. Spoon into punch bowl; pour in champagne. Float strawberries on top.

Wassail Punch

1 gallon cider
1 quart pineapple juice
1 quart orange juice
1 cup lemon juice
1 cup sugar
24 whole cloves
4 sticks cinnamon
   Orange and lemon slices to garnish

Stir together cider, pineapple juice, orange juice, lemon juice and sugar. Pour into large pan. Tie cloves and cinnamon in cheesecloth; place in pan. Heat and simmer for 10 minutes. Remove cheesecloth bag. Serve warm in punch bowl with orange and lemon slices floating. Great for hayrides.

Spiced Coffee

6 cups water
½ cup packed brown sugar
⅓ cup instant coffee
1 tablespoon ground cinnamon
2 teaspoons cocoa
½ teaspoon ground cloves
½ teaspoon vanilla

Bring water, brown sugar, coffee, cinnamon, cocoa and cloves to boiling; reduce heat. Simmer uncovered 10 minutes. Stir in vanilla.

Rosy Wassail Cheer

½ cup brown sugar
¼ cup instant tea powder
3 whole allspice
3 whole cloves
1 cinnamon stick
1 (1-quart) bottle cranberry juice cocktail
2 cups water
¼ cup lemon juice

In large saucepan, combine all ingredients. Bring to a boil, then simmer 10 minutes; remove spices. Serve in cups or mugs and garnish, if desired, with additional cinnamon sticks. Makes about 10 (5-ounce) servings.

Creamy Cider-Up

½ cup milk
2½ cups cider
½ cup sugar
1 teaspoon vanilla
1 pint whipping cream
Nutmeg to garnish

In large bowl or blender, beat milk, cider, sugar and vanilla together. Beat whipping cream until stiff; fold into milk mixture and beat until frothy. Serve in tall glasses and sprinkle with nutmeg.

Banana Smash

1 cup sugar
2 cups water
1 (46-ounce) can pineapple juice
1 (12-ounce) frozen orange juice, thawed
1 (6-ounce) can frozen lemonade
5 blended bananas
2 quarts lemon lime pop

Bring water and sugar to boil and boil until sugar is dissolved. Add pineapple juice, orange juice, lemonade and bananas; blend well. Freeze. Thaw about 45 minutes before party. Add pop to frozen punch mix and serve slushy.

Cranberry Rum Cocktail

1 (6-ounce) can concentrated cranberry juice
2 (6-ounce) cans water
1 (6-ounce) can rum

Mix together cranberry juice, water and rum. Stir gently; serve.

Santa's Pleasure Punch

½ cup lemon-flavored iced tea mix
2 (12-ounce) cans apricot nectar
2 cups pineapple juice
2 (7-ounce) bottles ginger ale, chilled

In large pitcher, combine all ingredients except ginger ale. Just before serving, add ginger ale. Serve in tall ice-filled glasses. Serves 6.

Hot Apple Cider

1 gallon apple cider
1 stick cinnamon
1 teaspoon whole cloves
1 teaspoon whole nutmeg

Place cider, cinnamon. cloves and nutmeg in slow cooker. When hot, serve.

Hot Mocha Mix

1 cup unsweetened cocoa
2 cups sugar
2 cups dry milk powder
½ cup instant coffee
2 cups non-dairy coffee creamer
1 vanilla bean, cut in quarters

Mix together cocoa, sugar, milk powder, coffee, coffee creamer and vanilla bean. Store in refrigerator at least 1 week before using. Use 3 tablespoons mix per serving. Add hot water and stir.

Wassail

1 gallon apple cider
2 teaspoons whole cloves
2 teaspoons whole allspice
2 (3-inch) sticks cinnamon
⅔ cup sugar
2 oranges, studded with cloves

Bring cider, cloves, allspice, cinnamon and sugar to boiling; reduce heat. Cover; simmer 20 minutes. Strain punch and pour into punch bowl. Float oranges in bowl.

Christmas Wassail

6 cups apple cider
2 cups cranberry juice
¼ cup sugar
1 teaspoon whole allspice
3 sticks cinnamon
14 whole cloves
1 teaspoon rum flavoring

Combine cider, juice and sugar in saucepan. Heat on stove until almost boiling. Wrap allspice, cinnamon and cloves in cheesecloth and place in slow cooker along with cider mixture. Add rum flavoring.

Sangria

1 (25½-ounce) bottle dry red wine, chilled
½ cup brandy
½ cup fresh orange juice
1 (6-ounce) can frozen lemonade concentrate, thawed
2 cups ginger ale, chilled
1 orange, thinly sliced
1 lemon, thinly sliced

Mix together wine, brandy, orange juice and lemonade concentrate. Refrigerate no longer than 24 hours. Stir in ginger ale. Pour over ice; garnish with orange and lemon slices.

Hot Buttered Rum

1½ ounces rum
Boiling water
3 dashes bitters
3 teaspoons sugar
3 teaspoons butter
3 cloves

Pour ½ ounce rum in mug; leave spoon in mug and pour in boiling water. Stir in 1 dash bitters, 1 teaspoon sugar, 1 teaspoon butter and 1 clove per mug. Makes 3 servings.

Chocolate Cherries

1 (7¼-ounce) package vanilla wafers finely crushed
½ cup confectioners' sugar
½ cup chopped walnuts
¼ cup boiling water
2 tablespoons butter
1 tablespoon light corn syrup
2 teaspoons instant coffee
30 maraschino cherries with stems
2 (6-ounce) packages semisweet chocolate bits

Mix together cookie crumbs, sugar and walnuts. Combine water, butter, corn syrup and coffee; mix in with cookie mixture. Shape ½ tablespoon of this mixture around each cherry. Cover and refrigerate at least 1 hour.

Melt chocolate over warm water. Holding stem, dip coated cherries into chocolate, coating carefully and completely. Place on waxed paper. Refrigerate. Makes 2½ dozen.

Chocolate Meringues

2 egg whites
1/8 teaspoon salt
1/8 teaspoon cream of tartar
1 teaspoon vanilla
3/4 cup sugar
1 (6-ounce) package semisweet chocolate chips
1/4 cup chopped nuts

Beat egg whites, salt, cream of tartar and vanilla until soft peaks form. Gradually add sugar, beating until peaks are stiff. Fold in chocolate chips and nuts. Drop mixture by rounded teaspoonfuls on well-greased cookie sheet. Bake at 300 degrees for 25 minutes.

Divinity

2 cups sugar
1/3 cup water
1/3 cup light corn syrup
1/4 teaspoon salt
2 egg whites
1 teaspoon vanilla
1/2 cup chopped nuts

Combine sugar, water, corn syrup and salt, cover. Microwave on HIGH for 5 minutes. Stir well. Microwave uncovered on HIGH for 3–4 minutes until a hard ball forms when a small amount is dropped into cold water. Cool 3–4 minutes.

Beat egg whites until very stiff. Pour in sugar mixture in a steady stream. Beat constantly, until mixture holds its shape and starts to lose its gloss. Add vanilla and nuts. Drop onto waxed paper by teaspoonfuls. Makes 3 dozen.

Turtles

28 caramels
2 tablespoons cream
1 1/4 cups pecans
6 ounces milk chocolate chips

Melt caramels with cream; add pecans. Stir until well mixed. Drop by spoonfuls on cookie sheet. Melt chocolate chips in double boiler. Spread over top of caramels.

Chocolate-Pecan Fudge

1/2 cup butter
3/4 cup cocoa
4 cups confectioners' sugar
1 teaspoon vanilla
1/2 cup evaporated milk
1 cup pecan pieces

Melt butter; remove from heat; stir in cocoa. Stir in confectioners' sugar and vanilla; add evaporated milk. Stir constantly over low heat until warm and smooth; add pecan pieces. Pour into greased 8-inch square pan; chill. Keep refrigerated. Makes 5 dozen squares.

Peanut Brittle

1 cup sugar
1/2 cup light corn syrup
Dash of salt
1 1/2 cups shelled raw peanuts
1 tablespoons butter
1 1/2 teaspoons baking soda
1 teaspoon vanilla

Thoroughly grease baking sheet. Combine sugar, corn syrup and salt in a 3-quart casserole. Add peanuts. Microwave on HIGH until light brown, 8–10 minutes, stirring once or twice.

Stir in butter, baking soda and vanilla. until light and foamy. Spread as thinly as possible on the greased baking sheet. Cool. Break into pieces. Makes 1 pound.

Dena's Caramel Corn

3 big poppers of popcorn
1 stick margarine
3 cups brown sugar
1/2 cup corn syrup
1 teaspoon baking soda

Sort out all unpopped popcorn kernels. In a large, heavy saucepan melt margarine; add brown sugar and corn syrup. Bring to a boil and boil for exactly 5 minutes. Remove from heat; add 1 teaspoon baking soda and stir until foamy and color changes. Pour caramel sauce over popped corn. Spread popped corn on 3 well-greased cookie sheets. Heat in 200-degree oven for 45 minutes, until golden. Store in airtight containers.

Favorite Fudge

3 cups semisweet chocolate chips
1 (14-ounce) can sweetened condensed milk
1/4 cup butter *or* margarine
1 cup chopped walnuts

Mix together chocolate chips, milk and margarine. Microwave at MEDIUM (50 percent) for 3–5 minutes, until chocolate chips are melted. Stir once or twice during the cooking time. Stir in nuts. Pour into greased 8-inch square baking pan. Refrigerate. Makes 2 pounds.

Yum Yum Fudge

2/3 cup evaporated milk
1 1/2 cups sugar
1/4 cup butter
1/2 teaspoon salt
32 large marshmallows
1 (12-ounce) bag semisweet chocolate chips
1 teaspoon vanilla
1/2 teaspoon peppermint extract

Place milk, sugar, butter, salt and marshmallows in pan. Cook over low heat, stirring constantly, until marshmallows are melted. Add chocolate pieces, stirring until melted. Add vanilla and peppermint extract; pour into buttered 8 x 8 x 2-inch pan. Chill for several hours. Cut into 1-inch squares.

Rocky Road

1 (6-ounce) package milk chocolate chips
2 tablespoons half-and-half
1 teaspoon vanilla
2 cups miniature marshmallows
1 1/2 cups chopped nuts
1 cup shredded coconut

Microwave chocolate chips and half-and-half at MEDIUM-HIGH (70 percent), stirring once, just until the chocolate chips are melted. Add vanilla and remaining ingredients. Stir until coated. Press into 8-inch square greased baking pan. Chill. Makes 2 dozen cookies.

Breads

TO MAKE

Three-Way Refrigerator Dough

- 3 cups bread flour, divided
- 3 tablespoons sugar
- 1 teaspoon salt
- 1 (¼-ounce) package regular dry yeast
- 1 cup hottest tap water
- 2 tablespoons shortening
- 1 large egg

Into a large bowl measure 1½ cups flour, sugar, salt and yeast. Mix briefly with dry beaters on low speed.

Measure 1 cup hottest tap water in pint pitcher; add shortening; whisk vigorously until smooth. Slowly pour into dry ingredients while beating on low speed; beat 2 minutes on low. Add egg; beat 1 minute on high. Mix in enough flour to make a firm dough, about 1¼ cups. (I do this with a sturdy spatula.) When thoroughly mixed, cover and let rest 10–15 minutes.

Sprinkle the remaining ¼ cup flour on pastry cloth; knead dough 5–10 minutes. For the best-quality bread, knead in as little additional flour as possible.

Spray a medium bowl with pan release or grease; drop in ball of dough; turn to coat; cover; refrigerate. After 2 hours, punch down by turning dough over in bowl and gently pressing out bubbles. Cover; store in refrigerator 2 hours to several days; use in the following recipes.

Dinner Rolls

Half of refrigerator dough makes 10 rolls.

To make rolls I lightly roll part of the dough into a rectangle 8 inches wide. It should be somewhat thick, about ½ inch. Spread generously with melted butter. With pastry shell or knife, cut strips about ¾ inch wide. Twist and coil into well-greased muffin cups. I use tall tulip-shaped custard cups. (Sprinkle with poppy or sesame seed if desired.)

Cover; let rise until double, about 1 hour. Bake in preheated 400-degree oven until nicely brown, about 15 minutes. Turn out onto a rack to cool. While still hot I rub tops with real butter.

Sticky Cinnamon Buns

Half of refrigerator dough makes 10 rolls.

Grease custard cups or muffin tins. In bottom of each, mix 1 teaspoon soft butter, 2 teaspoons brown sugar and ¼ teaspoon water. Sprinkle in 1 teaspoon chopped pecans.

To make cinnamon buns, flatten dough as for Dinner Rolls; spread generously with melted butter; sprinkle with cinnamon and brown or granulated sugar and chopped pecans, if desired. Fold dough over to enclose filling and make a 4-inch-wide rectangle; cut into strips about ¾-inch wide; twist; coil into prepared cups. Cover; let rise to double, about 1 hour. Bake at 400 degrees until brown, about 15 minutes. Set cooling rack over plate; turn out buns on rack carefully so sticky glaze coats sides of buns. Serve warm with plenty of butter

Pizza Dinner for Two

Prepare Tomato Sauce given below. Preheat oven to 475 degrees.

Pat a scant half of refrigerated dough evenly in a greased 12- or 13-inch pizza pan. Rub crust lightly with oil—olive oil is a flavorful choice. Spoon on 1 cup of tomato sauce. I top it with lots of lightly sautéed onion slices, crumbled crisply cooked bacon and shredded mozzarella cheese. Use whatever topping items you like. No rising is necessary. Bake on lowest oven rack at 475 degrees until crust is brown at edge, 15–20 minutes.

Tomato Sauce

- 1 tablespoon bacon drippings or margarine or olive oil
- 1 medium onion, chopped
- 1 clove garlic, mashed
- 1 (8-ounce) can tomato sauce
- 1 teaspoon oregano
- 1 teaspoon basil

In small saucepan heat bacon drippings or other fat. Add onion and garlic; cook on low until soft; stir in tomato sauce, oregano and basil. Cook gently, stirring often, until it thickens a bit. Makes 1 cup.

Pumpkin Bread

- 3⅓ cups flour
- 2 teaspoons baking soda
- 1½ teaspoons salt

1 teaspoon cinnamon
3 cups sugar
1 teaspoon nutmeg
1 cup oil
4 eggs
2/3 cup water
2 (No. 303) cans pumpkin
1 cup chopped walnuts

Mix together flour, baking soda, salt, cinnamon and nutmeg; add oil, eggs, water, pumpkin and sugar. Stir in nuts. Bake at 350 degrees for 1 hour. Makes 3 loaves.

Corn Bread

1 cup yellow cornmeal
1 cup flour
2 tablespoons sugar
4 teaspoons baking powder
1/2 teaspoon salt
1 cup milk
1/4 cup margarine
1 egg

Preheat oven to 425 degrees. Melt margarine in oven in 8–9-inch cast iron skillet; coat pan. Combine cornmeal, flour, sugar, baking powder and salt. Stir in milk, melted margarine and egg. Mix for 1 minute. Pour into skillet. Bake for 20–25 minutes or until golden brown.

Apple-Raisin Muffins

1 3/4 cups flour
1/4 cup sugar
2 teaspoons baking powder
1/2 teaspoon salt
1/2 teaspoon cinnamon
1 egg, beaten
3/4 cup milk
1/3 cup cooking oil
1 cup apples, chopped and peeled
1/4 cup raisins

In large bowl, stir together flour, sugar, baking powder, salt and cinnamon. Combine egg, milk and oil. Add egg mixture all at once to flour mixture. Stir just until moistened; batter should be lumpy. Fold in apples and raisins.

Grease muffin cups or line with paper baking cups; fill 2/3 full. Bake at 400 degrees for 20–25 minutes or until golden. Remove from pans and serve hot or warm. Makes 10–12 muffins.

Creamed Chicken a la King Over Biscuits

1 (6-ounce) can sliced mushrooms, drained, reserving 1/4 cup liquid
1/2 cup butter
1/2 cup flour
1 teaspoon salt
1/4 teaspoon pepper
2 cups light cream
1 3/4 cups chicken broth
2 cups cooked cubed chicken
Baking Powder Biscuits (recipe follows)

In large skillet, cook and stir mushrooms in butter for 5 minutes. Blend in flour, salt and pepper. Cook over low heat, stirring until mixture is bubbly. Remove from heat. Stir in cream, broth and reserved mushroom liquid. Heat to boiling, stirring constantly. Boil and stir 1 minute. Stir in chicken, heating thoroughly. Serve over Baking Powder Biscuits.

Baking Powder Biscuits

2 cups flour
1/4 cup shortening
3 teaspoons baking powder
3/4 cup milk
1 teaspoon salt

Preheat oven to 450 degrees. Combine flour, baking powder and salt; cut in shortening thoroughly until mixture looks like meal. Stir in milk. Knead lightly 20–25 times on floured board. Roll 1/2 inch thick; cut with floured biscuit cutter. Bake 10–12 minutes on ungreased baking sheet.

Sweet Muffins

1 egg, slightly beaten
1/2 cup milk
1/4 cup vegetable oil
1 1/2 cups flour
1/2 cup sugar
2 teaspoons baking powder
1/2 teaspoon salt

Mix together egg, milk and oil. Sift together flour, sugar, baking powder and salt; stir in egg mixture just until moistened. Batter will be lumpy. Do not overmix. Fill muffin cups 2/3 full. Bake at 400 degrees for 20–25 minutes until golden brown.

Blueberry Orange Muffins

1 1/3 cups flour
1 cup rolled oats
1/4 cup firmly packed brown sugar
1 tablespoon baking powder
1/2 teaspoon baking soda
1/2 teaspoon salt
3/4 cup fresh or frozen blueberries
2/3 cup milk
1/3 cup orange juice
1/4 cup oil
1 egg, beaten
2 teaspoons grated orange peel

Combine flour, oats, brown sugar, baking powder, baking soda and salt. Gently stir in blueberries. Combine milk, orange juice, oil, egg and orange peel; stir into flour mixture just until moistened. Fill 12 greased muffin cups 2/3 full. Bake at 400 degrees for 18–20 minutes or until golden brown. Makes 1 dozen muffins.

Apple Streusel Muffins

2 cups flour
1 cup sugar
1 tablespoon baking powder
1 1/4 teaspoons cinnamon
1/2 teaspoon salt
1/2 teaspoon baking soda
2 large eggs, beaten
1 cup dairy sour cream
1/4 cup butter, melted
1 cup finely diced apples
1/4 cup sugar
3 tablespoons flour
1/4 teaspoon cinnamon
2 tablespoons butter

Stir together 2 cups flour, 1 cup sugar, baking powder, 1 1/4 teaspoons cinnamon, salt and baking soda; set aside. Beat eggs, sour cream and 1/4 cup butter; add to dry ingredients with apples. Stir just until moistened. Fill well-greased muffin tins 2/3 full.

Combine 1/4 cup sugar, 3 tablespoons flour, 1/4 teaspoon cinnamon and butter. Sprinkle on top of muffins. Bake at 400 degrees for 20–25 minutes. Makes 18 muffins.

German Blue Ribbon Stollen

½ cup raisins
½ cup currants
1 cup grated mixed citrus peel
½ cup whole candied cherries, half red and half green
½ cup brandy
2 packages dry yeast
¼ cup lukewarm water
½ teaspoon sugar
1 cup milk, room temperature
¾ cup sugar
5 cups flour
¼ teaspoon cardamom
½ teaspoon salt
2 eggs, beaten
1 teaspoon grated lemon rind
½ teaspoon almond extract
¾ cup butter, softened
1 cup chopped almonds
2 tablespoons flour
¼ cup butter, melted
Icing (recipe follows)

Soak raisins, currants, citrus peel and cherries in brandy overnight. Dissolve yeast in warm water with ½ teaspoon sugar; set aside 5 minutes; add milk. Combine ¾ cup sugar, flour, salt and cardamom; stir in yeast mixture. Mix together eggs, lemon rind and extract; add to dough.

Knead pieces of butter into dough; knead for 20 minutes. Drain fruit and pat dry; add almonds. Sprinkle with 2 tablespoons of flour; knead into dough. Place in buttered bowl; butter top. Cover and let rise in a warm spot for 2 hours.

Punch dough down and divide in half. Roll each half to a 10 x 16-inch rectangle. Brush with melted butter. Fold 1 long side to the center ⅔ of the first side. Point both ends to shape. Brush cookie sheet with butter. Brush stollen top with butter. Place stollen on cookie sheet. Let rise 1 hour. Bake at 375 degrees for 40–45 minutes.

Ice with confectioners' sugar icing when cool or sprinkle top with sifted confectioners' sugar. Makes 2 large stollens.

Icing

1 cup confectioners' sugar
2 tablespoons milk

Mix together sugar and milk until smooth.

Christmas Stollen

¾ cup warm water
1 package active dry yeast
½ cup sugar
½ teaspoon salt
3 eggs
1 egg yolk
1 egg white
½ cup margarine
3½ cups flour, divided
½ cup chopped blanched almonds
¼ cup chopped citron
¼ cup chopped candied cherries
¼ cup golden raisins
1 tablespoon grated lemon rind
4 tablespoons margarine
1 tablespoon water
confedtioners' sugar glaze
blanched almonds (garnish)
citron (garnish)
candied cherries (garnish)

Place water in bowl; sprinkle in yeast; stir to dissolve. Add sugar, salt, 3 whole eggs, egg yolks, ½ cup margarine and half the flour. Beat for 10 minutes at medium speed of an electric mixer. Blend in remaining flour, almonds, fruits and lemon rind. Cover, let rise in warm place until double in size, about 1 hour, 30 minutes. Stir down batter by beating 25 strokes. Cover tightly and refrigerate overnight.

Divide dough in half; press each half into 10 x 7-inch oval. Spread each with 2 tablespoons margarine. Fold each oval in half lengthwise, firmly pressing folded edges only. Place on greased baking sheets; brush with slightly beaten egg white blended with 1 tablespoon water. Let rise in warm place until doubled, about 1 hour.

Bake at 375 degrees for 15–20 minutes or until done. Frost with confectioners' sugar glaze and decorate with blanched almonds, citron and candied cherries.

Apple Muffins

2 cups flour
3 teaspoons baking powder
1½ cups sugar
½ teaspoon salt
3 tablespoons shortening
⅓ cup nuts
1 egg, beaten
¾ cup milk
1 cup apples, chopped, peeled
⅓ cup brown sugar
½ teaspoon cinnamon

Sift together flour, baking powder, sugar and salt; cut in shortening. Combine egg and milk with flour mixture. Mix only until flour is dampened; do not overmix. Fold in apples. Fill muffin tins half full. Combine brown sugar, cinnamon and nuts. Sprinkle on top of muffins. Bake at 400 degrees for 25 minutes. Makes 18 muffins.

Cinnamon Apple Muffins

1 egg, slightly beaten
¼ cup milk
2 tablespoons oil
¼ cup apple, grated
¾ cup flour
¼ cup sugar
1 teaspoon baking powder
¼ teaspoon cinnamon
⅓ cup brown sugar
⅓ cup broken nuts
½ teaspoon cinnamon

Stir together egg, milk, oil and apple. Sift together flour, sugar, baking powder and cinnamon. Add milk mixture to flour mixture until just moistened. Fill greased muffin cups ½ full. Combine brown sugar, nuts and cinnamon in a small bowl. Cover all the filled muffins with topping mixture. Bake at 400 degrees for approximately 25 minutes.

Bread Sticks

1¼ cups warm water
1 package dry yeast
2 tablespoons oil
3 cups flour
2 tablespoons sugar
1 teaspoon salt

Dissolve yeast in water. Add oil, flour, sugar and salt; mix well. Knead briefly until dough loses stickiness. Divide dough into 16 pieces; roll each piece into stick about 8 inches long. Bake on lightly oiled baking sheets at 425 degrees for 12 minutes.

Holiday Oatmeal Bread With Honey Butter

1 cup quick-cooking oats
⅓ cup butter
2 cups boiling water
½ cup honey
1 tablespoon salt
2 (¼-ounce) packages active dry yeast
2 eggs
6¼ to 7¼ cups all-purpose flour
1 egg, slightly beaten
1 tablespoon water
3 tablespoons quick-cooking oats

Honey Butter
½ cup butter, softened
2 tablespoons honey

In large mixer bowl combine 1 cup oats, butter, boiling water, honey and salt. Cool to warm (105–115 degrees). Stir in yeast. Add 2 eggs and 2½ cups flour. Beat at medium speed, scraping bowl often, until smooth (1–2 minutes). Stir in enough remaining flour to make dough easy to handle.

Turn dough onto lightly floured surface; knead until smooth and elastic (about 10 minutes). Add more flour as needed until dough no longer sticks. Place in greased bowl; turn greased side up. Cover; let rise in warm place until double in size (about 1 hour).

Dough is ready if indentation remains when touched. Punch down dough; divide into thirds. Shape each third into loaf. Place loaves in 3 greased 8 x 4-inch loaf pans. Cover; let rise until double in size (about 1 hour).

In small bowl combine 1 egg and water; gently brush over top of loaves. Sprinkle each loaf with 1 tablespoon oats. Heat oven to 350 degrees. Bake for 25–35 minutes, or until loaf sounds hollow when tapped. Remove from pans immediately.

In small bowl stir together honey butter ingredients; serve with bread. Makes 3 loaves and ½ cup honey butter.

Eggnog Bread

3 cups flour
½ cup sugar
4 teaspoons baking powder
½ teaspoon salt
½ teaspoon nutmeg
1 egg, beaten
1¾ cups eggnog
½ cup oil
½ cup chopped pecans
½ cup golden raisins
½ cup confectioners' sugar
2–3 teaspoons eggnog

In large bowl, stir together flour, sugar, baking powder, salt and nutmeg. Combine egg, eggnog, and oil; add to dry mixture. Stir in nuts and raisins. Pour into a 9 x 5-inch greased loaf pan.

Bake at 350 degrees for 60–70 minutes. Cover with foil after 50 minutes, if browning too much. Cool 10 minutes; remove from pan. Stir together confectioners' sugar and eggnog; drizzle over bread.

Apricot Muffins

2 cups flour
4 teaspoons baking powder
½ teaspoon salt
¼ cup sugar
1 egg, beaten
¼ cup shortening, melted
1 cup milk
½ cup finely chopped dried apricots,

Sift together flour, baking powder, salt and sugar; add apricots. Mix together egg, shortening and milk; add to flour mixture stirring just enough to dampen flour. Fill greased muffin pans ⅔ full. Bake at 400 degrees for 25 minutes. Makes 12–15 muffins.

Failproof Popovers

1 cup milk
1 cup flour
2 eggs
½ teaspoon salt

Mix together milk, flour, eggs and salt just until blended. Batter will be lumpy. Pour into well-greased custard cups. Fill half full. Place in cold oven. Set the oven for 450 degrees and time for 30 minutes.

Banana Nut Bread

½ cup salad oil
1 cup sugar
2 eggs, beaten
3 ripe bananas, mashed
2 cups flour
½ teaspoon baking powder
½ teaspoon salt
3 tablespoons milk
½ teaspoon vanilla
1½ cups chopped nuts
cream cheese (optional)

Beat together oil and sugar; add eggs and bananas and beat well. Sift together flour, baking powder and salt; add to banana mixture. Stir in milk and vanilla; mix well; stir in nuts. Pour into greased and floured 9 x 5 x 3-inch loaf pan. Bake at 350 degrees for 1 hour. Cool well and store overnight before cutting. May spread with cream cheese for tea sandwiches..

Berry Quick Nut Bread

1 package nut bread mix
1 cup flour
1 tablespoon grated orange peel
1 teaspoon cinnamon
½ teaspoon nutmeg
2 eggs
1 (10-ounce) package frozen cran–berry-orange relish, thawed

Combine bread mix, flour, orange peel, cinnamon, nutmeg, eggs and relish. Stir until dry particles are moistened. Pour batter into greased 9 x 5-inch pan. Bake at 375 degrees for 60–65 minutes. Cool 10 minutes before removing from pan.

Egg Bread

½ cup butter
8 cups cubed day-old bread
3 eggs, beaten
½ cup milk
½ teaspoon salt
⅛ teaspoon black pepper

In large skillet, melt butter over low heat; stir in bread and toss until lightly browned. Mix together milk, eggs, salt and pepper. Pour mixture over bread cubes; cook over medium heat until it is set and browned on the bottom. Serve.

Pecan Loaf

2 cups flour
1 cup sugar
2½ teaspoons baking powder
¾ teaspoon salt
½ cup shortening
¾ cup milk
1 teaspoon vanilla
½ teaspoon orange extract
2 unbeaten eggs
½ cup finely chopped pecans

Sift together flour, sugar, baking powder and salt. Drop in shortening. Add ⅔ of milk, vanilla and orange extract; mix thoroughly. Add remaining milk and eggs; mix until well beaten. Stir in pecans. Bake in greased and floured pan at 350 degrees for 45 minutes.

Apricot Nut Bread

2½ cups flour
½ cup sugar
½ cup firmly packed brown sugar
3½ teaspoons baking powder
1 teaspoon salt
3 tablespoons vegetable oil
1¼ cups milk
1 egg
1 tablespoon grated orange peel
1 cup finely cut dried apricots
1 cup chopped nuts

Mix together flour, sugar, brown sugar, baking powder and salt; set aside. Blend in oil, milk, egg, orange peel, apricots and nuts. Bake at 350 degrees in 9 x 5 x 3-inch pan greased on bottom only for 55–65 minutes, until toothpick comes out clean. Cool slightly before removing from pan. Makes 1 loaf.

Apple-Molasses Bread

½ cup butter *or* margarine
1 cup sugar
3 eggs
2 cups sifted all-purpose flour
1 teaspoon baking powder
½ teaspoon salt
½ teaspoon cinnamon
½ teaspoon nutmeg
1 cup canned applesauce
¼ cup molasses

1 cup raisins
½ cup chopped pecans

Cream together butter and sugar. Add eggs, 1 at a time, beating well after each addition. Sift together flour, baking powder, salt, cinnamon and nutmeg. Combine applesauce and molasses. Add flour mixture, alternating with apple-sauce mixture, to egg mixture. Beat well after each addition. Fold in raisins and nuts. Pour into greased and floured 9 x 5 x 3-inch loaf pan. Bake at 350 degrees for 1 hour.

Microwave Banana Nut Bread

½ cup salad oil
1 cup sugar
2 eggs, beaten
3 ripe bananas, mashed
2 cups flour
1 teaspoon baking powder
1 teaspoon salt
3 tablespoons milk
½ teaspoon vanilla
1½ cups chopped nuts, divided
3 tablespoons firmly packed brown sugar,
Caramel Glaze (recipe follows)

Beat together oil and sugar; add eggs and banana pulp. Stir in flour, baking powder and salt; add milk and vanilla. Blend in 1 cup nuts.

Generously butter a 10-inch microwave fluted ring mold. Combine remaining ¼ cup nuts and brown sugar. Coat the fluted ring with nut mixture. Pour batter into prepared mold.

Microwave at MEDIUM-HIGH 11–13 minutes. Let stand on counter to cool 5 minutes before removing from pan. Top with Caramel Glaze.

Caramel Glaze

2 tablespoons butter
2 tablespoons milk
¼ cup firmly packed dark brown sugar
½ cup sifted confectioners' sugar
Cream cheese (optioanal)

Combine butter, milk and brown sugar in a 4-cup glass measuring cup. Microwave on HIGH 1½–2 minutes or until boiling. Stir in confectioners' sugar. Pour over cooled Banana Nut Bread.

Bran Banana Bread

2 cups flour
1 teaspoon baking powder
½ teaspoon baking soda
½ teaspoon salt
1½ cups mashed ripe bananas
2½ cups raisin bran cereal
½ cup margarine, softened
¾ cup sugar
2 eggs
½ cup coarsely chopped nuts (optional)

Sift together flour, baking powder, baking soda and salt; set aside. Mix together bananas and cereal; let stand 2 minutes. Cream margarine and sugar; stir in eggs and cereal mixture. Mix in flour mixture and nuts.

Spread in greased 9 x 5 x 3-inch loaf pan. Bake at 350 degrees for 55–60 minutes or until toothpick comes out clean. Let cool 10 minutes before removing from pan. Makes 1 loaf.

Coconut Bread With Whipped Butter

2 cups pancake mix
1 cup coconut
¼ cup sugar
¾ cup chopped pecans,
1 teaspoon cinnamon
2 eggs, beaten
1½ cups milk
3 tablespoons margarine, melted
Whipped Butter (recipe follows)

Combine pancake mix, coconut, sugar, pecans and cinnamon; mix well. Beat together eggs, milk and margarine; add to dry ingredients. Mix until moistened. Pour into a loaf pan that has been greased and bottom lined with waxed paper; grease again. Bake at 350 degrees for 50–55 minutes. Remove from pan and cool. Serve with Whipped Butter. Makes 1 loaf.

Whipped Butter

½ cup butter *or* margarine
½ cup maple syrup

Beat butter until light and fluffy; gradually beat in syrup.

Gingerbread With Orange Crusty Topping

1/2 cup butter, melted
1 1/2 cup sugar
1/2 cup molasses
2 cups flour
1/2 teaspoon salt
1 teaspoon baking soda
1 teaspoon ginger
1 teaspoon cinnamon
1 cup hot water
1 tablespoon butter, melted
3 tablespoons sugar
1/3 cup chopped nuts
2 tablespoons grated orange rind

Combine 1/2 cup butter, 1/2 cup sugar and molasses. Sift in flour, salt, baking soda, ginger and cinnamon. Blend in hot water. Pour into 8 x 8 x 2-inch pan. Combine 1 tablespoon butter, 3 tablespoons sugar, nuts and orange rind. Sprinkle over gingerbread. Bake at 350 degrees for 35–40 minutes.

Orange-Honey Crescents (Melomacarona)

1 1/2 cups salad oil
9 tablespoons frozen orange juice concentrate, divided
1/3 cup sugar
1 1/2 teaspoons grated orange peel
3 1/2 cups sifted flour
1 teaspoon cinnamon
3/4 cup baking powder
3/4 teaspoon soda
1/4 teaspoon salt
1/4 teaspoon cloves
1/4 teaspoon nutmeg
1 1/4 cups chopped pecans, divided
3/4 cup honey

Combine salad oil, 6 tablespoons orange juice concentrate, sugar and orange peel. Sift dry ingredients; add to orange juice mixture. Stir in 3/4 cup chopped pecans. Dough can be chilled. Shape into crescents. Bake at 350 degrees for 15–18 minutes. Cool. Combine honey and remaining orange juice concentrate; drizzle over cookies. Sprinkle with remaining pecans. Makes 3 1/2 dozen.

Old-Fashioned Apple Loaf

2 cups flour
2 teaspoons baking powder
3/4 teaspoon cinnamon
    Dash ground nutmeg
    Dash ground cloves
1/2 teaspoon salt
1/4 teaspoon baking soda
2/3 cup chunky applesauce
1/2 cup sugar
2 eggs
1/4 cup oil
2 tablespoons milk
2 tablespoons walnuts, chopped
2 teaspoons butter *or* margarine
1 teaspoon brown sugar, packed

Preheat oven to 350 degrees. Oil and flour 8 x 4-inch loaf pan. Set aside. Mix flour, baking powder, cinnamon, nutmeg, cloves, salt and baking soda in medium mixing bowl. Set aside.

Combine applesauce, sugar, eggs, oil and milk into large mixing bowl. Mix well. Add dry ingredients. Beat at medium speed with electric mixer just until combined, scraping bowl occasionally. Pour into prepared pan. Combine walnuts, butter and brown sugar in small mixing bowl. Mix with fork until crumbly. Sprinkle down center of loaf.

Bake at 350 degrees for 35–45 minutes or until golden brown and wooden pick inserted in center comes out clean. Immediately remove from pan. Cool on wire rack.

Easy Cranberry Nut Bread

3/4 cup sugar
1 egg
1 1/4 cups orange juice
1 tablespoon grated orange rind
3 cups biscuit mix
3/4 cup chopped nuts
1 cup chopped cranberries

Combine sugar, egg, orange juice, orange rind and biscuit mix. Beat for 30 seconds. Stir in nuts and cranberries. Pour into greased 9 x 5 x 3-inch pan. Bake for 55–60 minutes until toothpick comes out clean.

Chocolate Almond Zucchini Bread

3 eggs
2 cups sugar
1 cup vegetable oil
1 teaspoon vanilla
2 cups grated zucchini
2 squares baking chocolate, melted
3 cups flour
1 teaspoon salt
1 teaspoon cinnamon
1/4 teaspoon baking powder
1 teaspoon baking soda
1 cup chopped almonds

Beat eggs until lemon colored. Beat in sugar and oil. In large bowl, combine egg mixture, vanilla, zucchini and chocolate. Sift together flour, salt, cinnamon, baking powder and baking soda; stir into zucchini mixture. Stir in almonds. Pour into 2 greased 9 x 5 x 3-inch loaf pans. Bake at 350 degrees for 1 hour and 20 minutes or until toothpick comes out clean. Cool 15–20 minutes before removing from pans.

Muffin Extravaganza

1 1/2 cups flour
2 1/2 teaspoons baking powder
1/4 teaspoon salt
1 cup oat bran
1/2 cup firmly packed light brown sugar
1 cup milk
1/3 cup oil
2 eggs, lightly beaten
1 teaspoon vanilla extract
1 (3-ounce) package cream cheese, cut into 12 pieces
3/4 cup jam of choice

Sift together flour, baking powder and salt; stir in oat bran and brown sugar; set aside. Combine milk, oil, eggs and vanilla; stir into dry ingredients just until moistened.

Spoon 1/2 batter in greased muffin cups filling 2/3 full; spoon 1 tablespoon jam on top of batter and 1 piece of cream cheese on top of that. Spoon remaining batter over jam and cheese until each cup is 2/3 full. Bake at 425 degrees for 14–16 minutes or until browned.

Apple Kuchen

1 package yeast
2 tablespoons warm water
2 tablespoons butter
2 tablespoons sugar
1 teaspoon salt
½ cup milk, scalded and cooled
1 egg
2½ cups flour, sifted
3 cups apples, sliced
1 cup sugar
1½ teaspoons cinnamon
2 tablespoons butter, softened
1 egg
⅓ cup half-and-half

Soften yeast in warm water. Combine butter, sugar, salt and milk. Stir in unbeaten egg and softened yeast. Add flour gradually in 3 parts, beating well after each addition. Cover, let rise in a warm place until doubled in size—45–60 minutes.

Prepare apples. Combine sugar, cinnamon and soft butter; mix well. Punch down dough and spread or pat into a well-greased jelly roll pan. Arrange apple slices in rows over dough. Sprinkle half of the cinnamon-sugar-butter mixture over it. Cover and let rise for 30 minutes.

Bake at 375 degrees for 20–25 minutes. Blend egg and cream and pour over coffee cake. Sprinkle top with remaining cinnamon-sugar-butter mixture. Bake 15 minutes more. Serve warm.

Apple Pull-Apart Bread

1 cup milk
¼ cup raisins
¼ cup butter, divided
3½ cups flour, divided
½ cup sugar, divided
1 package rapid-rising dry yeast
½ teaspoon salt
1 large egg
1 teaspoon vanilla extract
2 large Delicious apples, peeled, cored, sliced in eighths
2 teaspoons lemon juice
½ teaspoon ground cinnamon
¼ teaspoon ground nutmeg

⅛ teaspoon ground cloves

Heat milk until bubbles form around side of pan; remove from heat. Add raisins and 2 tablespoons butter; set aside to cool.

Combine 3 cups flour, ¼ cup sugar, yeast and salt. Lightly beat egg and vanilla; gradually beat in cooled milk. Add milk mixture to flour mixture; stir until smooth dough forms. Knead as much of remaining ½ cup flour into bread as necessary. Cover dough and let rise until double in size, about 30 minutes.

Thinly slice each apple slice crosswise; toss with lemon juice. Combine remaining ¼ cup sugar, cinnamon, nutmeg and cloves. Punch down dough; cut into 32 pieces.

In saucepan, melt remaining 2 tablespoons butter. Add dough pieces, sugar mixture and melted butter to apples in large bowl. Toss to coat; place in greased and floured 10-inch tube pan. Let rise, uncovered, until double in size, about 35–40 minutes.

Bake at 350 degrees for 45–50 minutes or until golden brown. Cool before serving.

Pumpkin Bread With Orange Butter

⅔ cup shortening
2⅔ cups sugar
4 eggs
1 (16-ounce) can pumpkin
⅔ cup water
3⅓ cups flour
2 teaspoons baking soda
1½ teaspoons salt
½ teaspoon baking powder
1 teaspoon cinnamon
1 teaspoon cloves
⅔ cup coarsely chopped nuts
⅔ cup raisins
Orange Butter (recipe follows)

Cream together shortening and sugar; mix in eggs, pumpkin and water. Combine flour, baking soda, salt, baking powder, cinnamon and cloves; mix into pumpkin mixture. Stir in nuts and raisins. Bake in 2 9 x 5 x 3-inch pans

greased on bottom at 350 degrees for 60–70 minutes. Cool slightly before removing from pans. Serve with Orange Butter. Makes 2 loaves.

Orange Butter

½ cup butter, softened
1 tablespoon orange juice
1 teaspoon finely grated orange peel

Mix together butter, orange juice and orange peel until smooth.

Apple Muffins

1½ cups flour
1½ teaspoons baking powder
½ teaspoon salt
½ teaspoon nutmeg
½ cup sugar
⅓ cup shortening
1 egg, beaten
¼ cup milk
½ cup apple, grated
½ cup butter, melted
⅓ cup sugar
1 teaspoon cinnamon

Mix together flour, baking powder, salt, nutmeg and sugar. Cut in shortening until mixture is fine. Mix together egg, milk and apple. Add all at once to dry ingredients; mixing quickly but thoroughly. Fill greased muffin pans. Bake at 350 degrees for 20–25 minutes or until golden brown. Remove from pans. Immediately roll in melted butter, then in sugar and cinnamon which has been mixed together.

Easy Gingerbread

½ cup shortening
2 tablespoons sugar
1 egg
1 cup dark molasses
1 cup boiling water
2¼ cups flour
1 teaspoon baking soda
½ teaspoon salt
1 teaspoon ginger
1 teaspoon cinnamon

Cream together shortening, sugar and egg. Blend in molasses and water. Stir in flour, baking soda, salt, ginger and cinnamon. Beat until smooth. Pour into greased and floured 9-inch square pan and bake at 325 degrees for 45–50 minutes.

Frosty Orange Muffins

2 cups sifted self-rising flour*
1/3 cup sugar
1 tablespoon grated orange peel
1 egg
3/4 cup orange juice
1/4 cup vegetable oil
Orange Icing (recipe follows)

Preheat oven to 400 degrees. Grease muffin cups. Stir together flour, sugar and orange peel in mixing bowl. Beat egg in separate bowl; stir in orange juice and oil. Add liquid mixture to dry ingredients, stirring just until blended. Batter will be slightly lumpy.

Spoon batter into prepared muffin cups, filling each 2/3s full. Bake for 18–20 minutes, or until golden brown. Remove muffins from pan and cool for 5 minutes. Spread with Orange Icing. Makes about 12 medium muffins.

*If using all-purpose flour, sift 1 tablespoon baking powder and 3/4 teaspoon salt with flour.

Orange Icing

1 (3-ounce) package cream cheese, softened
2 tablespoons sugar
1 teaspoon grated orange peel
2 teaspoons orange juice

Combine cream cheese, sugar and orange peel in small bowl; blend well. Add orange juice and stir until smooth.

Baked Brown Bread

1 cup cornmeal
1/3 cup evaporated milk
1/3 cup water
2/3 cup flour
2 tablespoons white vinegar
1/3 cup sugar
1 teaspoon baking soda
1/2 teaspoon salt
1 egg
2/3 cup light molasses
1/2 cup raisins (optional)

Blend cornmeal with evaporated milk and water; set aside for 15–20 minutes. Sift together flour, sugar, baking soda, and salt. Add raisins; stir to coat. Beat egg; add with molasses and vinegar to cornmeal mixture. Add all at once to flour mixture. Stir only until moistened. Pour into greased and floured 8 x 4 x 3-inch loaf pan. Bake at 350 degrees for 55–60 minutes until toothpick comes out clean.

Applesauce Oatmeal Muffins

1 1/2 cups rolled oatmeal
1 1/4 cups flour
3/4 teaspoon cinnamon
1 teaspoon baking powder
3/4 teaspoon baking soda
1 cup applesauce
1/2 cup milk
1/2 cup brown sugar
3 tablespoons oil
1 egg
1/4 cup rolled oats
2 tablespoons brown sugar
1/4 teaspoon cinnamon
1 tablespoon margarine, melted

Combine oats, flour, cinnamon, baking powder and baking soda. Add applesauce, milk, brown sugar, oil and egg; mix just until dry ingredients are moistened. Line muffin cups with paper baking cups. Fill muffin cups almost full. For topping, combine oats, brown sugar, cinnamon and melted margarine; sprinkle evenly over muffins before baking. Bake at 350 degrees for 20–22 minutes. Serve warm. Makes 12 muffins.

Marvelous Bran Muffins

4 1/2 cups bran cereal
3 cups sugar
3 cups flour
5 teaspoons baking soda
2 teaspoons salt
1 cup butter, melted
4 eggs, well-beaten
1 quart buttermilk

Mix together cereal, sugar, flour, baking soda and salt; stir in butter, eggs and buttermilk. Refrigerate 1 hour. Pour into greased muffin cups filled 2/3 full. Bake at 375 degrees for 15–20 minutes.

Cranberry Banana Bread

2 cups fresh cranberries
1 cup sugar
1 cup water
1/3 cup shortening
2/3 cup sugar
2 eggs
1 3/4 cup flour
2 teaspoons baking powder
1/2 teaspoon salt
1/4 teaspoon baking soda
1 cup mashed bananas
1/2 cup coarsely chopped nuts

Combine cranberries, 1 cup sugar and 1 cup water. Cook over medium heat for 5 minutes or until cranberries begin to pop. Drain and set aside. Cream shortening with 2/3 cup sugar and eggs. Combine flour, baking powder, salt and baking soda; add to creamed mixture alternately with bananas.

Fold in cranberries and nuts. Bake at 350 degrees in greased and floured 9 x 5 x 3-inch loaf pan for 60–65 minutes or until toothpick comes out clean. Cool for 10 minutes before removing from pan. Makes 1 loaf.

Apricot-Date Bread

1 1/2 cups boiling water
1 cup cut up dried apricots
1/2 cup cut up dates
1 1/2 cups flour
1 cup whole-wheat flour
1 cup chopped nuts
3/4 cup firmly packed brown sugar
3 tablespoons vegetable oil
3 teaspoons baking powder
2 teaspoons finely shredded lemon peel
1/2 teaspoon nutmeg
1 egg

Mix together boiling water, apricots and dates; cool. Beat in flours, nuts, sugar, oil, baking powder, lemon peel, nutmeg and egg. Pour into a 9 x 5 x 3-inch pan that has been greased on the bottom only. Bake at 350 degrees for 55–65 minutes, until toothpick comes out clean. Cool slightly before removing from pan. Makes 1 loaf.

Pop-Up Poppy Seed Cheddar Cheese Bread

3 –3½ cups all-purpose flour, divided
1 (¼-ounce) package active dry yeast
½ cup milk
½ cup water
½ cup vegetable oil
¼ cup sugar
1 teaspoon salt
1 tablespoon poppy seed
2 eggs, beaten
1 cup (4 ounces) shredded cheddar cheese

Combine 1½ cups flour and yeast. Heat milk, water, oil, sugar and salt until warm (120–130 degrees), stirring to blend. Add to flour mixture along with eggs and cheese. Stir in poppy seed.

Beat with electric mixer until batter is smooth. Using a spoon, mix in remaining flour (batter will be stiff.)

Divide batter into 2 portions; spoon into 2 clean 1-pound coffee cans. Cover with plastic lids. Let rise in warm place until batter is ¼–½ inch below lids. Remove lids. Bake at 375 degrees for 30–35 minutes. Cool 15 minutes in cans. Remove from cans and finish cooling on wire rack. Makes 2 loaves.

At Christmastime omit the poppy seed and use 1 tablespoon each diced sweet red and green peppers to make it festive.

French Bread

2 packages yeast
1 teaspoon sugar
¼ cup warm water
2 tablespoons shortening
2 tablespoons sugar
2 ½ teaspoons salt
2 cups boiling water
6 cups flour
1 egg, beaten

Dissolve yeast in ¼ cup warm water with 1 teaspoon sugar. Let stand until yeast is softened. Add shortening, 2 tablespoons sugar and salt to boiling water; stir to mix. Cool. Add to yeast mixture; add half

of flour. Beat until smooth. Gradually mix in the rest of flour; wait 10 minutes. Knead dough for 12 minutes until dough is smooth and elastic. Oil dough and let rise until double in size; punch down and let rise again.

Divide dough into 2 balls; let rest 10 minutes. Roll each ball into a rectangle ½ inch thick. Roll up like a jelly roll. Roll ends into points. Place on greased cookie sheet. Make crosswise slashes with knife every 2 inches along length of the loaves. Brush tops with beaten egg. Let rise again until double in size. Bake at 400 degrees until golden brown.

Golden Pumpkin Bread

1½ cups all-purpose flour
1 cup firmly packed brown sugar
1 cup cooked pumpkin
½ cup butter, softened
2 eggs
1 teaspoon baking powder
1 teaspoon baking soda
1 teaspoon salt
1½ teaspoons cinnamon
½ teaspoon cloves
½ teaspoon ginger

Heat oven to 350 degrees. In large mixer bowl, combine all ingredients. Beat at medium speed, scraping bowl often, until well-mixed (2–3 minutes). Pour into greased 9 x 5-inch loaf pan or 3 greased 5¾ x 3-inch miniature loaf pans.

Bake for 45–55 minutes for 9 x 5-inch loaf, or 30–35 minutes for miniature loaves, or until wooden pick inserted in center comes out clean. Cool 10 minutes; remove from pan. Cool completely; store refrigerated. Makes 1 (9 x 5-inch) loaf or 3 (5¾ x 3-inch) miniature loaves.

Maple-Flavored Gingerbread

2½ cups flour
1½ teaspoons baking soda
1 teaspoon cinnamon
1 teaspoon ginger
½ teaspoon cloves
½ teaspoon salt
½ cup shortening

½ cup sugar
1 egg
½ cup molasses
½ cup maple-flavored syrup
1 cup hot water
Whipped cream

Combine flour, baking soda, spices and salt; set aside. Cream shortening and sugar until light and fluffy. Add egg, beating well. Gradually beat in molasses and syrup. Add dry ingredients alternately with hot water, beating well after each addition.

Pour batter into greased 13 x 9 x 2-inch pan. Bake at 350 degrees for 30 minutes or until done. Cool thoroughly in pan. Serve with whipped cream.

Cherry Pecan Bread

¾ cup sugar
½ cup butter or margarine
2 eggs
1 teaspoon vanilla
1 cup buttermilk
2 cups flour
1 teaspoon baking soda
½ teaspoon salt
1 (10-ounce) jar maraschino cherries, drained, chopped
1 cup chopped nuts

Cream together sugar, butter and eggs until light and fluffy. Sift flour, baking soda and salt; add to creamed mixture with buttermilk. Beat until blended. Stir in nuts, cherries and vanilla. Bake in 9 x 5 x 3-inch greased loaf pan. Bake at 350 degrees for 55 minutes or until toothpick comes out clean. Makes 1 loaf.

Hush Puppies

1½ cups cornmeal
½ cup flour
½ teaspoon baking soda
¾ cup buttermilk
2 teaspoons salt
1 large onion, finely diced

Combine cornmeal, flour and baking soda. Stir in buttermilk and beat until batter is smooth. Stir in salt and onion. Drop heaping tablespoons of batter into a deep fryer; fry until golden brown. Drain.

Banana-Chocolate Tea Bread

1 cup butter, softened
2 cups sugar
4 eggs
3 cups flour
4 tablespoons cocoa
2 teaspoons baking soda
6 bananas, mashed
1 teaspoon cinnamon
2 teaspoons vanilla
1 cup sour cream
1 cup chopped pecans
1 cup semisweet chocolate chips

Cream together butter, sugar and eggs. Stir in flour, cocoa, baking soda and cinnamon; blend well. Add vanilla, bananas, sour cream, nuts and chocolate chips. Spoon batter into 2 greased and floured 8 x 3 x 2-inch loaf pans. Bake at 350 degrees for 55 minutes or until toothpick comes out clean. Cool for 10 minutes before removing from pan. Makes 2 loaves.

Irish Soda Bread

1 cup whole-wheat flour
1 cup flour
1/2 teaspoon baking soda
2 teaspoon baking powder
1/2 teaspoon salt
1 tablespoon sugar
3 tablespoons butter, softened
1/4 cup raisins
1/4 cup dried currants
1 teaspoon caraway seeds
1 cup buttermilk plus 3 tablespoons

Place flours, baking soda, baking powder, salt and sugar into food processor bowl. Add butter; pulse 6–8 times. In another bowl combine processed food, raisins, currants and caraway seeds. Add 1 cup buttermilk, mixing until dough forms into a ball.

On greased cookie sheet, mold dough into domed 8–9-inch circle. Lightly brush top with remaining buttermilk and cut a shallow X across the top. Bake for 5 minutes at 450 degrees; reduce heat to 325 degrees and bake an additional 30–40 minutes, until toothpick comes out clean.

Applesauce Bread

1 1/4 cups applesauce
1 cup sugar
1/2 cup oil
3 tablespoons milk
2 eggs
1/2 teaspoon cinnamon
1/4 teaspoon nutmeg
1/4 teaspoon allspice
1/4 teaspoon salt
1 teaspoon baking soda
1/2 teaspoon baking powder
2 cups flour
1/2 cup pecans
1/4 cup pecans, finely chopped
1/4 cup brown sugar
1/2 teaspoon cinnamon

Stir together applesauce, sugar, oil, milk and eggs. Sift spices, salt, baking soda, baking powder and flour; stir into applesauce mixture. Stir in 1/2 cup pecans. Pour into greased and floured loaf pan. For topping, stir together 1/4 cup pecans, brown sugar and 1/2 teaspoon cinnamon; sprinkle over loaf before baking. Bake at 350 degrees for 60 minutes. Makes 1 loaf.

Best-Yet Banana Bread

1/2 cup margarine
1 cup sugar
2 eggs
2 large ripe bananas, mashed
2 cups flour
1 teaspoon baking soda
1/8 teaspoon salt
1/4 cup sour cream
1/2 cup chopped walnuts

Beat together butter, sugar and eggs until light and fluffy; stir in bananas. Sift together flour, baking soda and salt; add to banana mixture. Stir in sour cream; mix until smooth.

Pour into well-greased 9 x 5 x 3-inch loaf pan. Sprinkle with walnuts. Bake at 375 degrees for 55–60 minutes or until center springs back when lightly touched. Cool 10 minutes before removing from pan.

Spicy Tomato Bread

2 1/2 cups flour
1 tablespoon baking powder
3/4 teaspoon salt
1 teaspoon garlic salt
1/8 teaspoon cayenne
1 teaspoon oregano
3/4 tablespoon sugar
1/2 cup grated cheese
1/4 cup grated Parmesan cheese
Milk
1 (16-ounce) can stewed tomatoes, drained, coarsely chopped, reserve liquid
2 eggs
1/4 cup vegetable oil

Stir together flour, baking powder, salt, garlic salt, cayenne, oregano, sugar and cheeses. Add enough milk to reserved tomato juice to make 2/3 cup. Add eggs and oil and stir to blend well; mix with flour mixture.

Fold in chopped tomatoes. Batter will be thick. Bake in greased 8 x 4 x 3-inch loaf pan at 350 degrees for 60 minutes or until toothpick comes out clean.

Luscious Strawberry Bread

3 cups mashed strawberries
3 cups flour
1 teaspoon baking soda
1 teaspoon cinnamon
2 cups sugar
1 teaspoon salt
1 1/4 cups oil
4 eggs, well beaten
1 (8-ounce) package cream cheese, softened

Drain 1/2 cup strawberry juice from mashed strawberries; save for topping. Mix together flour, baking soda, cinnamon and salt. Make a well in center of mixture; add strawberries and remaining juice, oil and eggs. Mix until thoroughly combined. Pour into 2 greased 9 x 5 x 3 inch loaf pans. Bake at 350 degrees for 50–60 minutes. Remove from pans; cool thoroughly. Mix together cream cheese and reserved strawberry juice; blend until smooth. Drizzle over loaves.

Poppy Seed Bread

3 eggs, well-beaten
1⅛ cups oil
2¼ cups sugar
3 cups flour
1½ teaspoons salt
1½ teaspoons baking powder
1½ cups milk
1½ teaspoons almond extract
1½ teaspoons butter flavoring
1½ teaspoons vanilla
1¼ tablespoons poppy seeds
Orange Glaze (recipe follows)

Mix together eggs, oil and sugar. Sift together flour, salt and baking powder; blend alternately with egg mixture and milk. Stir in almond extract, butter flavoring, vanilla and poppy seeds. Bake in greased loaf pan at 325 degrees for 60 minutes. Top with glaze and let sit, wrapped, for at least 24 hours.

Orange Glaze

¼ cup orange juice
¾ cup sugar
1½ teaspoons almond extract
½ teaspoon butter flavoring
½ teaspoon vanilla

Heat orange juice, sugar, almond extract, butter flavoring and vanilla over medium heat until dissolved.

Peanut Butter Bread

¾ cup peanut butter, smooth *or* chunky style
¼ cup margarine, softened
2 cups all-purpose flour
½ cup sugar
2 teaspoons baking powder
1 teaspoon salt
1 egg
1¼ cups milk
1 tablespoon grated orange peel

Beat peanut butter and margarine together until fluffy; add flour, sugar, baking powder and salt. Mix until crumbly. In a small bowl, combine egg, milk and orange peel. Stir into crumbly mixture just until moistened. Bake in a greased 9 x 5 x 3-inch loaf pan at 350 degrees for about 1 hour. Makes 1 loaf.

German Sauerkraut Rolls

1½ large cans sauerkraut
¾ cup shortening
Pepper, to taste
3 cups flour
Salt, to taste
4 eggs
½ teaspoon salt
¼ cup water

Drain juice from sauerkraut. In skillet, heat shortening; stir in kraut; add pepper to taste. Fry about 20 minutes, or until browned; cool. Mix together flour and ½ teaspoon salt; add eggs and water. Knead until dough is smooth and elastic.

Roll to ¼-inch thickness on floured board. Spread cooled sauerkraut on top; roll up like jelly roll. Slice cross-wise; place cut pieces in frying pan. Cover with small amount of water; add salt. Cook over medium heat for 1 hour.

Basic Batter White Bread

1 package active dry yeast
1¼ cups warm water
2 tablespoons honey
2 tablespoons margarine
1 teaspoon salt
3 cups flour

Dissolve yeast in water; stir in honey. Add margarine, salt and 2 cups flour; mix well. Add remaining flour. Grease dough, cover and let rise in warm place until doubled in bulk, about 45 minutes. Punch down bread; spoon into greased 8 x 4-inch loaf pan. Let rise, covered, in warm place for 30–40 minutes or until batter rises to edge of pan. Bake at 375 degrees for 35 minutes. Makes 1 loaf.

Popovers

2 eggs, slightly beaten
1 cup flour
1 cup milk
½ teaspoon salt

Combine eggs, flour, milk and salt; beat just until smooth, do not overbeat. Fill 8 greased medium muffin cups ¾ full. Bake at 450 degrees for 20 minutes. Lower temperature to 350 degrees and bake 15 minutes longer. Makes 6–8 popovers.

Apple Bread

1 cup sugar
½ cup shortening
2 eggs
1 teaspoon vanilla
2 cups flour
1 teaspoon baking powder
1 teaspoon baking soda
1 teaspoon cinnamon
½ teaspoon salt
2 cups pared and chopped apples
½ cup chopped nuts
1 tablespoon sugar
¼ teaspoon cinnamon

Cream 1 cup sugar and shortening; add eggs and vanilla. Stir in flour, baking powder, baking soda, 1 teaspoon cinnamon and salt; mix well. Blend in apples and nuts.

Place in 9 x 5 x 3-inch greased and floured loaf pan. Mix together 1 tablespoon sugar and ¼ teaspoon cinnamon; sprinkle over batter. Bake at 350 degrees for 50–60 minutes, until toothpick in center comes out clean. Makes 1 loaf.

Peanut Butter Banana Muffins

1 cup flour
¾ cup rolled oats
⅓ cup firmly packed brown sugar
1 tablespoon baking powder
1 cup milk
½ cup peanut butter
½ cup ripe mashed banana
1 egg, beaten
2 tablespoons oil
1 teaspoon vanilla
¼ cup rolled oats
¼ cup flour
2 tablespoons margarine, melted
2 tablespoons firmly packed brown sugar

Combine flour, oats, brown sugar and baking powder. Whisk together milk, peanut butter, banana, egg, oil and vanilla; add to dry ingredients, mixing just until moistened. Fill greased muffin cups ¾ full. Combine oats, flour, margarine and brown sugar. Sprinkle on muffins. Bake at 375 degrees for 16–18 minutes or until golden brown. Makes 1 dozen muffins.

Orange Cranberry Bread

½ cup butter, softened
¾ cup sugar
1 egg
1 teaspoon grated orange peel
2½ cups all-purpose flour
⅔ cup orange juice
⅓ cup milk
1 tablespoon baking powder
1 teaspoon salt
¾ cup coarsely chopped fresh *or* frozen cranberries
⅓ cup chopped pecans

Heat oven to 350 degrees. In large mixer bowl combine butter, sugar, egg and orange peel. Beat at medium speed, scraping bowl often, until well-mixed (1–2 minutes). Add remaining ingredients, except cranberries and pecans. Continue beating, scraping bowl often, until well-mixed (1–2 minutes). By hand, stir in cranberries and pecans.

Spoon into greased 9 x 5-inch loaf pan or 3 greased 5¾ x 3-inch miniature loaf pans. Bake for 50–60 minutes for 9 x 5-inch loaf or 30–40 minutes for miniature loaves, or until wooden pick inserted in center comes out clean. Cool 10 minutes; remove from pan. Makes 1 (9 x 5-inch) loaf or 3 (5¾ x 3-inch) miniature loaves.

Arab Bread

5½ cups flour
1 package dry yeast
1 tablespoon sugar
1 teaspoon salt
2 cups very warm water
2 tablespoons shortening
2 tablespoons cornmeal
(use to flour board with)

Mix thoroughly 2 cups flour, yeast, sugar and salt; set aside. Pour warm water over shortening, stirring to melt; gradually add to dry ingredients. Beat 2 minutes. Stir in enough additional flour to make a soft dough. Knead on lightly floured board until smooth and elastic.

Place in greased bowl, greasing top of bread also. Cover and let rise in warm place until double in size, about 1 hour.

Punch down; turn out onto lightly floured board, cover and let rise 30 minutes.

Divide dough into sixths and form each portion into a ball. Roll each on lightly floured board into an 8–9-inch circle about ¼-inch thick. Let rise 30–45 minutes. Bake at 500 degrees on greased baking sheet until puffed and lightly browned, for 9–10 minutes. Makes 6 loaves.

Applesauce Nut Bread

2 cups sifted flour
¾ cup sugar
3 teaspoons baking powder
½ teaspoon cinnamon
1 teaspoon salt
½ teaspoon baking soda
1 cup nuts, chopped
1 egg
1 cup applesauce
2 teaspoons butter, melted

Sift together flour, sugar, baking powder, cinnamon, salt and baking soda. In mixing bowl, beat egg; add applesauce and melted butter; blend together. Add dry mixture, stirring just enough to blend. Fold in nuts. Pour into greased large loaf pan. Bake at 350 degrees for 60 minutes. Makes 1 large loaf.

Apple Rolls

4 cups flour
6 teaspoons baking powder
1 teaspoon salt
4 teaspoons shortening
Milk
Butter
1 quart apples, thinly sliceed
Sugar
Cinnamon
1 cup sugar
2 tablespoons butter, melted
Cinnamon

Mix together flour, baking powder, salt and shortening. Add just enough milk to make a nice biscuit dough. Roll on board until ½-inch thick; spread on butter.

Spread apples over rolled dough; sprinkle with sugar and cinnamon. Roll up

dough and cut every half inch. In 13 x 9-inch pan, put 1 cup sugar, melted butter and enough water to fill pan 1/2-inch in bottom of pan. Put in rolls; sprinkle cinnamon over top. Bake until done. Serve with milk. Makes 10 servings.

Oatmeal Applesauce Nut Bread

1½ cups whole-wheat pastry flour
½ teaspoon cinnamon
1 teaspoon baking powder
1 teaspoon baking soda
1 teaspoon salt
½ teaspoon nutmeg
⅓ cup butter
½ cup brown sugar
1½ cups applesauce
2 eggs
1 cup rolled oats
1 cup nuts, chopped
½ cup raisins

Preheat oven to 350 degrees. Grease a 9 x 5-inch loaf pan. Sift together flour, cinnamon, baking powder, baking soda, salt and nutmeg. Cream butter and sugar. Beat in applesauce and eggs. Add dry ingredients. Stir in oats, nuts and raisins. Bake for 55–60 minutes. Makes 1 loaf.

Light-as-Foam Rolls

1 cup milk
½ cup shortening
2 teaspoons salt
¼ cup sugar
1 package yeast
¼ cup lukewarm water
1 egg, beaten
3¼ cups flour

Combine milk, shortening, salt and sugar in 2-quart saucepan. Scald. Cool to lukewarm and add yeast dissolved in warm water. Add egg; stir. Add flour. Mix well; cover and let rise 1½ hours. Stir down. Cover and let rise ½ hour longer. Stir down again and spoon into greased muffin tins. Let rise 20 minutes. Bake at 425 degrees for 12–18 minutes. Makes 12–15 rolls.

Apple Bread

1 cup sugar
½ cup shortening
2 eggs
1 teaspoon vanilla
2 cups flour
1 teaspoon baking powder
1 teaspoon baking soda
1 teaspoon cinnamon
½ teaspoon salt
2 cups pared and chopped apples
½ cup nuts, chopped
1 tablespoon sugar
¼ teaspoon ground cinnamon

Preheat oven to 350 degrees. Grease and flour a loaf pan. Mix sugar, shortening, eggs and vanilla. Stir in flour, baking powder, baking soda, cinnamon and salt in a large bowl until smooth (batter will be thick). Stir in apples and nuts. Spread in pan. Mix 1 tablespoon sugar and ¼ teaspoon cinnamon; sprinkle over batter.

Bake until wooden pick inserted in center comes out clean, about 50–60 minutes. Remove from pan immediately. Cool completely before slicing. Store tightly covered. Makes 1 loaf.

Whole Grain Pumpkin Muffins

¾ cup flour
½ cup whole-wheat flour
½ cup toasted wheat germ
2 tablespoons sugar
2½ teaspoons baking powder
½ teaspoon salt
½ teaspoon ground cinnamon
½ teaspoon ground nutmeg
2 egg whites
¾ cup skim milk
½ cup canned pumpkin
¼ cup cooking oil
1 teaspoon vanilla

Mix together flour, whole-wheat flour, wheat germ, sugar, baking powder, salt, cinnamon and nutmeg. Make a well in center. Combine egg whites, milk, pumpkin, oil and vanilla; add all at once to dry ingredients. Stir just until moistened. Spoon into greased muffin cups. Bake at 400 degrees for 20–25 minutes. Cool 2 minutes in pan before removing. Makes 12 muffins.

Pecan Applesauce Bread

1 cup sugar
1 cup applesauce
¼ cup oil
3 egg whites
3 tablespoons skim milk
½ teaspoon salt
½ teaspoon cinnamon
¼ teaspoon nutmeg
2 cups flour
1 teaspoon baking powder
1 teaspoon baking soda
½ cup pecans, chopped

Combine sugar, applesauce, oil, egg whites and milk. Mix together salt, cinnamon, nutmeg, flour, baking powder and baking soda; add to applesauce mixture. Stir in pecans. Spread batter in oiled and floured 9 x 5-inch loaf pan. Bake at 350 degrees for 60–70 minutes. Makes 1 loaf.

Rich Wheat Bread

1 package dry yeast
¼ cup lukewarm water
1½ cups whole-wheat flour
1½ cups bread flour
¼ cup nonfat dry milk
3 tablespoons margarine, softened, cut in 4 parts
2 tablespoons sugar
1 teaspoon salt
1 egg, slightly beaten
¾ cup lukewarm water
Margarine, melted

In measuring cup, mix yeast with ¼ cup lukewarm water. Allow to stand 10 minutes. Using your food processor, position knife blade in the bowl; add the flours, dry milk, margarine, sugar and salt. Process to mix, about 5 seconds. With processor running, add yeast mixture, egg and ½–¾ cup lukewarm water (just enough water to make a soft ball). Stop the processor.

Turn dough onto a well-floured board and gently knead about 10 times until smooth. Now follow the simple instructions above to "proof" your bread. When your loaf is ready, bake at 375 degrees for 35–40 minutes. Remove from pan and brush top lightly with melted margarine. Makes 1 loaf.

Bran Yeast Rolls

1 cup shredded bran cereal
1 cup shortening
¾ cup sugar
2 teaspoons salt
1 cup boiling water
2 fresh yeast cakes
1 cup lukewarm water
2 eggs, beaten
5–6 cups flour
Butter

Combine cereal, shortening, sugar and salt; pour on boiling water and stir until shortening melts and mixture is well-blended. Cool to lukewarm. Crumble yeast cakes; stir in lukewarm water. Let stand until yeast dissolves, about 10 minutes. Whisk eggs; mix ½ cup flour and eggs into bran mixture; stir in yeast mixture and mix well.

Add enough flour to form stiff but slightly sticky dough. Knead on floured surface until smooth, about 5 minutes. Butter dough ball; cover and let rise in warm place until dough is doubled, about 50 minutes.

Punch down dough; knead on lightly floured surface until smooth, about 3 minutes.

Roll small pieces of dough into 1-inch balls. Place 3 balls into buttered muffin tins. Cover and let rise until almost doubled in volume, about 20 minutes. Preheat oven to 450 degrees; place tins in oven and turn temperature to 400 degrees for 15 minutes or until golden brown.

Rhubarb Bread

1½ cups brown sugar
⅔ cup salad oil
1 egg
1 teaspoon vanilla
¼ teaspoon salt
1 teaspoon baking soda
1 cup sour milk
1½ cups diced rhubarb
2½ cups flour
¼ cup wheat germ (optional)

Mix together sugar, salad oil, egg, vanilla and salt. Mix baking soda into sour milk; add to egg mixture. Stir in flour and wheat germ; mix well; fold in rhubarb. Bake in 2 greased 4 x 8-inch loaf pans for 60 minutes at 350 degrees.

Whole-Wheat Bread

1 package dry yeast
¼ cup lukewarm water
¼ cup honey
¼ cup oil
1 tablespoon salt
1 cup boiling water
1 (8-ounce) carton plain yogurt
3 cups whole-wheat flour
3 cups bread flour
   Margarine, melted

Soften yeast in lukewarm water. In large bowl, using an electric mixer, combine honey, oil, salt and boiling water. Add yogurt to cool the mixture. Cool to lukewarm. Stir in yeast and gradually add flours to form a stiff dough.

Knead lightly until smooth and satiny, adding more flour, if needed. Follow the easy steps for "proofing" your bread. When bread is ready, bake at 350 degrees for 50–60 minutes. Remove from pans and brush tops with melted margarine. Makes 2 loaves.

Jo's Wheat Sandwich Buns

3½ cups whole-wheat flour
4 cups flour
1 scant cup sugar
½ teaspoon salt
2½ cups warm water
1 package dry yeast
½ cup corn oil

Mix 1 cup whole-wheat flour with 1 cup white flour, sugar, salt and yeast. Stir in water and oil; beat 2 minutes on medium speed. Add 1 cup whole-wheat flour, beat 2 minutes on high speed. Add rest of flours with spoon to make a stiff dough. Knead 7–10 minutes. Place in greased bowl; cover and let rise until double in size.

Punch down dough and shape small amounts into buns. Place on greased cookie sheets. Cover with waxed paper that has been wiped with butter or oil to prevent sticking. Cover waxed paper with towels or plastic wrap. Let rise overnight at room temperature. Bake at 350 degrees for 15–20 minutes.

Miniature Date Loaves

½ cup boiling water
1½ cups cut up dates
2 tablespoons shortening
1 tablespoon grated orange peel
½ cup orange juice
1 egg, beaten
2 cups sifted flour
⅓ cup sugar
1 teaspoon baking powder
1 teaspoon baking soda
½ teaspoon salt
½ cup chopped nuts

Pour boiling water over dates; add shortening; cool to room temperature. Stir in orange peel, orange juice and egg. Sift together flour, sugar, baking powder, baking soda and salt; add to date mixture, stirring just until mixed. Mix in nuts. Pour into 4 greased 4½ x 2¾ x 2-inch loaf pans. Bake at 325 degrees for 40–45 minutes. Remove from pans immediately; cool.

Christmas Carrot Loaf

1¼ cups flour, sifted
½ teaspoon baking powder
½ teaspoon baking soda
½ cup sugar
1 teaspoon cinnamon
½ teaspoon nutmeg
½ teaspoon ginger
¼ teaspoon salt
2 eggs, beaten
¼ cup oil
¼ cup milk
1 cup shredded carrots
¾ cup coconut
¼ cup maraschino cherries, chopped and drained
¼ cup raisins
¼ cup chopped pecans

Sift together flour, baking powder and soda; add sugar, cinnamon, nutmeg, ginger and salt. Combine eggs, oil and milk; mix well; add to dry ingredients. Stir in the carrots, coconut, maraschino cherries, raisins and pecans. Spoon into greased loaf pan. Bake at 350 degrees for 50–60 minutes.

Christmas Wreath

2–3 cups flour, divided
1 package active dry yeast
¾ cup milk
3 tablespoons sugar
3 tablespoons butter
¼ teaspoon salt
1 egg
   Milk
   Pecan halves

Combine 1 cup flour and yeast. Heat milk, sugar, butter and salt just until warm and butter starts to melt, stirring constantly. Add flour mixture; stir in egg. Beat on low speed with an electric mixer for ½ minute. Beat for 3 minutes at high speed.

Stir in as much remaining flour as you can mix in with a spoon. Knead in enough remaining flour to make dough smooth and elastic. Place in greased bowl; cover; let rise until double, about 1 hour.

Punch down dough, divide into 3 portions; shape into balls; cover and let rest 10 minutes. Roll each ball to 20-inch rope. Grease outside of a 6-ounce custard cup and invert the dish in the center of greased baking sheet. Starting at center, braid ropes loosely to ends. Wrap braid around custard cup, stretching as necessary to join ends, pinch to seal.

Cover, let rise until nearly double, about 30 minutes. Brush carefully with milk, tuck pecan halves in braid. Bake at 375 degrees for 20 minutes. Cool on wire rack. Loosen braid from custard cup with narrow spatula, removing cup.

Indian Fry Bread

4 cups flour
1 cup water
2¼ teaspoons baking powder
   Pinch salt
   Oil

Mix together flour, water, baking powder and salt until well-blended; knead 1 minute. Cover and let rise 15–20 minutes. Pat bread out to ½-inch thickness. Cut in wedges. Make a 1-inch slice in middle of each wedge. Heat 1½ inches of oil in large skillet. Fry wedges until golden brown.

Buttermilk Banana Nut Bread

2 cups flour
1 teaspoon baking soda
½ teaspoon salt
½ cup butter *or* margarine
1 cup sugar
2 eggs
1 cup bananas, mashed
⅓ cup buttermilk
1 teaspoon lemon juice
½ cup nuts, chopped

Sift together flour, baking soda and salt. Cream butter or margarine, gradually adding sugar. Add eggs and bananas, blending thoroughly. Combine buttermilk and lemon juice. Add sifted dry ingredients to banana mixture, alternately with buttermilk mixture, beginning and ending with the dry ingredients. Stir in nuts.

Spoon mixture into a 9 x 5 x 3-inch loaf pan, greased only on the bottom. Bake at 350 degrees for 60–70 minutes. Remove from oven and cool slightly. Remove from pan and cool right side up. Makes 1 loaf.

Sesame Seed Ring

1 cup milk, scalded
¼ cup sugar
4 tablespoons butter
1 teaspoon salt
2 tablespoons sesame seeds
1 egg, beaten
1 package dry yeast
½ cup warm water
3 ¾ cups flour
½ cup brown sugar
2 tablespoons flour
½ teaspoon cinnamon
½ cup currants

Dissolve yeast in warm water. Melt butter in hot milk; add sugar, salt and sesame seeds. Cool to lukewarm; add egg and yeast, stirring well. Mix in 3¾ cups flour. Cover with damp towel and allow to rise until double in size. Stir down and roll out on floured board into a rectangle; spread with melted butter.

Mix together brown sugar, 2 tablespoons flour, cinnamon and currants; spread evenly over buttered dough. Start at 1 end and roll tightly and evenly. Place into a ring on lightly greased baking sheet. Wet ends lightly and seal together. With sharp knife, cut slits in top of ring diagonally. Cover with damp towel and let rise to double in bulk. Bake at 400 degrees for 20 minutes.

Shredded Wheat Bread

2 (large size) shredded wheat cereal biscuits
3 tablespoons shortening
2 cups boiling water
½ cup molasses
1 heaping teaspoon salt
2 packages dry yeast
½ cup warm water
3 tablespoons sugar
6 cups flour

Mix together wheat biscuits, shortening, water, molasses and salt; cool. Dissolve yeast in warm water with sugar; add to biscuit mixture. Stir in flour; mix well. Knead until shiny and elastic. Place in greased bowl, cover and let rise in warm place until double in size. Punch dough down. Shape into 2 loaves. Place into 2 greased bread pans. Cover and let rise 1 hour, or until double in bulk. Bake at 425 degrees for 25–30 minutes. Makes 2 loaves.

Rye Bread With Beer

2 cups rye flour
12 ounces beer
2 packages yeast
2 tablespoons sugar
1 teaspoon salt
2 tablespoons shortening
1 large egg
3 cups flour
1 tablespoon caraway seeds

Combine rye flour, beer and yeast; cover with plastic wrap. Leave overnight. Add sugar, salt, shortening and egg; beat with mixer. Add caraway seeds. Stir in flour to make soft dough until it leaves side of bowl. Knead until smooth, approximately 10 minutes.

Grease dough and let rise in warm place 1 hour. Punch down, divide in half and make rounds. Place on baking sheets sprinkles with cornmeal. Let rise 30 minutes. Bake at 400 degrees for 30 minutes.

Mashed Potato Biscuits

1 teaspoon salt
1 ¾ cups flour
1 cup butter, chilled
2 tablespoons sour cream
1 cup cold mashed potatoes
4 egg yolks

Combine salt and flour; cut in butter. Add cream, potatoes and 3 egg yolks; blend. Knead together; form into a ball. Chill until firm. Repeat kneading and chilling process. After chilling, roll out to ¼-inch thickness. Brush with remaining egg yolk; cut with 2-inch biscuit cutter. Bake at 400 degrees for 15 minutes or until golden in color.

Caramel-Topped Raisin Bran Muffins

6 tablespoons butter
6 tablespoons firmly packed brown sugar
¼ cup corn syrup
1 cup raisin and bran cereal
¾ cup milk
¼ cup unprocessed wheat bran
¾ cup molasses
¼ cup oil
1 egg, beaten
2 cups flour
1 tablespoon baking powder
2 teaspoons cinnamon
½ teaspoon baking soda
½ teaspoon salt
½ cup raisins

Heat butter, brown sugar and corn syrup over medium heat until sugar is dissolved; bring to a boil without stirring. Pour 2 tablespoons of mixture into 6 large greased muffin cups; set aside.

Mix together cereal, milk and wheat bran; set aside for 10 minutes.

Blend in molasses, oil and egg; add flour, baking powder, cinnamon, baking soda and salt just until combined. Stir in raisins. Place batter in reserved muffin cups dividing evenly between the 6 cups. Bake at 400 degrees for 25 minutes until toothpick comes out clean. Makes 6 large muffins.

English Raisin Bread

2 packages yeast
½ cup warm water
1½ cups lukewarm milk
¼ cup sugar
1 tablespoon salt
3 eggs
¼ cup shortening
7½ cups flour
2 cups raisins

Dissolve yeast in warm water. Stir in milk, sugar, salt, eggs, shortening and 3½ cups flour; beat until smooth. Mix in raisins and enough of the remaining flour to make dough easy to handle. Turn the dough onto a lightly floured board and knead until smooth and elastic, about 5 minutes. Let rise in covered, greased bowl until doubled, about 1½ hours.

Punch down dough and divide in half. Roll each half into a rectangle 18 x 9 inches. Roll up, beginning at the short side, using side of your hand, press down on each end to seal Fold under loaf. Place loaf seam side down in a greased loaf pan 9 x 5 x 3 inches.

Let rise until double, about 1 hour. Bake at 400 degrees for 25–30 minutes or until golden brown. Frost with confectioners' sugar glaze, if desired. Makes 2 loaves.

Blueberry Wild Rice Muffins

3 tablespoons butter, softened
1 cup sugar
½ cup water
½ cup evaporated milk
2 cups flour
1 teaspoon salt
2 teaspoons baking powder
1½ cups blueberries
1 cup cooked wild rice

Cream together butter and sugar; add water, milk, flour, salt and baking powder. Stir until smooth. Fold in blueberries and rice. Fill greased muffin tins ⅔ full and bake at 350 degrees for 25 minutes. Makes 2 dozen muffins.

Casserole Rye Bread

1 cup milk
3 tablespoons sugar
1 teaspoon salt
1½ tablespoons margarine
1 cup warm water
2 packages dry yeast
3 cups flour
1½ cups rye flour

Heat milk, sugar, salt and margarine together and cool to lukewarm. Measure warm water and dry yeast into a bowl. Stir until dissolved. Stir in lukewarm milk mixture and flours. Beat until well-blended. Cover and let rise in warm place 50 minutes or until double in size.

Stir batter down and beat vigorously about half a minute. Turn into 1½-quart well-greased casserole dish. Brush carefully with milk and bake uncovered for 50–60 minutes at 375 degrees. Butter top well after baking.

Vanilla-Poppy Seed Muffins

1½ cups biscuit mix
½ cup sugar
1 tablespoon poppy seeds
¾ cup chopped raisins
1 egg, beaten
¾ cup sour cream
1 teaspoon vanilla

Mix together biscuit mix, sugar and poppy seeds. Make a well in center of mixture; stir in raisins, egg, sour cream and vanilla. Stir just until moistened. Fill greased muffin cups ½ full. Bake at 400 degrees for 20 minutes or until toothpick comes out clean. Makes 1 dozen muffins.

Drop Biscuits

2 cups flour
3 teaspoons baking powder
1 teaspoon salt
¼ cup shortening
1 cup milk

Mix together flour, baking powder, salt, shortening and milk. Drop by spoonfuls into a 10-inch greased baking pan. Bake at 450 degrees for 10–12 minutes.

Fresh Apple Bread

2 cups flour
1 teaspoon soda
1 teaspoon baking powder
½ teaspoon salt
½ cup shortening
1 cup sugar
2 eggs
2 cups chopped apples (3 medium)
½ cup chopped nuts
1 teaspoon vanilla flavoring
¼ cup sugar
1½ teaspoons cinnamon

Sift first 4 ingredients together; cream sugar and shortening. Add eggs and beat well. Add apples, nuts and vanilla. Stir in flour mixture. Pour batter into well-greased bread pan and sprinkle with ¼ cup sugar and 1½ teaspoons cinnamon. Bake for 1 hour at 350 degrees.

Turn pan on side to cool after removing from oven. Do not slice until bread is cool. Makes 1 loaf.

Eat and enjoy; it is delicious!

Lightning Sweet Rolls

1 package refrigerator rolls
3 tablespoons margarine, melted
¼ cup sweetened condensed milk
¼ cup seedless raisins
¼ cup chopped nuts

Pour margarine in 8-inch baking pan; spread to coat. Mix together milk, raisins and nuts; pour into pan. Separate biscuits and place on top. Bake at 400 degrees for 12 minutes. Turn out onto hot platter so fruit and nuts are on top.

Quick Cheddar Bread

3⅓ cups biscuit mix
2½ cups grated sharp cheddar cheese
2 eggs, slightly beaten
1¼ cups milk

Combine biscuit mix with cheese. Mix together eggs and milk; stir into cheese mixture, mixing just enough to moisten. Bake in greased and floured 9 x 5-inch loaf pan at 350 degrees for 55 minutes.

Easy Herbed Rolls

2½ cups flour
1 package dry yeast
½ teaspoon celery seed
1 teaspoon dry tarragon, crushed
½ teaspoon dried basil
1 cup warm water
2 tablespoons sugar
2 tablespoons corn oil
½ teaspoon salt
1 egg

Combine 1½ cups flour, yeast, herbs and celery seed. Stir together water, sugar, oil and salt; add to flour mixture; stir in egg. Beat on low speed for 30 seconds. Beat 3 minutes on high speed. Stir in remaining flour with spoon.

Cover dough; let rise until doubled, 30 minutes. Spoon into greased muffin cups, filling each slightly more than half full. Cover. Let rise until nearly doubled, 30 minutes. Bake at 375 degrees for 15–18 minutes. Makes 1 dozen.

Cranberry Orange Bread

2 cups flour
1 cup sugar
1½ teaspoons baking powder
½ teaspoon baking soda
1½ teaspoons salt
¼ cup butter *or* margarine
1 egg, beaten
1 teaspoon grated orange peel
¼ cup orange juice
1½ cups raisins
1½ cups chopped cranberries

Sift together flour, sugar, baking powder, salt and baking soda. Cut in butter until mixture is crumbly. Add egg, orange peel and orange juice. Stir just until moist. Fold in raisins and cranberries. Baked in greased 9 x 5 x 3-inch pan. Bake at 350 degrees for 70 minutes or until toothpick comes out clean.

Orange-Pecan Bread

½ cup water
1½ cups orange peel, cut into ½-inch pieces
¾ cup sugar
2 cups flour
⅔ cup sugar
⅔ cup milk
1 tablespoon plus 1 teaspoon oil
2 teaspoons baking powder
1 egg
½ teaspoon salt
⅔ cup finely chopped pecans

Blend water and orange peel in blender on medium speed until finely chopped. Heat orange peel mixture and ¾ cup sugar to boiling. Stir until thickened, 10–12 minutes. Cool.

Mix orange mixture with flour, ⅔ cup sugar, milk, oil, baking powder, egg and salt. Stir in nuts. Bake in greased 9 x 5 x 3-inch pan at 325 degrees for 50–60 minutes. Cool in pan for 10 minutes before removing from pan. Makes 1 loaf.

Jalapeño Corn Bread

2 eggs
¼ cup salad oil
1–4 canned jalapeños, seeds removed, finely chopped
1 (9-ounce) can cream-style corn
½ cup sour cream
1 cup yellow cornmeal
½ teaspoon salt
2 teaspoons baking powder
2 cups shredded sharp cheddar cheese

Beat eggs and oil until well-blended. Combine jalapeños and egg mixture.

Mix in corn, sour cream, cornmeal, salt, baking powder and 1½ cups of the cheese, stirring until well-blended. Pour batter into greased 8 or 9-inch pan. Sprinkle with remaining cheese. Bake at 350 degrees for 1 hour, or until a toothpick comes out clean.

Apple-Raisin Muffins

1¾ cups flour
¼ cup sugar
2½ teaspoons baking powder
¾ teaspoon salt
½ teaspoon cinnamon
1 cup peeled, chopped apples
¼ cup raisins
1 egg, beaten
¾ cup milk
⅓ cup oil

Mix together flour, sugar, baking powder, salt, cinnamon, apples and raisins. Make a well in the center. Combine egg, milk and oil; add all at once to flour mixture. Stir just until moistened; batter will be lumpy. Fill greased muffin cups ⅔ full. Bake at 400 degrees for 20–25 minutes or until golden brown. Makes 10–12 muffins.

Carrot & Bran Muffins

1½ cups bran cereal
¼ cup wheat germ
1 cup whole-wheat flour
1 teaspoon baking powder
1 teaspoon baking soda
½ teaspoon salt
1 cup shredded carrots
½ cup chopped nuts
1 cup raisins
1 egg
¾ cup milk
½ cup honey
3 tablespoons oil

Mix together bran, wheat germ, whole-wheat flour, baking powder, baking soda and salt. Stir in carrots, nuts and raisins. Combine egg, milk, honey and oil; add to flour mixture. Stir to moisten. Fill greased muffin cups and bake at 400 degrees for 15–20 minutes. Makes 18 muffins.

Quick Pumpkin Bread

1 (16-ounce) package pound cake mix
1 cup pumpkin pie filling
2 eggs
⅓ cup milk
½ teaspoon cinnamon
½ teaspoon nutmeg

Combine cake mix, pumpkin, eggs, milk, cinnamon and nutmeg; mix well. Bake in greased 9 x 5-inch loaf pan at 300 degrees for 1¼ hours or until bread springs back when touched lightly. Cool 20 minutes in pan before removing.

Plum Nut Bread

3 cups flour
4 teaspoons baking powder
1 teaspoon salt
1 cup sugar
1 cup walnuts, chopped
2 ½ cups coarsely chopped fresh pitted plums
1 egg, well-beaten
¾ cup milk
⅓ cup orange juice
3 teaspoons grated orange rind
3 tablespoons salad oil

Sift together flour, baking powder, salt and sugar; fold in nuts and plums. Mix together egg, milk, orange juice, orange rind and oil; blend with flour mixture, stirring just until blended. Place in greased 2-quart loaf pan; spread batter into corners, leaving a slight hollow in center. Cover with lightly greased pan of the same size. Allow to rest 20 minutes. Bake at 350 degrees for 20 minutes. Remove top pan carefully. Bake an additional 60 minutes until toothpick comes out clean.

Aunt Sarah's Spiced Apple Muffins

1 egg, beaten
1 cup milk
4 tablespoons margarine, melted
2 cups flour
½ cup sugar
4 teaspoons baking powder
½ teaspoon salt
1 cup apples, finely chopped
2 tablespoons sugar
½ teaspoon cinnamon

Add egg, milk and margarine to flour, ½ cup sugar, baking powder and salt. Add chopped apples; stir together. Fill greased muffin tins. Mix 2 tablespoons sugar and cinnamon together. Sprinkle over the top of muffins. Bake at 400 degrees for 25–30 minutes.

Pumpkin Muffins

2½ cups flour
2 teaspoons baking soda
2 teaspoons baking powder
½ teaspoon salt
½ cup shortening
½ cup butter
2 cups brown sugar
2 eggs
2 cups pumpkin
1 teaspoon vanilla
¾ cup chopped dates
¾ cup chopped nuts

Sift together flour, baking soda, baking powder and salt; set aside. Cream shortening, butter, brown sugar and eggs. Fold dry ingredients alternately with pumpkin into egg mixture. Add vanilla, dates and nuts. Fill greased muffin cups ⅔ full. Bake at 350 degrees for 30 minutes.

Pineapple-Pumpkin Muffins

½ cup pumpkin
1 large egg
½ cup milk
½ stick butter, melted
½ cup crushed pineapple, drained
2 teaspoons baking powder
1½ cups flour
⅔ cup sugar
¾ teaspoon salt
½ teaspoon cinnamon
½ teaspoon nutmeg
¼ cup brown sugar

Combine pumpkin, egg, milk and butter. Mix together flour, baking powder, sugar, salt, cinnamon and nutmeg. Make well in center of flour mixture and pour in pumpkin mixture, blend well. Fold in pineapple. Fill buttered muffin cups ⅔ full. Sprinkle with brown sugar. Bake at 425 degrees for 20–25 minutes.

Spectacular Sweet Potato Muffins

2 tablespoons firmly packed brown sugar
1 teaspoon cinnamon
1½ cups flour
2 teaspoons baking powder
1 teaspoon cinnamon
½ teaspoon salt
½ teaspoon baking soda
½ teaspoon allspice
⅓ cup firmly packed brown sugar
1 cup cooked, mashed sweet potatoes
¾ cup buttermilk
¼ cup oil
1 egg, beaten

Mix together 2 tablespoons brown sugar and cinnamon; set aside. Sift together flour, baking powder, cinnamon, salt, baking soda, allspice and ⅓ cup brown sugar; set aside. Mix together sweet potatoes, buttermilk, oil and egg; stir into dry ingredients.

Fill greased muffin cup ⅔ full. Sprinkle each muffin with ½ teaspoon of reserved cinnamon mixture. Bake at 425 degrees for 14–16 minutes or until toothpick comes out clean. Makes 12 muffins.

Cornmeal Dumplings

2 cups white cornmeal
1 tablespoon baking soda
1 teaspoon salt
½ cup raw diced sweet potatoes
½ cup flour
4 quarts water

Mix together cornmeal, baking soda, salt, sweet potatoes and flour. Bring 4 quarts water to a rapid boil. Add enough water to dry ingredients so they stick together like biscuit dough. Pinch off dough into small pieces; mold like a biscuit and drop in hot water. Cook until they float.

Canadian Banana Bread

1 cup brown sugar
½ cup margarine, softened
1 teaspoon vanilla
3 large ripe bananas, mashed
2 eggs, well-beaten
2 cups whole-wheat flour
3 teaspoons baking powder
½ teaspoon salt
½ cup chopped nuts

Cream together sugar and margarine; add vanilla, bananas and eggs. Mix together flour, baking powder, salt and nuts; mix with creamed mixture. Pour into 1 large greased loaf pan. Bake at 350 degrees for 1 hour.

Icebox Muffins

2 cups boiling water
2 cups rolled oats
2 cups bran cereal
2 cups shredded wheat cereal, broken
3 cups sugar
1 heaping cup shortening
4 eggs
1 teaspoon salt
1 quart buttermilk
5 cups flour
5 teaspoons baking soda

Soak oats and cereals in boiling water; set aside. Cream together sugar, shortening and eggs; mix in salt, buttermilk, flour and baking soda. Blend in cereal mixture. Refrigerate for up to 3 months in tightly covered bowl leaving enough room for rising. Fill greased muffin cups 2/3 full; bake at 350 degrees for 20 minutes.

Norwegian Rye Bread

2 packages yeast
1/3 cup warm water
2 cups buttermilk
1 1/2 teaspoons salt
2/3 cup light molasses
2 tablespoons caraway seed
1/3 cup butter, melted
2 cups flour
2 cups rye flour
2 cups whole-wheat flour

Dissolve yeast in warm water. Heat buttermilk in pan. Add salt, molasses, caraway seed, butter and dissolved yeast. Gradually stir in flours until stiff. Turn dough onto floured board and knead until smooth. Place in buttered bowl, cover, and let rise until double in bulk, about 1 1/4 hours. Place in 2 buttered 8-inch loaf pans. Let rise 1 1/2 hours or until double in size. Bake at 325 degrees for 45 minutes.

Spiral Breadsticks

1 (8-count) package refrigerated breadsticks
8 (10–12-inch) metal skewers
2 teaspoons milk
1/2 teaspoon sesame seed

Unwind dough to form strips. Cut 4 strips in half crosswise; tie into knots. Place on greased baking sheet. Cut 4 remaining strips in half lengthwise. Grease skewers. Roll 1 strip around each skewer, stretching dough slightly and leaving about 1/4 inch of space between dough twists. Place on greased baking sheet, tucking ends under to secure. Brush rolls with milk; sprinkle with seeds. Bake at 325 degrees for 15–20 minutes or until golden. Serve warm.

Glazed Apple Bread

1/2 cup shortening
1 cup sugar
1/4 teaspoon salt
1 teaspoon vanilla
2 eggs
2 cups flour
2 teaspoons baking powder
2 tablespoons milk
1/4 cup nuts
1 cup apples, chopped
1/2 cup confectioners' sugar
2 tablespoons butter, melted
1 tablespoon water

Cream shortening with sugar; add salt, vanilla and eggs; mix thoroughly. Sift together flour and baking powder and add to sugar mixture with milk. Add nuts and chopped apples. Bake in greased 9 x 5 x 5-inch loaf pan, for 50–60 minutes at 350 degrees. Cool. Combine confectioners' sugar, butter and water. Pour over bread.

Boston Gingerbread

1 cup molasses
1 cup sour milk
2 1/4 cups flour
1 3/4 teaspoons baking soda
2 teaspoons ginger
1/2 teaspoon salt
1 egg, beaten
1/2 cup shortening, melted

Mix together molasses and milk; set aside. Sift together flour, baking soda, ginger and salt; stir in molasses mixture, egg and shortening. Pour into greased 9-inch square pan and bake for 350 degrees for 30 minutes or until toothpick comes out clean.

Lemon Blueberry Muffins

2 cups flour
1/2 cup sugar
3 teaspoons baking powder
1/4 teaspoon salt
1 (8-ounce) carton lemon yogurt
2 eggs
1 teaspoon vanilla
2 tablespoons oil
2 tablespoons milk
1 cup frozen blueberries

Mix together flour, sugar, baking powder and salt; set aside. Combine yogurt, eggs, vanilla, oil and milk. Make a well in dry ingredients; add liquid ingredients and frozen blueberries. Stir just until blended. Spoon in 12–14 greased muffin cups 2/3 full. Bake at 425 degrees for 15 minutes.

Pluckets

1 package yeast
1/4 cup warm water
1 cup milk
3 eggs
1/3 cup sugar
1/3 cup margarine *or* butter
1/2 teaspoon salt
4 cups flour
1 cup sugar
3 teaspoons cinnamon
1 cup nuts

Dissolve yeast in warm water. Scald milk; add sugar, margarine and salt to milk. When lukewarm add dissolved yeast and eggs. Stir well then add 2 cups flour. Add rest of the flour 1 cup at a time, beating well after each addition. Grease bowl and cover and let rise in warm place until double.

Punch down and let rise again. Punch down; take about 1 teaspoon of the dough and dip into mixture of sugar, cinnamon and nuts. Place balls into greased angel food cake pan. Let rise. Bake at 350 degrees until done, about 45 minutes. Keep checking. When done, turn pan upside down and pluck'em out and eat them.

Cherry Coffee Cake

1 packet dry yeast
1/4 cup warm water
1/3 cup sugar
1/3 cup butter
2 teaspoons salt
1/2 cup milk, scalded
2 eggs
4 cups flour
1 (1-pound, 5-ounce) can cherry pie filling
1/4 cup sugar

Soften yeast in water. Combine sugar, butter, salt and milk; cool to lukewarm. Stir in eggs and softened yeast. Gradually add up to 4 cups flour to form a stiff dough. Knead 5–7 minutes. Cover and place in greased bowl; let rise until doubled.

Roll out half of dough. Spread butter down center third; top with half of cherry pie filling. Sprinkle 1/4 cup sugar over cherries. Fold 1 side of dough over filling; fold over other side; seal edges. Place 1 end, seam side down, in center of greased 9-inch pan; wind into pan to make a flat coil. Flatten slightly. Make deep slashes from center to within 1/2 inch of outside edge, 1 inch apart. Sprinkle with sugar. Repeat with remaining dough.

Let rise until doubled, about 1 hour. Bake at 350 degrees for 30–35 minutes until golden brown. Cool slightly before removing from pans.

Italian Bread Dumplings

2 slices stale bread
1 egg
1/4 cup Romano grated cheese
2 tablespoons chopped parsley
2 teaspoons crumbled basil
1 clove minced garlic
1 teaspoon salt

Soak bread in water for 5 minutes; squeeze almost dry. Mix in egg, cheese, parsley, basil, garlic and salt. Shape into 1/2 inch balls. Drop into boiling chicken or beef bouillon; cook, covered, for 15 minutes.

Ginger Mint Loaf

2 1/4 cups flour
1 1/4 teaspoons baking soda
1 teaspoon salt
1/2 cup sugar
1/2 teaspoon ginger
1/2 teaspoon cinnamon
1/4 teaspoon cloves
2 eggs, beaten
1/2 cup milk
1/2 cup light molasses
1/2 cup oil
2 (8 1/2-ounce) cans crushed pineapple, drained
1/4 teaspoon peppermint extract

Sift together flour, baking soda, salt, sugar, ginger, cinnamon and cloves. Blend eggs, milk, molasses, oil, pineapple and peppermint extract; stir into dry ingredients. Pour into greased 9 x 5-inch loaf pan and bake at 350 degrees for 50–55 minutes. Makes 1 loaf.

Orange Nut Bread

2 1/4 cups sifted flour
3/4 cup sugar
2 1/4 teaspoons baking powder
3/4 teaspoon salt
1/4 teaspoon baking soda
3/4 cup chopped walnuts
1 tablespoon grated orange peel
1 egg, beaten
3/4 cup orange juice
2 tablespoons salad oil

Mix together flour, sugar, baking powder, salt and baking soda. Stir in walnuts and orange peel; set aside. Mix together egg, orange juice and salad oil; add to dry ingredients; stir until moistened.

Pour into a greased 9 1/2 x 4 1/2 x 2 1/2-inch loaf pan. Bake at 350 degrees for 55 minutes or until toothpick comes out clean. Remove from pan immediately and cool on rack.

Corn Sticks

1 cup sifted flour
1/4 cup sugar
4 teaspoons baking powder
3/4 teaspoon salt
1 cup yellow cornmeal
2 eggs
1 cup milk
1/4 cup shortening

Mix together flour, sugar, baking powder and salt; stir in cornmeal. Add eggs, milk and shortening. Beat until just smooth. (Do not overbeat.) Pour into greased corn-stick pans, filling 2/3 full. Bake at 425 degrees for 12–15 minutes. Makes 18.

Peanut Butter Bacon Bread

1 cup sugar
1 tablespoon melted shortening
1 cup milk
1 egg, well beaten
1 cup peanut butter
1/2 teaspoon salt
2 cups flour
3 teaspoons baking powder
1 cup chopped unsalted peanuts
1 cup finely chopped fried bacon

Mix together sugar, shortening and milk with egg. Add peanut butter. Mix in salt, flour and baking powder. Add nuts and bacon. Let stand in a greased and floured loaf pan for 20 minutes. Bake at 350 degrees for 1 hour or until toothpick comes out clean.

Apple Corn Bread

2 cups yellow cornmeal
1/4 cup sugar
1 1/2 teaspoons salt
2 cups buttermilk
2 tablespoons shortening, melted
2 teaspoons baking soda
1 tablespoons water
2 eggs, well beaten
1 cup apple, chopped

Mix cornmeal, sugar, salt, buttermilk and shortening in top part of double boiler. Cook over hot water 10 minutes, stirring frequently. Cool. Dissolve baking soda in cold water; combine with eggs and apples. Stir together cornmeal mixture and baking soda mixture. Bake in greased 8 x 8-inch pan at 400 degrees for 20–25 minutes. Serves 8.

Whole-Wheat Carrot Banana Bread

½ cup butter or margarine
1 cup packed brown sugar
2 eggs
1 cup flour
1 cup whole-wheat flour
1 teaspoon baking soda
½ teaspoon baking powder
½ teaspoon ground cinnamon
½ teaspoon salt
1 cup ripe, mashed banana
1 cup finely shredded carrots
½ cup walnuts

Beat butter for 30 seconds; add sugar and beat until fluffy. Beat in eggs; combine flours, baking soda, baking powder, cinnamon and salt. Add dry ingredients and banana alternately to butter mixture, beating after each addition. Fold in carrots and nuts. Pour into 2 greased 71/2 x 33/4 x 2-inch loaf pans. Bake at 350 degrees for 40–50 minutes. Makes 2

Zucchini Parmesan Bread

3 cups flour
1 cup shredded zucchini
⅓ cup sugar
3 tablespoons grated Parmesan cheese
½ teaspoon baking soda
1 teaspoon baking powder
1 teaspoon salt
⅓ cup butter, melted
1 cup buttermilk
2 eggs, beaten
1 tablespoon grated onion

Combine flour, zucchini, sugar, cheese, baking soda, baking powder and salt; set aside. Stir butter into buttermilk. Mix together eggs with buttermilk mixture and onion; stir into flour mixture. Bake in greased and floured 9 x 5 x 3-inch loaf pan at 350 degrees for 1 hour.

Sopapillas

3 cups lukewarm water
1¼ tablespoons salt
2 tablespoons shortening

1 package dry yeast
5–6 cups flour
1 tablespoon sugar

Add sugar to water; sprinkle in yeast and let stand until yeast dissolves. Add salt, shortening and 1 cup flour to yeast mixture. Mix well. Continue adding flour, a cup at a time, mixing well after each addition, until dough no longer sticks to hands. Knead 5 minutes. Grease dough with small amount of shortening and cover, letting rise in warm place for 1 hour.

Roll a small amount of dough at a time to ⅛ inch thickness. Cut into 3–4 squares. Fry squares a few at a time in deep hot oil in heavy pot until sopapillas are golden on both sides. Drain on paper towels and serve hot.

Polish Doughnuts

1 cake yeast
2 cups milk, scalded
7 cups flour
4 egg yolks
1 egg
½ cup sugar
½ teaspoon vanilla
Rind of lemon, grated
1 teaspoon salt
½ cup butter, melted

Dissolve yeast in lukewarm milk; add 2 cups flour. Let stand in warm place about ½ hour. Beat together egg yolks, egg, sugar, vanilla, lemon rind and salt until light; add to flour mixture. Stir in butter and remaining flour; beat well. Cover and let rise until doubled in size.

Place on floured board; pat until dough is 1-inch thick. Cut with doughnut cutter and let rise. Fry in deep fat of 365 degrees for about 3 minutes.

Cowboy Rolls

3 cups warm water
1 cup warm milk
1 cup sugar
½ cup shortening
½ teaspoon salt
4 tablespoons yeast
2 eggs, beaten
½ cup whole-wheat flour
1 cup oatmeal

3 cups flour
Brown sugar
Cinnamon

Mix water, milk, sugar, shortening, salt, yeast and eggs together in a large mixing bowl. Add whole-wheat flour, oatmeal and flour; mix well. Let set approximately 10 minutes. Add more flour if needed until it's springing but holds together. Knead well; let rise 2 times. Roll out and sprinkle with brown sugar and cinnamon. Roll up and cut in 1–1½-inch slices. Let rise then bake at 350–375 degrees for 15–20 minutes. Frost with favorite icing.

Sweet Rolls

1 cup milk
1 stick margarine
⅓ cup sugar
1 package yeast
2 eggs, beaten
½ teaspoon salt
4 cups flour

Scald milk. Place margarine and sugar in large bowl. Stir in milk, stirring to melt margarine. Add eggs, yeast and salt. Mix well. Add 2 cups flour beating very well. Add rest of flour. Knead well. Let rise in warm place. Punch down. Make into rolls, cinnamon rolls or tea ring. Let rise again until double. Bake at 350 degrees until golden brown and done (30–40 minutes).

To Make Cinnamon Rolls

½ cup margarine, melted
3 teaspoon cinnamon
1½ cups sugar

Roll out dough. Brush with margarine and sprinkle with cinnamon and sugar mixture.

Spoon Rolls

1 package dry yeast
2 tablespoons warm water
2 cups warm water
¾ cup oil
4 cups self-rising flour
1 egg
1 tablespoon sugar

Dissolve yeast in 2 tablespoons water. Combine 2 cups water, oil, flour, egg and sugar; add yeast mixture and blend well. Spoon into greased muffin tins and bake at 400 degrees for 15–20 minutes. Makes 2–3 dozen rolls.

Applesauce Gingerbread

2 cups flour
½ cup sugar
1 teaspoon ginger
2 eggs
1 cup applesauce
½ cup molasses

Sift together flour, sugar and ginger. Add eggs, applesauce and molasses; stir well. Do not overbeat. Pour batter into a greased bread pan. Bake at 350 degrees for 35–45 minutes, or until toothpick inserted comes out clean.

Pineapple Pecan Bread

¼ cup butter *or* margarine
¾ cup brown sugar
1 egg
1¾ cups flour
¼ cup wheat germ
1 teaspoon baking powder
½ teaspoon salt
1 (6-ounce) can frozen orange juice concentrate, thawed
1 (8¾-ounce) can crushed pineapple
½ cup chopped pecans

Cream butter, sugar and egg until light and fluffy. Sift together flour, wheat germ, baking powder and salt; add flour mixture alternately with orange juice concentrate. Stir in pineapple and nuts. Bake in greased and floured 9-inch loaf pan for 60 minutes at 350 degrees.

Southern Buttermilk Biscuits

⅓ cup shortening
2 cups flour
2 teaspoons sugar
2 teaspoons baking powder
1 teaspoon salt
½ teaspoon baking soda
⅔ cup buttermilk

Cut shortening into flour, sugar, baking powder, salt and baking soda. Stir in almost all the buttermilk until the mixture rounds up into a ball and no dry ingredients remain in bowl. Dough should not be sticky. Knead lightly 20–25 times on lightly floured board.

Roll ½-inch thick; cut with floured 2-inch biscuit cutter. Bake on ungreased cookie sheet about 1 inch apart at 450 degrees for 10–12 minutes or until golden brown. Makes 1½ dozen biscuits.

Honey Orange Loaf

2 tablespoons shortening
1 cup honey
1 egg, beaten
1½ tablespoons grated orange rind
¾ cup orange juice
2¼ cups flour
2¼ tablespoons baking powder
½ teaspoon salt
¾ cup chopped pecans

Cream together shortening and honey. Add egg and orange rind. Sift together flour, baking powder and salt; add alternately with orange juice. Add chopped nuts. Pour into greased loaf pan and bake at 350 degrees for 1 hour and 10 minutes or until nicely browned.

Surprise Bran Muffins

2 cups whole bran cereal
2 cups buttermilk
2 eggs
½ cup oil
2 cups flour
⅔ cup firmly packed brown sugar
2 teaspoons baking powder
2 teaspoons baking soda
1 teaspoon salt
Orange marmalade

Mix cereal with buttermilk; let stand 3 minutes. Beat in eggs and oil; stir in flour, brown sugar, baking powder, baking soda and salt, mixing until moistened. Fill greased muffin tins ½ full. Drop 1 teaspoon orange marmalade in center of each; add enough batter to fill cups ⅔ full. Bake at 400 degrees for 15–20 minutes. Makes 2 dozen muffins.

Soda Cracker Dumplings

2 packages crackers, coarsely crumbled
2 tablespoons butter, melted
3 dashes nutmeg
2 tablespoons flour
2 eggs
¾ cup milk
chicken gravy

Mix together cracker crumbs, butter, nutmeg and 2 tablespoons flour with a fork. Add eggs and milk. Mixture will feel like hamburger. Shape into golf-ball-size balls. Place in chicken gravy. Cover and simmer 12 minutes. Makes 24 dumplings.

Date Nut Bread

¾ cup flour
½ teaspoon salt
½ teaspoon baking powder
1 cup chopped dates
½ cup chopped nuts
2 eggs
1 cup firmly packed brown sugar
Confectioners' sugar

Sift together flour, salt and baking powder; stir in dates and nuts to coat. Beat eggs until light. Gradually beat in sugar; stir in dry ingredients. Bake in well-greased shallow pan at 350 degrees for 30 minutes. Cool and cut in strips. Roll in confectioners' sugar.

Strawberry Bread

3 cups flour
1 teaspoon baking soda
½ teaspoon salt
1 tablespoon cinnamon
2 cups sugar
3 eggs, beaten
1 cup oil
2 (10-ounce) packages frozen strawberries, slightly thawed

Combine flour, baking soda, salt, cinnamon and sugar. Stir together eggs, oil and strawberries; add to flour mixture, mixing well. Bake in 2 greased and floured 8 x 5 x 3-inch loaf pans at 350 degrees for 60 minutes or until toothpick comes out clean.

Brunch FARE

Pumpkin Waffles

- 2 large eggs
- 2 tablespoons brown sugar
- 1 cup half-and-half
- 4 tablespoons butter, melted and cooled
- 1 cup all-purpose flour
- 1½ teaspoons baking powder
- ½ teaspoon salt
- ¼ teaspoon pumpkin pie spice
- ½ cup canned pumpkin purée
- ½ Granny Smith apple, pared, cored and cut into small pieces
- ½ cup chopped, toasted walnuts

Whisk eggs and brown sugar together in mixing bowl. Add half-and-half and butter; whisk until blended. Mix flour, baking powder, salt and pie spice in another bowl. Add to egg mixture and stir just until blended. Stir in pumpkin; fold in apple and walnuts.

Heat waffle iron as directed and make waffles. Use generous ¾ cup batter for large iron. Serve with butter and warm maple syrup.

Apple Fritters

- 2 cups milk
- 3 eggs
- ½ teaspoon salt
- 2 cups flour
- 1 teaspoon baking powder
  Sliced apples

Mix together milk and eggs; add salt, flour and baking powder. Dip apple slices in batter and fry in butter. *Variation:* Chop apples and add to batter; deep fry. You can either glaze them or roll in cinnamon sugar.

Peach Coffee Cake

- 2⅓ cups flour
- 1⅓ cups sugar
- ¾ teaspoon salt
- ¾ cup shortening
- 2 teaspoons baking powder
- ¾ cup milk
- 2 eggs
- 1 teaspoon vanilla
- 1 (3-ounce) package cream cheese, softened
- 1 (14-ounce) can sweetened condensed milk
- ⅓ cup lemon juice
- 2 teaspoons ground cinnamon, divided
- 1 (29-ounce) can sliced peaches, well drained, chopped
- 1 cup chopped nuts, divided
- ⅓ cup firmly packed brown sugar

Combine flour, sugar and salt; cut in shortening until crumbly; reserve 1 cup crumb mixture. To remaining crumb mixture add baking powder, then milk, eggs and vanilla. Beat on medium speed with an electric mixer for 2 minutes.

Spread into greased 13 x 9-inch baking pan. Bake at 350 degrees for 25 minutes. Beat cream cheese until fluffy; gradually beat in milk; stir in lemon juice, then peaches, ½ cup nuts and 1 teaspoon cinnamon. Combine reserved crumb mixture, remaining ½ cup nuts, 1 teaspoon cinnamon and brown sugar.

Spoon peach mixture evenly on top of cake. Sprinkle with crumb mixture. Bake 35 minutes longer until set. Cool. Serve warm.

French Toast With Brandied Lemon Butter

- 4 eggs
- 2 tablespoons and 1 teaspoon sugar
- ½ teaspoon salt
- 1 cup whole milk
- ¼ teaspoon vanilla extract
- 12 thick slices bread (cut and left overnight to dry out)
  Butter
  Confectioners' sugar
  Brandied Lemon Butter (recipe follows)

In shallow dish, beat eggs, sugar, salt, milk and vanilla. Soak bread in the mixture. Heat butter over medium-high heat and cook each slice until slightly brown on each side.

Serve with Brandied Lemon Butter and lemon slices, if desired. Sprinkle with confectioners' sugar. Serves 6.

Brandied Lemon Butter

- ½ cup butter *or* margarine
- 1 cup sugar
  Juice of 2 lemons
- 4 teaspoons grated lemon rind
- 3 ounces rum *or* brandy

Melt butter over low heat. Spoon off any foam that forms. Pour into a dish, leaving sediment in the pan. Wash pan. Pour in the clarified butter and sugar. Stir continuously until sugar dissolves. Add rind, juice and rum; stir until smooth. Pour over hot toast.

Fresh Strawberry Bread

- 1 pint fresh strawberries
- 1¼ cups flour
- 1 teaspoon baking soda
- ¾ teaspoon salt
- ½ teaspoon cinnamon
- ¼ teaspoon baking powder
- 1 cup sugar
- ⅓ cup shortening
- 2 eggs
- ¼ teaspoon vanilla
- ⅓ cup water
- ½ cup chopped walnuts
- Cream cheese, optional

Crush enough berries to make 1 cup; pour into saucepan and heat to boiling. Cook 1 minute, stirring constantly; cool. Slice remaining strawberries; chill. Combine flour, baking soda, salt, cinnamon and baking powder; set aside. Cream together sugar, shortening, eggs and vanilla until light and fluffy; add dry ingredients alternately with water. Stir in crushed strawberries. Fold in walnuts.

Spread batter in greased 9 x 5 x 3-inch loaf pan. Bake at 350 degrees for 50–60 minutes; cool 10 minutes before removing from pan. To serve; slice, spread with cream cheese and top with reserved sliced strawberries.

Danish Apple Coffee Cake

- 1 packet active dry yeast
- ¼ cup warm water
- 2¾ cups flour
- 1 teaspoon salt
- ½ cup butter
- ½ cup sour cream
- 2 eggs
- 1 cup sugar
- 2 teaspoons cinnamon
- 2 tablespoons bread crumbs
- Butter
- Apple Filling (recipe follows)

Soften yeast in warm water. Combine flour with salt; cut in butter until crumbly. Add sour cream, eggs and softened yeast. Mix to form dough. Cover. Chill 2 hours. Combine sugar and cinnamon. Sprinkle 2 tablespoons on rolling surface. Roll out half of dough, to a 12 x 8-inch rectangle. Sprinkle with 2 tablespoons sugar-cinnamon mixture. Fold in half.

Repeat rolling and folding 2 more times, adding sugar-cinnamon as necessary. Roll out again. Sprinkle 1 tablespoon bread crumbs down center third of rectangle. Place half of Filling over crumbs.

Sprinkle with 1 tablespoon bread crumbs; dot with butter. Fold 1 side of dough over Filling, then fold opposite side to overlap. Seal edges. Place, seam side up, on greased cookie sheet. Make deep diagonal slashes across top about 3 inches apart and to within ½ inch of edge. Repeat with other half of dough. Let rise 30 minutes. Bake at 350 degrees for 30–35 minutes until golden brown.

Apple Filling

- 1 (1-pound, 4-ounce) can apple pie slices
- ½ cup sugar
- 2 teaspoons cinnamon
- 1 teaspoon grated lemon rind
- ¼ teaspoon nutmeg

Drain apples on paper towels. Combine with sugar, cinnamon, lemon rind and nutmeg.

Bacon-Nut Bread

- 2 cups flour
- ⅓ cup sugar
- 2½ teaspoons baking powder
- 1 teaspoon salt
- 2 (3-ounce) packages cream cheese, softened
- 1 egg
- ¼ cup bacon drippings
- ¾ cup milk
- ¾ cup chopped walnuts
- ¼ cup chopped green peppers
- ¼ cup chopped onion
- 5 strips bacon, crisply fried, crumbled

Sift together flour, sugar, baking powder and salt; set aside. Stir together cream cheese, egg and bacon drippings; cream well. Gradually add milk. Stir in nuts, green pepper, onion and bacon; blend in dry ingredients. Stir until dry particles are moistened. Place in a 9 x 5 x 3-inch pan greased on bottom. Bake at 350 degrees for 60–65 minutes. Let stand at least 4 hours before slicing.

Raspberry Cream Cheese Coffee Cake

- 3 ounces cream cheese
- ¼ cup margarine
- 2 cups biscuit mix
- ⅓ cup milk
- ½ cup raspberry preserves
- Confectioners' Sugar Glaze (recipe follows)

Cut cream cheese and margarine into biscuit mix until crumbly; blend in milk. Turn onto floured surface and knead 8–10 strokes. On waxed paper, roll dough to a 12 x 8-inch rectangle. Turn onto greased baking sheet and remove paper. Spread preserves down center of dough. Make 2½-inch cuts at 1-inch intervals on long sides. Fold strips over filling. Bake 12–15 minutes. at 375degrees. Drizzle with glaze while still warm.

Confectioners' Sugar Glaze

- 1½ cups confectioners' sugar
- 2 tablespoons butter
- 1½ teaspoons vanilla
- 1–2 tablespoons hot water

Beat together sugar, butter, vanilla and enough water for a good spreading consistency.

Apple Rolls

- 4 cups flour
- 1 teaspoon salt
- 3 tablespoons shortening
- 4 tablespoons sugar
- 8 teaspoons baking powder
- Milk
- Butter
- Chopped apples
- 3 cups sugar
- 2 cups hot water
- 2 tablespoons flour
- 1 teaspoon salt

Mix together flour, 1 teaspoon salt, shortening, 4 tablespoons sugar and baking powder with enough milk to make a soft dough. Roll out, then spread with butter and chopped apples. Roll up and cut into pieces. Make a syrup out of the remaining sugar, water, flour and salt. Pour hot syrup over rolls and bake for 40–45 minutes at 350 degrees.

Breakfast Bubble Buns

- 1/3 cup sugar
- 1/2 teaspoon cinnamon
- 1/2 cup finely chopped walnuts
- 1 (10-count) package refrigerated biscuits
- 1/3 cup mayonnaise

Combine sugar, cinnamon and walnuts. Separate biscuits; cut into quarters; shape into balls. Coat each with mayonnaise; roll in walnut mixture. Place 4 balls in 10 greased muffin cups. Bake at 400 degrees for 15–17 minutes, or until browned. Makes 10 buns.

Eggs Benedict Casserole

- 2 1/2 cups dried cooked smoked ham
- 10 eggs
- 1/4 teaspoon pepper
  Mornay Sauce (recipe follows)
- 1 cup crushed cornflake cereal
- 1/4 cup margarine, melted

Arrange ham in ungreased 13 x 9 x 2-inch baking dish. Heat 1 1/2–2 inches water to boiling; reduce to simmering. Holding egg close to water, carefully slip egg into water. Cook until egg is just set, 3 minutes. Remove from water; place on ham. Repeat with remaining eggs.

Sprinkle eggs with pepper. Pour Mornay Sauce over eggs. Combine cornflakes with margarine, sprinkle over casserole. Bake, uncovered, at 350 degrees for 25–30 minutes.

Mornay Sauce

- 1/4 cup margarine
- 1/4 cup flour
- 1/2 teaspoon salt
- 1/8 teaspoon ground nutmeg
- 2 1/2 cups milk
- 1 1/2 cups shredded Swiss cheese
- 1/2 cup grated Parmesan cheese

Melt margarine over low heat; blend in flour, salt and nutmeg. Cook over low heat, stirring constantly, until smooth and bubbly; remove from heat. Stir in milk. Heat to boiling, stirring constantly. Boil and stir 1 minute. Add Swiss and Parmesan cheeses; cook and stir until cheese is melted and mixture is smooth.

Huckleberry-Pecan Bread

- 2 cups flour
- 2/3 cup sugar
- 1 1/2 teaspoons baking powder
- 1/2 teaspoon baking soda
- 1/2 teaspoon salt
  Juice of 1 orange
  Rind of 1 orange, grated
- 2 tablespoons butter, melted
- 1/2 cup boiling water
- 1 cup huckleberries
- 1 1/2 cups chopped pecans

Sift together 1 3/4 cup flour, sugar, baking powder, baking soda and salt. In measuring cup, add juice, grated rind and melted butter; add enough boiling water to make 3/4 cup. Blend liquid with dry ingredients; mix well; set aside. Combine berries, pecans and remaining 1/4 cup flour; gently add this into batter to keep from mashing berries.

Spoon into 9 x 5-inch greased waxed-paper–lined pan. Bake at 350 degrees for 1 hour or until pick comes out clean. Remove loaf from pan and cool on rack. Makes 1 loaf.

Breakfast Pizza

- 3/4 cup spaghetti sauce
- 1/2 pound pork sausage, browned, drained
- 1 (4-ounce) package refrigerated crescent rolls
- 1 cup cooked brown rice
- 1/4 cup shredded mild cheddar cheese, shredded
- 4 eggs, beaten
- 1/4 cup milk
- 1/2 teaspoon salt
- 1/8 teaspoon pepper
- 2 tablespoons grated Parmesan cheese

Mix together eggs, milk, salt and pepper; set aside. Combine sausage with brown rice. Place crescent rolls in lightly greased electric skillet. Spoon rice mixture and spaghetti sauce over rolls and top with cheddar cheese. Pour egg mixture over this. Sprinkle with Parmesan cheese and bake at 300 degrees for 30 minutes. Cut in wedges or squares to serve.

Coffee Praline Muffins

- 1 3/4 cups flour
- 1/3 cup brown sugar
- 1 tablespoon baking powder
- 1/4 teaspoon salt
- 1/2 cup chopped pecans
- 2 tablespoons instant coffee
- 1 egg
- 3/4 cup milk
- 1 1/4 teaspoon vanilla
- 1/2 cup butter, melted
- 1 tablespoon sugar
- 2 tablespoons chopped pecans

Combine flour, brown sugar, baking powder, salt and pecans; set aside. Mix together instant coffee, egg, milk, vanilla and butter; blend with dry ingredients just until moistened. Pour into 8–12 greased muffin tins and sprinkle with mixture of 1 tablespoon sugar and 2 tablespoons pecans. Bake at 375 degrees for 18–20 minutes. Makes 8–12 muffins.

Old-Fashioned Doughnuts

- 2 1/2 cups flour
- 1/2 teaspoon salt
- 3 teaspoons baking powder
- 1/2 teaspoon cinnamon
- 1/4 teaspoon nutmeg
- 1/2 cup sugar
- 1 egg, beaten
- 1/2 cup milk
- 1 teaspoon grated lemon rind
- 2 tablespoons butter, melted
  Shortening
  Confectioners' sugar

Sift together flour, salt, baking powder, spices and sugar. Mix together egg; stir in milk, lemon rind and butter. Blend into flour mixture, stirring until all flour is moistened. Chill 15 minutes. Roll dough out to 1/2-inch thickness on well-floured board. Cut with 3-inch doughnut cutter. Heat shortening to 375 degrees. Gently drop doughnuts into 1–2 inches of shortening, 3–4 at a time. As they rise to surface, turn with fork to brown other side, about 3 minutes. Drain. Dust with confectioners' sugar. Makes 1 dozen doughnuts.

Morning Glory Muffins

3 eggs
1 cup oil
2 teaspoon vanilla
2 cups grated carrots
½ cup chopped nuts
1 apple, peeled, grated
½ cup coconut
1 cup raisins
2 cups flour
2 teaspoon baking soda
¼ teaspoon nutmeg
½ cup brown sugar
½ cup sugar
2 teaspoons cinnamon
¼ teaspoon salt

Mix together eggs, oil and vanilla. Add carrots, apple, nuts, coconut and raisins. Mix well; add flour, baking soda, nutmeg, brown sugar, sugar, cinnamon and salt. Use paper liners and fill muffin cups ⅔ full. Bake at 350 degrees for 15–20 minutes until they spring back to the touch. Makes 24 muffins.

Quick Hot Cross Buns

1 (8-ounce) package cream cheese, softened
1 egg
2 tablespoons sugar
¼ cup raisins
2 packages buttermilk refrigerator biscuits
1 cup confectioners' sugar
1 egg white, beaten

In blender, purée cream cheese, egg and sugar. Stir in raisins; set aside. Press 2 biscuits together; flatten to make a 4-inch square. Repeat to make 9 more squares. Spoon cream cheese mixture filling onto center of dough. Pull diagonal corners together over filling and pinch to seal. Repeat with the other 2 corners.

Arrange buns in greased 9-inch pie plate. Bake at 400 degrees for 25–30 minutes. Cool. Combine confectioners' sugar with egg white. Drizzle onto buns to resemble crosses. Serve warm.

Pumpkin Doughnut Drops

1½ cups flour
⅓ cup sugar
2 teaspoons baking powder
½ teaspoon salt
¼ teaspoon cinnamon
¼ teaspoon nutmeg
¼ teaspoon ginger
¼ cup milk
½ cup canned pumpkin
2 tablespoons oil
½ teaspoon vanilla
1 egg
½ cup sugar
1 teaspoon cinnamon

Combine flour, sugar, baking powder, salt, cinnamon, nutmeg and ginger. Stir in milk, pumpkin, oil, vanilla and egg with a fork just until dry ingredients are moistened.

Drop by teaspoonfuls into 375-degree oil 5–6 at a time. Fry doughnuts for 1–1½ minutes on each side until deep golden brown. Drain. Mix together ½ cup sugar and 1 teaspoon cinnamon; roll warm doughnut balls in sugar mixture. Makes 30–36 doughnut balls.

Cake Doughnuts

4½ cups flour
1 cup sugar
3 teaspoons baking powder
1 teaspoon baking soda
1 teaspoon salt
½ teaspoon nutmeg
1 cup buttermilk
¼ cup margarine, melted
1 teaspoon vanilla
2 eggs, slightly beaten
Oil

Combine flour, sugar, baking powder, baking soda, salt and nutmeg. Stir in buttermilk, margarine, vanilla and eggs just until dry ingredients are moistened.

Heat 2–3 inches oil in skillet to 375 degrees. Toss dough on well-floured surface until no longer sticky. Roll half the dough at a time to ⅜-inch thickness. Cut with doughnut cutter. Fry doughnuts 1½ minutes on each side or until deep golden brown. Drain. Makes 30 doughnuts.

Banana Doughnuts

3 cups shortening
4 cups flour
¾ cup sugar
4 teaspoons baking powder
1 teaspoon salt
½ teaspoon cinnamon
½ teaspoon nutmeg
¼ cup butter
1 cup mashed ripe bananas
2 eggs, well-beaten
Topping (recipe follows)

In deep-fat fryer, heat shortening to 375 degrees. Mix together flour, sugar, baking powder, salt, cinnamon and nutmeg. Cut in butter. Make a well in center and add bananas and eggs; mix well. On lightly floured board roll dough to ½-inch thickness. Cut with 2½-inch doughnut cutter. Deep-fry until golden brown. Drain. Combine topping and dip warm doughnuts in the mixture. Makes 22 doughnuts.

Topping

¾ cup sugar
2 teaspoons cinnamon

Blend sugar and cinnamon.

Fresh Peach Muffins

1 cup whole-wheat flour
1 cup flour
1½ teaspoons baking powder
½ teaspoon baking soda
½ teaspoon cinnamon
1 egg
⅔ cup brown sugar
¾ cup buttermilk
¼ cup corn oil
½ teaspoon almond extract
1 cup finely chopped fresh peaches
Dash nutmeg

Combine flours, baking powder, baking soda and cinnamon; set aside. Mix together egg, brown sugar, buttermilk, corn oil and almond extract; blend well. Gently fold dry ingredients into liquid ingredients; fold in peaches. Fill 12 greased muffin cups. Bake at 375 degrees for 20–25 minutes. Sprinkle with nutmeg.

Cream Cheese Pumpkin Coffee Cake

1 (8-ounce) package cream cheese
1/4 cup sugar
1/2 teaspoon vanilla
1 cup packed brown sugar
3/4 cup sugar
2/3 cup vegetable oil
2 eggs
3/4 cup buttermilk
3/4 cup cooked *or* canned pumpkin
2 cups flour
1/2 teaspoon baking powder
1/2 teaspoon baking soda
1/2 teaspoon salt
1 teaspoon cinnamon
1 teaspoon nutmeg
1/4 teaspoon ginger

Microwave cream cheese on HIGH for 30–45 seconds; blend in sugar and vanilla until creamy; set aside. Combine sugars and oil in large bowl; blend well. Beat in eggs 1 at a time; beat well after each addition. Blend in buttermilk and pumpkin; add flour, baking powder, soda, salt, cinnamon, nutmeg and ginger; beat just until smooth.

Use tube microwave springform pan; spray lightly with non-stick cooking spray. Pour cake batter into pan; spread evenly. Spoon cream cheese mixture by teaspoonfuls onto batter, staying away from edge of pan.

Microwave on MEDIUM (50 percent) power, uncovered, 15–16 minutes; rotate pan once. Microwave on HIGH 5–6 minutes; rotate pan twice, if necessary. Let stand 10 minutes. When springform pan is not available use a 12 x 8-inch baking dish. Top with cream cheese mixture; swirl lightly, microwave on MEDIUM (50 percent) power for 12 minutes; rotate dish once. Microwave on HIGH 6–8 minutes.

Streusel Coffee Cake

1 box yellow cake mix
1 package yeast
1 cup flour
2/3 cup warm water
2 eggs
5 tablespoons margarine, melted and cooled
2 teaspoons sugar
1 can pie filling

Beat 1 1/2 cups cake mix, yeast, flour, eggs and water with an electric mixer for 2 minutes. Spread in 9 x 13-inch greased pan. Mix remaining cake mix with cooled margarineand sugar until mixture resembles coarse crumbs. Top dough with any pie filling desired and top with crumb mixture. Bake at 375 degrees for 30 minutes.

Walnutty Pancakes

2 cups biscuit baking mix
2 eggs
1 cup milk
1 teaspoon maple-flavored extract
1/2 cup chopped walnuts
Maple syrup

Beat biscuit mix, eggs, milk and extract together. Add walnuts. Pour 1/4 cupfuls of batter onto hot greased griddle. Cook until dry around edges. Turn; cook until golden in color. Makes 13 pancakes. Serve with maple syrup.

Honey-Filled Biscuits

1 cup flour
1/4 cup sugar
1/4 teaspoon salt
1/3 cup butter *or* margarine
2 egg yolks
1 cup finely chopped candied fruits
Honey
Confectioners' sugar

Make a smooth paste of sugar, salt, butter and egg yolks; stir in flour until well-blended. Mix in fruits. Chill 2 hours. Roll dough 1/8 inch thick on lightly floured board; cut in 2-inch fluted rounds.

Bake on ungreased baking sheet at 350 degrees for 8–10 minutes or until tinged with brown. Cool; put together, sandwich fashion, with honey as filling. Sprinkle tops with confectioners' sugar. Makes 2 dozen biscuits.

One-Rise Cinnamon Rolls

1 cup whipping cream
1 cup brown sugar
3 1/2 cups flour
1 package yeast
1/4 cup sugar
1 teaspoon salt
1 cup hot water
2 tablespoons butter, softened
1 egg
1/2 cup sugar
2 teaspoons cinnamon
1/2 cup butter, softened

Mix together whipping cream and brown sugar; pour into 9 x 13-inch pan. Mix together 1 1/2 cups flour, yeast, sugar, salt, water, butter and egg. Beat on medium speed for 3 minutes. Stir in remaining 1 1/2–2 cups flour. Knead on floured board for 1 minute. Roll out dough into 15 x 7-inch rectangle.

Mix together sugar, cinnamon and butter. Sprinkle filling over dough. Roll up jelly roll fashion, starting at long end. Cut into 1–1 1/2-inch sections. Place rolls onto cream mixture. Cover and let rise for 30–45 minutes or until double in size. Bake at 400 degrees for 25 minutes. Cool for 10–15 minutes before inverting onto serving tray.

Key Lime Muffins

2 cups flour
1 cup sugar
1 tablespoon baking powder
1/2 teaspoon salt
1/4 cup milk
2 eggs, beaten
1/4 cup oil
1 teaspoon grated lime rind
1/4 cup plus 2 tablespoons lime juice

Sift together flour, sugar, baking powder and salt; set aside. Mix together milk, eggs, oil, lime rind and lime juice; add all at once to dry ingredients. Stir lightly with fork just until moistened. Batter will be lumpy. Spoon into greased muffin cups, filling 3/4 full. Bake at 400 degrees for 20 minutes.

Rhubarb Coffee Cake

½ cup margarine

1¼ cups sugar

1 egg

2 cups flour

1 teaspoon baking soda

½ teaspoon salt

1 cup buttermilk

1 teaspoon vanilla

2 cups chopped rhubarb

Dash cinnamon

1 teaspoon cinnamon

½ cup sugar

2 tablespoons margarine

½ cup chopped nuts

Cream together margarine and 1¼ cups sugar until light; beat in egg. Sift flour, baking soda and salt; alternately add to creamed mixture with buttermilk. Fold in vanilla, rhubarb and dash cinnamon. Pour into greased 9 x 13-inch pan. Combine 1 teaspoon cinnamon, ½ cup sugar, margarine and nuts; sprinkle over batter. Bake at 350 degrees for 40 minutes.

Croissant French Toast

⅔ cup half-and-half

3 eggs

⅓ cup orange juice

1 teaspoon sugar

1 teaspoon vanilla

1 teaspoon grated orange peel

¼ teaspoon ground cinnamon

⅛ teaspoon ground nutmeg

4 day-old croissants, halved lengthwise

2 tablespoons unsalted butter

Confectioners' sugar

Maple syrup

Whisk first 8 ingredients in medium bowl. Add croissants to egg batter and turn until thoroughly coated. Melt butter in heavy large skillet over medium-high heat. Add croissants and cook until golden brown on both sides, about 3 minutes per side. Sift confectioners' sugar over. Serve with maple syrup. Serves 4.

French Toast With Currant Jelly Sauce (Challah Egg Bread)

1 cup milk

½ cup half-and-half

2 eggs

2 tablespoons *plus* 1½ teaspoons sugar

2 teaspoons grated orange peel

½ teaspoon vanilla extract

½ teaspoon salt

¼ teaspoon ground cardamom

4 (1-inch-thick) slices egg bread *or* French bread

¼ cup butter

Currant Jelly Sauce (recipe follows)

Whisk first 8 ingredients in shallow dish to blend. Add bread and soak 15 minutes, turning once. Melt butter in heavy large skillet over medium-low heat. Add bread and cook until outside is golden brown, but inside is still custardlike, about 5 minutes per side. Transfer to plates. Spoon sauce over. Serves 2.

Currant Jelly Sauce

½ cup red currant jelly

¼ cup fresh orange juice

½ teaspoon (scant) ground cardamom

2 tablespoons butter *or* margarine

Melt jelly with orange juice and cardamom in heavy small saucepan over medium heat, stirring constantly. Boil until syrupy, about 3 minutes. Remove from heat and whisk in 2 tablespoons butter.

Fabulous French Toast

2 eggs

⅓ cup milk

¼ teaspoon salt

4 slices bread, 1 inch thick

Oil

Syrup

Beat eggs with milk and salt. Trim crusts from bread and cut in half; dip in egg mixture. Let set for a few seconds and then turn over. Fry in oil heated to 365 degrees for 2 minutes. Drain. Serve with syrup.

Pineapple Poppins

1 tablespoon baking powder

½ teaspoon salt

½ cup sugar

2 cups flour

1 cup crushed pineapple, drained, reserve juice

¼ cup margarine

¾ cup milk

1 egg, beaten

¼ cup pineapple juice

½ cup flour

⅓ cup brown sugar

¼ teaspoon cinnamon

¼ cup margarine, melted

Dash cinnamon

Chopped nuts

Maraschino cherries, halved

Sift together baking powder, salt, ½ cup sugar and 2 cups flour; set aside. Combine pineapple, margarine, milk, egg and pineapple juice; stir into sifted ingredients. Fill greased muffin cups ¾ full. Combine ½ cup flour, cinnamon, brown sugar and margarine; brush over unbaked poppins. Bake at 375 degrees for 20–25 minutes. Garnish with cherries and nuts.

Pumpkin Muffins

¼ cup vegetable oil

½ cup plain yogurt

¾ cup sugar

2 eggs

¾ cup canned pumpkin

2 cups flour

¼ teaspoon baking powder

¼ teaspoon baking soda

¼ teaspoon salt

1 teaspoon cinnamon

¼ teaspoon ginger

⅛ teaspoon cloves

Combine oil, yogurt, sugar and eggs; mix well; blend in pumpkin. Add flour, baking powder, soda, salt, cinnamon, ginger and cloves; mix until well-blended. Spoon mixture into paper-lined microwave muffin pan, filling cups⅔s full. Microwave on HIGH, 6 muffins at a time, uncovered, for 2–2½ minutes; rotate pan if needed. Continue with remaining batter. Makes 18 muffins.

Baked "Overnight" French Toast

¼ cup butter, room temperature
12 (¾-inch-thick) French bread slices
6 eggs
1½ cups milk
¼ cup sugar
2 tablespoons maple syrup
1 teaspoon vanilla
½ teaspoon salt
   Confectioners' sugar
   Maple-Walnut Syrup (recipe follows)

Spread butter over bottom of heavy large baking pan with 1-inch-high sides. Arrange bread slices in pan. In large bowl beat eggs, milk, sugar, syrup, vanilla and salt to blend. Pour mixture over bread. Turn bread slices to coat. Cover with plastic and refrigerate overnight.

Preheat oven to 400 degrees. Bake French bread 10 minutes. Turn bread over and continue baking until just golden, about 4 minutes longer. Transfer cooked toast to plates and sprinkle with confectioners' sugar. Serve at once, passing Maple-Walnut Syrup separately. Serves 6.

Maple-Walnut Syrup

2 cups maple syrup
1 cup chopped walnuts, toasted

Combine syrup and walnuts in heavy medium saucepan. Bring to simmer. Serve hot. Makes 3 cups.

"Highly Unorthodox" French Toast

6 eggs
¼ cup triple sec *or* orange liqueur
2 tablespoons maple syrup
1 tablespoon heavy cream
1 teaspoon ground cinnamon
3–4 tablespoons unsalted butter
1 (1-pound) loaf brioche or challah (egg bread), cut into 12 thick slices
   Confectioners' sugar
   Orange slices

Beat eggs, triple sec, maple syrup, cream and cinnamon in large bowl until smooth. Melt 1 tablespoon of the butter in large skillet over medium heat. Dip 4 slices of brioche in egg mixture until well-saturated. Sauté in butter, turning once, until golden brown on both sides, about 5 minutes. Transfer to warm serving platter. Dust with confectioners' sugar. Keep warm.

Repeat with remaining brioche slices, adding more butter to skillet as needed. Dust with sugar. Garnish with orange slices. Serves 6.

Blueberry Buttermilk Muffins

2½ cups flour
2½ teaspoons baking powder
1 cup sugar
¼ teaspoon salt
1 cup buttermilk
2 eggs, beaten
½ cup butter, melted and lightly browned
¼ teaspoon vanilla
1½ cup blueberries

Sift together flour, baking powder, sugar and salt; make a well in center and add buttermilk, eggs, butter and vanilla. Mix well. Fold in blueberries. Bake in greased muffin cups at 400 degrees for 20 minutes. Makes 24 muffins.

Farmer's Breakfast

6 slices bacon
½ cup green pepper, diced
¼ cup onion, diced
3 large potatoes, boiled, peeled and cubed
   Salt and pepper, to taste
½ cup desired cheese, grated
6 eggs

Fry bacon; cut in small strips. Save 3 tablespoons of grease in skillet. Place green pepper and onion in skillet. Place potatoes in skillet; sprinkle with salt and pepper. Fry until golden brown, stirring often. Sprinkle with grated cheese. Break 6 eggs over potatoes in pan and cook at low heat until eggs are set. Stir constantly. Serves 6.

Quick Coffee Cake

1 cup sugar
1½ cups flour
2 teaspoons baking powder
¼ teaspoon salt
¼ cup butter
1 egg, well beaten
½ cup milk
1½ teaspoons cinnamon
3 teaspoons sugar

Mix together 1 cup sugar, flour, baking powder and salt. Work in butter. Combine egg and milk and add to flour mixture. Pour into a buttered pan (sides and bottom). Bake for 20 minutes at 375 degrees. Mix together cinnamon and 3 teaspoons sugar and sprinkle on top of coffee cake.

Best-Ever French Toast

1 cup flour
1½ teaspoons baking powder
1½ teaspoons sugar
1 teaspoon salt
1 cup sweet milk
1 egg, beaten
   Bread slices

Stir together flour, baking powder, sugar and salt. Blend milk and egg; add to flour mixture and beat until smooth. Slightly dip bread slices into batter, coating both sides evenly. Fry in preheated 375-degree (hot) fat in heavy skillet until brown. Fry about 2 minutes on each side. Serve hot with butter and syrup.

Sage Pancakes

1½ cups quick-cooking oatmeal
½ cup flour
¼ teaspoon salt
½ teaspoon baking soda
2 tablespoons brown sugar
1½ teaspoons sage
1 cup heavy cream
½ cup buttermilk
2 tablespoons butter, melted

Mix together oatmeal, flour, salt, baking soda, brown sugar and sage; stir in cream, buttermilk and butter. Cook on lightly greased, hot griddle.

Pancakes

3 eggs
2 cups flour
1 teaspoon baking soda
Pinch of salt
1-2 cups thick sour milk

Beat eggs until fluffy. Add flour, baking soda, salt and sour milk; mix well. Fry in hot lard. Serve with syrup and butter.

Orange Doughnut Puffs

2 eggs, beaten
1½ cups sugar
1⅔ cups evaporated milk
2 tablespoons lemon juice
⅓ cup fresh orange juice
2 teaspoons grated orange rind
6 cups flour
½ teaspoon salt
2 teaspoons baking soda
Confectioners' sugar, sifted

Beat eggs with sugar; add evaporated milk, lemon juice, orange juice and rind; mix well. Sift flour, salt and baking soda into egg mixture just until dry ingredients are dampened. Do not overmix. Drop dough by teaspoonfuls into hot oil for 4–5 minutes or until golden brown. Sprinkle with confectioners' sugar; cool. Makes 6 dozen.

Baking Powder Biscuits

1¾ cups flour
4 teaspoons baking powder
½ teaspoon salt
¼ cup shortening
⅔ cup milk

Mix together flour, baking powder and salt. Cut in shortening until mixture is crumbly. Add enough milk to make a dough that leaves sides of bowl. Gently knead on floured board for 12 minutes. Roll out to ¾-inch thickness. Cut with cutter or knife. Bake on ungreased baking sheet at 450 degrees for 12 minutes or until a delicate brown. Makes 8–10 biscuits.

Fruit Crumble

2 cups diced red apples
Juice of ½ lemon
1 (1-pound 4-ounce) can crushed pineapple with juice
1 (1-pound) can cranberry sauce
1 cup quick-cooking rolled oats
¾ cup dark brown sugar
½ cup flour
1 teaspoon cinnamon
½ cup butter

In large baking dish, mix together the fruit with cranberry sauce and lemon juice. Combine half the sugar and the cinnamon; sprinkle over fruit. Cut butter into flour, remaining sugar and rolled oats until a crumble mixture is formed. Sprinkle crumble mixture evenly over top of fruit and bake in 350-degree oven for 35–40 minutes. Serve warm with whipped cream or topping.

Pumpkin Pancakes

2 cups biscuit mix
2 tablespoons firmly packed brown sugar
2 teaspoons ground cinnamon
1 teaspoon ground allspice
1½ cups evaporated milk
½ cup pumpkin
2 tablespoons oil
2 eggs
1 teaspoon vanilla

Combine biscuit mix, sugar, cinnamon and allspice; add milk, pumpkin, oil, eggs and vanilla. Beat until smooth. Pour ¼ cup batter on heated, lightly greased griddle. Cook until surface is bubbly; turn; cook until golden. Serve warm with syrup or honey.

Waffles From Heaven

2 cups biscuit mix
1 egg
½ cup oil
1⅓ cups club soda

Mix together biscuit mix, egg, oil and club soda. Cook in waffle iron.

Cinnamon Bread

¼ cup margarine
1 cup sugar
1 egg
1 cup buttermilk
1 teaspoon baking soda
2 cups flour
¼ teaspoon salt
⅓ cup sugar
1 tablespoon cinnamon

Cream together margarine, 1 cup sugar and egg; add buttermilk, baking soda, flour and salt; set aside. Mix together ⅓ cup sugar and cinnamon. In greased loaf pan, place ⅓ batter, then ½ cinnamon mixture, then ⅓ batter, then last half of cinnamon mix, then rest of batter. Bake at 375 degrees for 50 minutes.

Christmas Coffee Cake

2 (1-pound) loaves frozen bread dough
1 teaspoon cinnamon
2 cups sugar
2 sticks butter, melted
½ pound finely chopped nuts

Thaw bread thoroughly. Cut each loaf into approximately 30 pieces. Roll each into a ball about 1 inch in size. Dip pieces in melted butter, then into combined mixture of cinnamon and sugar.

Place in well-buttered 10-inch tube pan. Arrange balls in pan; they should just touch in each layer. Preheat oven to 350 degrees. Bake for 50 minutes. Carefully remove cake by inverting on plate.

Poached Eggs on Chicken Muffins

1 (4¾-ounce) can chicken spread
½ teaspoon thyme
3 English muffins, split and toasted
6 eggs, poached
Chives, chopped (optional)

Mix chicken with thyme and spread on English muffins. Top each muffin half with an egg and sprinkle with chives. Makes 6 servings.

Raisin Fritters

1 egg
¼ cup milk
1 cup pancake mix
¼ cup seedless raisins
1 (12-ounce) can whole-kernel corn
Oil

Blend together egg and milk. Add pancake mix and raisins; stir just until mixed. Fold in corn, do not overbeat. Drop by teaspoonfuls into hot cooking oil and fry until golden brown, about 4 minutes.

Banana Blueberry Muffins

3 ripe bananas, mashed
3 eggs
½ cup honey
1 cup melted butter
1 cup frozen blueberries
2 teaspoons vanilla
3½ cups whole-wheat flour
4 teaspoons baking powder
1 teaspoon cinnamon
¾ teaspoon salt

Combine bananas, eggs, honey and butter until well-blended. Stir in blueberries and vanilla; set aside. Mix together flour, baking powder, cinnamon and salt; make a well in center of dry ingredients. Pour banana mixture in center. Mix gently. Bake in greased muffin cups at 350 degrees for 25–30 minutes.

Buttermilk Pancakes

2 cups flour
2 cups buttermilk
1 teaspoon baking soda
1 teaspoon baking powder
1 tablespoon sugar
½ teaspoon salt
1 egg

Combine flour, buttermilk, baking soda, baking powder, sugar, salt and egg; mix thoroughly. Refrigerate overnight. Cook on greased griddle until underside of pancakes is full of bubbles. Makes 6 servings.

Quick-Bread English Muffins

1½ cups whole-wheat flour
½ cup cornmeal
1 teaspoon salt
2½ teaspoons baking powder
½ cup dried milk powder
2 tablespoons oil
2 tablespoons honey
1½ cups water

Mix together flour, cornmeal, salt, baking powder and dried milk; stir in oil and honey. Add 1 cup water and stir until moist. Add remaining water as necessary to produce a batter thicker than pancake batter, but still spreadable. Bake in covered skillet in 4-inch circles.

Beer Pancakes

2 cups biscuit mix
2 tablespoons sugar
½ teaspoon cinnamon
5 eggs, beaten
½ cup beer
2 tablespoons oil

Combine biscuit mix, sugar and cinnamon; add eggs, beer and oil. Stir until moistened. Batter will be lumpy. Add more beer for thinner pancakes. Using ¼ cup batter for each pancake, pour onto heated, greased griddle and cook on each side for 2 minutes, or until golden.

Stuffed French Toast

8 slices ¾-inch-thick heavy bread, cubed, crusts removed
2 (8-ounce) packages cream cheese, cubed
12 eggs, beaten
⅓ cup maple syrup, warmed
Dash cinnamon
Dash sugar

Place half the bread cubes in the bottom of a 9 x 13-inch baking pan. Top with cubed cheese. Put the rest of the bread cubes on top of this. Pour beaten eggs over all. Cover and refrigerate overnight. Bake at 375 degrees and serve with warmed maple syrup, cinnamon and sugar.

Cheese Soufflé

4 ounces grated cheddar cheese
1 (10-ounce) can cheddar cheese soup
6 eggs, separated

Heat cheese and soup until cheese is melted; remove from heat. Beat egg yolks until thickened and add to soup mixture. Beat egg whites until stiff. Fold into soup mixture. Pour into greased 2-quart soufflé dish. Bake at 400 degrees for 30–35 minutes or until golden brown.

Banana French Toast

6 slices bread
2 eggs
½ cup milk
½ teaspoon cinnamon
1 banana, chunked

Blend eggs, milk, cinnamon and banana in blender until well mixed. Dip slices of bread into mixture. Brown on both sides on hot greased griddle.

Sweet Cream Biscuits

1½ cups flour
3 teaspoons baking powder
2 tablespoons shortening
½ teaspoon salt
½ cup whipping cream
3 tablespoons milk

Sift together flour, baking powder and salt. Cut in shortening; add cream and milk. Knead 10–12 times until smooth. Roll out onto lightly floured surface to about ¼-inch thickness. Cut in rounds with biscuit cutter. Bake on slightly floured cookie sheet at 450 degrees for 10–12 minutes or until golden brown. Makes about 12–14 biscuits.

Strawberry Butter

1 cup strawberries
⅓ cup confectioners' sugar
2 cups butter
Dash vanilla

Blend strawberries, confectioners' sugar, butter and vanilla in food processor. Freeze extra strawberry butter.

Cakes TO BAKE

Mocha Cake Surprise

- ¾ cup sugar
- 1 cup sifted flour
- 2 teaspoons baking powder
- ⅛ teaspoon salt
- 1 (1-ounce) square unsweetened chocolate
- 2 tablespoons butter *or* margarine
- ¼ cup milk
- 1 teaspoon vanilla
- ½ cup firmly packed brown sugar
- ½ cup sugar
- 4 tablespoons breakfast cocoa, not instant
- 1 cup cold, double-strength coffee

Preheat oven to 350 degrees. Mix and sift first 4 ingredients. Melt chocolate and butter together over hot water; add to first mixture and blend well. Combine milk and vanilla; add and mix well. Pour into greased 8-inch square cake pan. Combine brown sugar, ½ cup sugar and cocoa. Sprinkle evenly over batter and pour coffee over top. Bake for 40 minutes. Serve warm.

Roman Apple Cake

- 1 cup sugar
- ½ cup brown sugar
- 1 cup margarine
- 2 eggs, beaten
- 1 teaspoon baking soda
- 1 cup sour milk
- 2½ cups flour
- 1 teaspoon baking powder
- 2 teaspoons cinnamon
- ½ teaspoon salt
- 2 cups apples, diced
- ½ cup sugar
- ½ cup nuts, chopped
- 1 teaspoon cinnamon

Cream together sugar, brown sugar and margarine; add eggs and beat. In a separate bowl, add baking soda to sour milk; set aside. Sift together flour, baking powder, cinnamon and salt. Alternately add milk and dry ingredients to creamed mixture. Fold in apples.

Pour into a 9 x 13-inch cake pan. Mix together ½ cup sugar, nuts and 1 teaspoon cinnamon. Sprinkle on top of cake. Bake at 350 degrees for 30–40 minutes.

Easy Sponge Cake

- 5 eggs, separated
- 5 tablespoons cold water
- 1 cup cake flour, sifted 3 times
- 1 cup superfine sugar
- 1 teaspoon cream of tartar
- 1 teaspoon vanilla extract
- 1 teaspoon lemon extract
- ½ teaspoon salt

Preheat oven to 300 degrees. Beat egg whites until foamy at medium speed with electric mixer; add cream of tartar and salt. Beat until stiff.

In another bowl, at medium speed, beat egg yolks, sugar and 5 tablespoons cold water until light yellow and fluffy. Add cake flour and vanilla and lemon extracts to yolk mixture. Blend well at low speed. Fold in egg whites and blend. Pour into an ungreased 10 x 4-inch tube pan. Bake 70 minutes. Turn upside down to cool.

Crunchy Apricot Cake

- 1 (22-ounce) can apricot pie filling
- 1 (1-layer-size) package white cake mix
- ⅓ cup water
- 1 egg
- ½ cup flaked coconut
- ½ cup chopped pecans
- ½ cup butter *or* margarine, melted

Heat oven to 350 degrees. Spread pie filling in bottom of 9 x 9 x 2-inch baking dish. Combine cake mix, water and egg. With electric mixer beat 4 minutes at medium speed. Pour over pie filling; sprinkle with coconut and pecans. Drizzle melted butter over top.

Bake for 40 minutes. Serve warm. Serves 9.

Hot Fudge Pudding Cake

- 1 cup buttermilk baking mix
- 1 cup sugar, divided
- ⅓ cup *plus* 3 tablespoons cocoa
- 1 teaspoon vanilla
- ½ cup milk
- 1⅔ cups *hot* tap water

Preheat oven to 350 degrees. In mixing bowl, combine baking mix, ½ cup sugar and 3 tablespoons cocoa. Stir in milk and vanilla. Spread in an 8-inch square pan. Sprinkle with remaining ⅓ cup cocoa and ½ cup sugar. Pour hot water over top. Do not stir! Bake for 40 minutes, or until top is firm. Pudding will form on bottom.

Banana Cake

2¼ cups flour
1¼ teaspoons baking powder
1 teaspoon baking soda
1 teaspoon salt
1 cup very ripe bananas, mashed
1 cup buttermilk at room temperature
⅔ cup shortening
1½ cups sugar
2 eggs at room temperature
1 teaspoon vanilla
Icing (recipe follows)

Combine flour, baking powder, baking soda and salt. Mix bananas with buttermilk. Cream shortening and sugar; add eggs 1 at a time. Alternately add flour and banana mixture. Bake at 350 degrees for 30 minutes.

Icing

1 (8-ounce) package cream cheese
½ cup corn syrup
½ cup peanut butter
Peanuts

Mix together cream cheese, corn syrup and peanut butter; ice cake; top with peanuts.

Apple Cake

2 cups sugar
2 eggs
1½ cups oil
2 teaspoons vanilla
3 cups apples, diced
1 cup nuts, chopped (optional)
3 cups flour
1 teaspoon baking soda
1 teaspoon salt
Icing (recipe follows)

Beat together sugar, eggs and oil. Add vanilla, apples and nuts. Sift together flour, baking soda and salt; add to apple mixture. Bake in a greased pan for 1 hour at 350 degrees. Ice cake while still warm.

Icing

2 cups confectioner's sugar
4 tablespoons water
1 teaspoon vanilla

Mix together confectioners' sugar, water and vanilla; pour over warm cake.

Blueberry Sour Cream Cake

½ cup butter
1 cup sugar
2 eggs
1 cup sour cream
2 cups sifted flour
1 teaspoon baking soda
½ teaspoon salt
1 teaspoon vanilla extract
2 cups fresh blueberries

Filling

½ cup firmly packed brown sugar
½ cup chopped nuts
½ teaspoon cinnamon

Preheat oven to 350 degrees. Grease and flour a 9 x 12-inch pan. In a bowl, cream butter until light and fluffy. Beat in sugar and cream again until light and fluffy. Beating until smooth after each, beat in eggs, 1 at a time. Stir in sour cream. When well-blended, beat in flour, baking soda, salt and vanilla. Fold in blueberries. Pour half of batter into prepared pan.

Mix brown sugar, nuts and cinnamon. Sprinkle evenly over batter in pan. Top with remaining batter.

Bake until cake begins to pull away from sides of pan, 40–45 minutes. Cool completely in pan. Cut into squares. If desired, dust lightly with confectioners' sugar before serving. Serves 12.

Amish Yellow Cake

4 cups flour
½ teaspoon salt
4 teaspoons baking powder
1 cup margarine
4 eggs, separated
1 cup milk
½ cup plus 2 teaspoons margarine

In bowl, mix together flour, salt, baking powder and margarine until coarsely blended. Reserve 1 cup crumbs; set aside. Beat egg yolks until thick; add yolks and milk to the crumb mixture.

Stir until just blended. Beat egg whites until soft peaks form; add to batter. Pour into greased 9 x 13-inch pan. Sprinkle with the reserved crumbs. Bake at 350 degrees for 30–40 minutes or until done. Melt ½ cup plus 2 teaspoons margarine and pour over top of baked cake.

Apple Cake

2 eggs
1½ cups sugar
½ cup oil
1 teaspoon vanilla
½ teaspoon salt
1 teaspoon baking soda
1 teaspoon cinnamon
2 cups flour
4 cups apples, finely chopped
½ cup nuts, chopped
Whipped cream, if desired

Mix together eggs, sugar and oil. Add vanilla, salt, baking soda, cinnamon and flour. Mix well, then add apple bits. Pour into a greased 9 x 13-inch pan. Sprinkle with nuts. Bake at 350 degrees for 45 minutes or until done. Serve with whipped cream.

Butterscotch Cake

½ cup (1 stick) butter
1 cup light brown sugar
1 egg
2 cups sifted flour
3 teaspoons baking powder
½ cup milk

Frosting

¾ cup brown sugar
2 tablespoons milk
Pinch salt
2 tablespoons butter
½ cup confectioners' sugar, sifted
Chopped brown almonds

Grease 8-inch layer pan. Cream butter and sugar until light and fluffy. Beat in egg. Fold in sifted flour and baking powder alternately with milk. Turn into pan. Bake at 375 degrees for about 45 minutes. Turn onto cooling rack. When cold, top with frosting.

To make frosting, place brown sugar, milk, salt and butter into saucepan, stir over low heat until mixture boils. Cook without stirring 5 minutes.

Remove from stove. While still just warm, stir in confectioners' sugar. Beat well and add extra, if necessary, to spreading consistency. Spread almonds on baking sheet; brown lightly under broiler. Watch carefully so they *do not* burn. Arrange almonds around edge of frosted cake. Serves 6–8.

True Love Cake

1 (18¼-ounce) package white cake mix
1 cup water
½ cup sour cream
¼ cup vegetable oil
3 egg whites
1 (8-ounce) cup glacé whole red cherries, chopped
  White Chocolate Buttercream Frosting (recipe follows)
  Glacé whole red cherries, halved

Beat cake mix, water, sour cream, oil and egg whites in medium bowl on low speed until combined. Then, beat at medium speed 2 minutes. Gently mix in chopped glacé cherries.

Pour batter into 8-cup puffed heart cake pan. Bake in preheated 350-degree oven 1 hour, or until toothpick inserted in center of cake comes out clean. Cool in pan on wire rack 15 minutes.

Using long sharp knife, slice off any cake that is above top of pan (cake will maintain heart shape without cracking). Invert cake onto wire rack. Cool completely.

Make White Chocolate Buttercream Frosting. Place cake on serving plate and frost. Decorate with glacé cherry halves.

Note: Cake may also be baked in 3-tiered heart-shaped pan or 2 (9-inch) heart-shaped or round cake pans. Bake about 35 minutes, or until toothpick inserted in center of cake comes out clean.

White Chocolate Buttercream Frosting

6 tablespoons butter *or* margarine, softened
4 ounces white chocolate, melted
1 (16-ounce) box confectioners' sugar
4–5 tablespoons whipping cream *or* half-and-half
  Pink paste food coloring

Beat butter in medium bowl until fluffy; beat in melted chocolate. Beat in confectioners' sugar, adding enough cream to make a good spreading consistency. Stir in small amount food color to turn frosting pink. Makes 3 cups.

Spice Apple Cupcakes

½ cup margarine
¾ cup sugar
1 egg
1½ cups flour
1 tablespoon baking powder
½ teaspoon salt
½ teaspoon cinnamon
  Pinch of nutmeg
½ cup milk
1 cup apples, finely chopped
¼ cup brown sugar
¼ cup nuts, chopped
½ teaspoon cinnamon

Cream together margarine and sugar; blend well. Add egg and beat until light (2 minutes). Combine flour, baking powder, salt, ½ teaspoon cinnamon and nutmeg. Alternately add dry ingredients and milk to creamed mixture. Fold in apples. Fill 12 large greased muffin cups half full. Mix together brown sugar, nuts and ½ teaspoon cinnamon. Sprinkle over muffins. Bake at 375 degrees for about 20 minutes.

Fruit Cocktail Cake

1½ cup sugar
2 cups flour
2 teaspoons baking soda
½ teaspoon salt
2 eggs
1 (No. 303) can fruit cocktail
¼ cup brown sugar
1 cup nuts, chopped
¾ cup sugar
½ cup Milnot
1 cup coconut, shredded
1 teaspoon vanilla
⅓ cup margarine

Mix together sugar, flour, baking soda and salt. Add fruit cocktail and eggs that have been beaten with a spoon for 3 minutes. Pour in a 9 x 13-inch pan. Mix brown sugar and nuts and sprinkle over the top of cake. Bake for 30–35 minutes at 350 degrees.

Meanwhile, mix together ¾ cup white sugar, Milnot, coconut, vanilla and margarine. Bring to a boil and boil for 2 minutes. Pour over cake while it is still hot.

Kahlúa-Chocolate Cherry Cheesecake

1 (11.2-ounce) package no-bake cheesecake mix
2 tablespoons sugar
⅓ cup butter *or* margarine, melted
1 (21-ounce) can cherry filling and topping
½ cup Kahlúa
½ cup milk
2 (1-ounce) squares unsweetened chocolate, melted

Prepare crumb crust, in a 9-inch pie plate, using crumb packet from cheesecake mix, sugar and melted butter or margarine, as directed on package. In a large mixing bowl, stir together cheesecake filling packet from mix, ¾ cup cherry filling, Kahlúa and milk. Stir in melted chocolate, mixing well until mixture thickens. Spoon mixture into prepared crust. Cover and chill at least 1 hour before serving time. When firm, spread remaining cherry filling over top of pie.

Holiday Fruit-Nut Cake

1 cup butter *or* margarine, softened
2 cups sugar
6 eggs, separated
4 cups all-purpose flour, divided
2 teaspoons baking powder
⅛ teaspoon ground nutmeg
1 cup whiskey
4 cups pecan halves
1 (8-ounce) package chopped dates
½ pound chopped candied cherries

Cream together butter and sugar. Add egg yolks, 1 at a time, beating well after each addition. Combine 3¾ cups flour, baking powder and nutmeg. Add alternately with whiskey to sugar mixture, mixing well. Combine remaining ¼ cup flour, pecans, dates and cherries. Stir into flour mixture.

Beat egg whites until stiff. Fold into cake batter. Spoon into greased and floured 10-inch tube pan. Bake at 350 degrees for 1 hour and 40 minutes. Cover top of cake with foil if needed to prevent overbrowning. Cool on wire rack. Makes 1 (10-inch) cake.

Crumb Cake

½ cup shortening
1 egg
2 cups brown sugar
1 cup sour milk
2 cups all-purpose flour
1 teaspoon baking soda
¼ teaspoon salt
1 teaspoon vanilla
   Cinnamon
   Raisins (optional)
   Chopped nuts (optional)

Blend shortening, sugar, flour and salt thoroughly; measure ¾ cup; set aside for topping.

To remaining mixture add egg and sour milk, to which the soda has been added. Add vanilla and stir. Pour batter into greased 7½ x 11-inch cake pan.

Sprinkle reserved crumbs over top. Cinnamon may be sprinkled over top, if desired. Raisins or chopped nuts or both may be added to batter. Bake at 350 degrees approximately 40 minutes.

Chocolate Plantation Cake

½ cup margarine
1¼ cups sugar
2 eggs
2 (1-ounce) squares bitter chocolate, melted
1¾ cups flour
1 teaspoon soda
   Salt to taste (optional)
1 cup buttermilk
   Vanilla to taste

Mocha Frosting

⅓ cup margarine
4 cups sifted confectioners' sugar
3½ tablespoons cocoa
¾ teaspoon salt, if desired
½ cup strong coffee
1 teaspoon vanilla
   Slivered almonds

Cream margarine with sugar until light; beat in salt (if desired), vanilla and eggs. Stir in chocolate. Sift dry ingredients together; add to creamed mixture alternately with buttermilk. Pour into 2 greased 8-inch round cake pans. Bake at 350 degrees for 30–35 minutes. Cool.

For frosting, cream margarine until light. Sift sugar, cocoa and salt, if desired, together. Add to margarine gradually with coffee. Beat until of desired spreading consistency. Spread between layers and top of cake; sprinkle with almonds and red hearts (cinnamon) if desired. Serves 10–12.

Milwaukee Cake

⅔ package zwieback, finely crushed
½ cup butter, melted
½ cup sugar
6 egg yolks
1 cup canned applesauce
1 can sweetened condensed milk
⅓ cup lemon juice
¼ teaspoon lemon extract
6 egg whites

Mix together zwieback crumbs with butter and sugar; pat in bottom of spring-form pan which has been well greased with butter. Mix egg yolks well; add a cup of canned applesauce, sweetened condensed milk, lemon juice and lemon extract. Beat egg whites and add to applesauce mixture.

Bake at 350 degrees for 10 minutes, then 200 degrees for 1 hour 50 minutes. Let stand at least 6 hours, remove sides of pan and serve with whipped cream. Serves 10.

Chocolate Salad Dressing Cake

1½ cups sugar
2 cups flour
2 tablespoons cocoa
2 teaspoons baking soda
1 cup warm water
1 teaspoon vanilla
1 cup salad dressing
   Pinch of salt

Mix sugar, flour, cocoa and baking soda. Add water and vanilla; beat well. Stir in salad dressing and salt. Bake at 300–325 degrees for 50–60 minutes, or until done. This is a very moist cake. Nestlé Quik can be used instead of cocoa.

Mom's Apple Cake

3 cups apples, peeled and sliced
1 cup nuts, chopped
3 eggs
2 cups sugar
3 cups flour, sifted
1 teaspoon baking soda
1 teaspoon cinnamon
1 cup oil
1 teaspoon salt
2 teaspoons vanilla
   Topping (recipe follows)

Stir together apples and nuts. Break eggs over apples, stirring well; set aside. Mix together sugar, flour, baking soda, cinnamon, salt, vanilla and oil. Add to apple mixture. Bake in 9 x 13-inch pan at 350 degrees for 1 hour or until done.

Topping

1 cup brown sugar
¼ cup milk
1 stick margarine

Combine brown sugar, milk and margarine. Bring to a boil and boil 3 minutes. Pierce cake with fork; pour topping over cake while cake is hot. Let stand 3 hours.

Nutmeg Pecan Cake

2 cups brown sugar
2 cups unbleached flour
½ cup butter
1 egg, lightly beaten
1 teaspoon nutmeg
1 cup sour cream
1 teaspoon baking soda
¾ cup chopped pecans

Mix together sugar and flour; cut butter into small pieces and work into sugar and flour with your fingers to make coarse crumbs. Put half of the crumbs in bottom of a 9-inch greased baking dish. Stir egg and nutmeg into remaining course crumbs.

Mix sour cream with soda and add to crumb mixture. Spoon batter into baking dish and top with nuts. Bake in a pre-heated 350-degree oven for 35–40 minutes. Serves 8–10.

Orange Party Girl Cake

1 stick sweet butter, softened
3/4 cup sugar
2 eggs, separated
Grated zest of 2 oranges
1 1/2 cups unbleached all-purpose flour
1 1/2 teaspoons baking powder
1/4 teaspoon soda
1/4 teaspoon salt
1/2 cup fresh orange juice
Orange Glaze (recipe follows)
Coconut (optional)

Cream butter; gradually add sugar. Beat in 2 egg yolks, 1 at a time. Add orange zest. Sift dry ingredients together. Add to batter alternately with orange juice. Beat egg whites until stiff peaks form and fold into batter. Pour into 9-inch layer cake pan; bake until cake shrinks from side of pan (20–25 minutes). Also test with toothpick. Cool 10 minutes in pan; turn out on rack and while still warm, pour on orange glaze.

Orange Glaze

1/4 cup orange juice
1/4 cup sugar

Simmer ingredients until syrupy. Also may sprinkle orange-tinted coconut on cake for added appeal.

This recipe is excellent in taste and appearance. Serves 8–10.

Daffodil Cake

White Batter

1 3/4 cups egg whites (12–14)
1 1/4 cups sifted cake flour (sift before measuring)
1 1/2 cups sugar
1/2 teaspoon salt
1 1/2 teaspoons cream of tartar
1 1/2 teaspoons vanilla extract

Yellow Batter

5 egg yolks
2 tablespoons cake flour
2 tablespoons sugar
2 tablespoons grated lemon peel

Preheat oven to 350 degrees. Beat egg whites, adding cream of tartar 1/2 teaspoon at a time. Add Vanilla. Combine cake flour, sugar and salt; fold into egg whites. Place in 9 x 13-inch pan.

Prepare yellow batter by adding flour, sugar and lemon peel to beaten yolks. Pour yellow batter on top of white batter. Using a knife cut through batter to give a yellow-white swirled effect. Bake 35–40 minutes. Serves 12.
Note: To get good volume, let egg whites warm to room temperature before beating. Be sure to use cake (not all-purpose) flour in this recipe. If you are baking the cake a day ahead, leave it in the pan overnight and remove it just before serving. Cut cake with a knife that has a serrated edge, using a light sawing motion. Nice served with ice cream. The absence of butter makes this recipe a plus for dieters.

Rosie's Apple Cake

1 cup sugar
1 egg
3 tablespoons butter
1 teaspoon baking soda
1/2 teaspoon cinnamon
1 cup flour
1/2 teaspoon salt
3 cups apples, sliced
1/4 cup nuts, chopped
1 teaspoon vanilla
1/2 teaspoon nutmeg

Cream together sugar, egg and butter. Sift nutmeg, baking soda, cinnamon, flour and salt. Add to creamed mixture. Blend in apples, nuts and vanilla. Pour in a 8 x 8-inch pan and bake for 45 minutes at 350 degrees.

Lazy Woman's Cake

2 cups sugar
3 cups flour
1 teaspoon salt
5 tablespoons cocoa
2 teaspoons baking soda
1 cup oil
1 tablespoon vanilla
2 tablespoons vinegar
2 cups cold water

In a large bowl, sift together sugar, flour, salt, cocoa and baking soda. Make 3 holes in the dry ingredients. Pour oil, vanilla and vinegar in each hole; pour water over all and stir with a fork until smooth. Pour into an ungreased loaf pan. Bake at 350 degrees for about 30 minutes.

Hickory Nut Cake

2 1/2 cups sifted cake flour
2 1/2 teaspoons baking powder
1/2 to 3/4 teaspoon salt
1/2 cup oil
1 cup milk
1 teaspoon vanilla
2 eggs
1 1/2 cups sugar
1 cup finely ground hickory nuts
Brown Sugar Icing (recipe follows)

Sift together flour, baking powder and salt in large mixing bowl. Add oil, milk and vanilla. Beat until it forms a very smooth batter. In small mixer bowl, beat eggs until thick and foamy. Gradually add sugar and continue beating until very well blended. Fold this egg and sugar mixture thoroughly into batter.

Lightly fold in nuts. Pour into 2 waxed-paper–lined and greased 9-inch pans. Bake at 375 degrees for 25–30 minutes. Frost with Brown Sugar Icing.

Brown Sugar Icing

1/2 stick margarine
1 cup brown sugar
1/2 cup milk
1 teaspoon vanilla
1 pound confectioners' sugar

Melt butter and sugar in pan; bring to boil. Add milk and boil for 2 minutes, stirring frequently. Cool; add vanilla and confectioners' sugar to make the right consistency for spreading.

Poor Man's Cake

1 cup sugar
1 cup salad dressing
2 teaspoons baking soda
1 cup warm water
2 cups flour
4 tablespoons cocoa
Pinch of salt
1 teaspoon vanilla

Cream sugar with salad dressing. Mix baking soda and water; add to creamed mixture. Sift flour and cocoa. Stir into creamed mixture and add salt and vanilla. Mix well. Bake at 350 degrees until done.

Valentine Red Cake

1½ cups unsalted butter, softened
1½ cups sugar
2 eggs
¼ cup red food coloring
1 teaspoon vanilla
2 tablespoons cocoa
1 teaspoon salt
1 cup buttermilk
2¼ cups sifted cake flour
1 teaspoon baking soda
1 teaspoon vinegar
Fluffy Frosting (recipe follows)

Preheat oven to 350 degrees. Beat butter with sugar until light and fluffy. Add eggs, 1 at a time, beating thoroughly after each egg. Stir food coloring, vanilla and cocoa together to form a paste. Beat into batter.

Stir salt into buttermilk; add to batter in 3 parts, alternating with flour. Stir baking soda into vinegar; add to batter. Pour batter into 2 prepared 9-inch pans. Bake about 30 minutes, or until done. Let cool completely before unmolding from pans. Cut each layer in half to form 4 layers. Frost cake with Fluffy Frosting

Fluffy Frosting

3 tablespoons flour
1 cup unsalted butter, softened
1 cup milk
1 cup sugar
1 teaspoon vanilla

Whisk flour and milk together slowly until smooth. Cook, stirring frequently, over medium heat until thick, about 3 minutes. Let cool. Beat butter with sugar until light and fluffy. Add vanilla slowly. Beat in cooled milk mixture. Makes enough to frost top and sides of 4 layers.

Chocolate Raisin Cake

1½ cups cold water
1 cup sugar
½ cup margarine
1 cup raisins
1 teaspoon cinnamon
½ teaspoon cloves

2 (1-ounce) squares unsweetened chocolate
½ cup flour
1 teaspoon baking soda
1 teaspoon vanilla
Creamy Almond Icing (recipe follows)

In saucepan, boil water, sugar, margarine, raisins, cinnamon, cloves and chocolate. Cool. Dissolve baking soda in 2 tablespoons cold water; add to cooled mixture. Add flour and vanilla. Mix well. Pour into a greased and floured 9-inch square pan. Bake at 350 degrees for 35 minutes. Cool. Serves 10.

Creamy Almond Icing

1 (8-ounce) package cream cheese
2 tablespoons confectioners' sugar
1 teaspoon almond extract

Combine all ingredients and spread icing over cooled cake.

Queen of Hearts Cake

1 cup chopped dates
1 cup boiling water
1 teaspoon soda
1 cup sugar
¼ cup butter *or* margarine
1 egg
1 teaspoon vanilla
1½ cups flour
1 teaspoon baking powder
⅓ teaspoon salt
½ cup chopped nuts
5 tablespoons butter
5 tablespoons milk *or* cream
½ cup brown sugar
Coconut
Chopped nuts

Add boiling water to chopped dates; when cool, add soda. Mix together sugar, butter, egg and vanilla. Sift together flour, baking powder and salt. Add date mixture and nuts. Bake in 9-inch greased pan. Bake in a 350-degree oven for 30 minutes.

When cool, boil together 5 tablespoons butter, 5 tablespoons milk or cream and ½ cup brown sugar. Spread on cake; sprinkle with coconut and chopped nuts. Place under broiler for 2 minutes.

Grandma's Apple Cake

2 eggs
2 cups sugar
1 cup oil
3 cups flour
½ teaspoon salt
1 teaspoon baking soda
3 cups apples, chopped
2 teaspoons vanilla
1 cup nuts, chopped
Icing (recipe follows)

Mix together eggs, sugar and oil. Sift together flour, salt and baking soda; add to egg mixture. Stir in apples, vanilla and nuts; mix well. Pour into greased 9 x 13-inch cake pan; bake 45 minutes at 350 degrees.

Icing

1 cup brown sugar
¼ cup milk
¼ cup butter

Combine brown sugar, milk and butter in saucepan; cook for 2½ minutes. Stir a little after removing from stove; do not beat. Dribble over cake while cake and icing are still hot.

Apple Coffee Cake

1 cup brown sugar
1 cup sugar
1 cup flour
1 stick butter
1 teaspoon cinnamon
½ cup nuts, chopped
1 cup apples, diced
2 eggs
1 cup flour
1 cup buttermilk
1 teaspoon baking soda

Mix together brown sugar, sugar, flour and butter. Take out 1 cup of this mixture and add cinnamon, nuts and apples; set aside. To remaining sugar/flour mixture add eggs, flour, buttermilk and baking soda; mix well. Pour batter evenly in 2 round, or 9 x 9-inch greased and floured cake pans. Cover with apple/nut mixture and bake at 350 degrees for 30 minutes.

Zucchini Cake

Frosting

- ⅓ cup sugar
- 1½ tablespoons cornstarch
- ⅓ cup milk
- ⅓ cup plain yogurt
- ½ teaspoon vanilla

Cake

- 1 cup sugar
- ½ cup plain yogurt
- ⅓ cup vegetable oil
- 1 teaspoon vanilla
- 1 egg
- 1½ cups flour
- 1 teaspoon baking powder
- ¼ teaspoon baking soda
- ½ teaspoon salt
- 1½ teaspoons cinnamon
- ½ teaspoon nutmeg
- 1½ cups unpeeled, shredded zucchini
- ⅓ cup chopped nuts

Combine sugar, cornstarch and milk for frosting in a glass measure. Mix until well-combined. Microwave on HIGH, uncovered, for 2–2½ minutes. Cool.

Combine sugar, yogurt, oil, vanilla and egg for cake; mix well. Add flour, baking powder, soda, salt, cinnamon, nutmeg, zucchini and nuts; mix just until well-combined.

Spoon into an 8-inch square glass baking dish, greased on bottom only, spread batter evenly. Microwave on MEDIUM (50 percent), uncovered, 10–11 minutes; rotate dish once. Microwave on HIGH, uncovered, for 2–4 minutes; rotate dish once, if needed. Cool.

Beat frosting mix until creamy; blend in yogurt and vanilla; spread on cake. Refrigerate until served.

Hidden Apple Coffee Cake

- ¾ cup sugar
- ⅓ cup nuts
- 1 teaspoon cinnamon
- 2 cans biscuits
- ¼ cup margarine, melted
- 1 apple, peeled and cored

- ½ cup confectioners' sugar
- ¼ teaspoon vanilla
- 2–3 teaspoon milk

Combine sugar, nuts and cinnamon. Separate biscuits and dip each one in melted margarine, then into sugar mixture. Arrange biscuits in greased 9-inch round cake pan, overlapping 15 biscuits around outer edge and 5 biscuits in center. Cut apple into 20 slices; place 1 slice of apple between each biscuit.

Bake at 400 degrees for 25–30 minutes or until golden brown. Remove from pan immediately. Combine confectioners' sugar, vanilla and milk and mix until smooth. Drizzle over warm coffee cake.

Amazing Corn Cake

- 1 (17-ounce) can cream-style corn
- ½ cup packed brown sugar
- ¾ cup sugar
- 3 eggs
- 1 cup oil
- 1 tablespoon baking powder
- 2¼ cups flour
- 1 teaspoon baking soda
- 1 teaspoon salt
- 1 teaspoon cinnamon
- ½ cup raisins
- ½ cup chopped nuts
- Caramel Frosting (recipe follows)

Heat oven to 350 degrees. Combine corn and sugars. Add eggs and oil. Beat until well-blended. Combine dry ingredients. Add to batter and mix well. Stir in raisins and nuts. Pour into a greased 13 x 9-inch pan. Bake for 30–35 minutes. Cool thoroughly; frost.

Caramel Frosting

- 4 tablespoons margarine
- ½ cup brown sugar
- ¼ cup milk
- 2–3 cups confectioners' sugar

Bring margarine and brown sugar to boil over medium heat. Remove from heat. Stir in milk. Stir in confectioners' sugar, a little at a time, until desired consistency. Frost cooled cake.

Mississippi Mud Sheet Cake

- 1 stick butter
- ½ cup oil *or* lard
- 4 tablespoons cocoa
- 1 cup water
- ⅓ cup buttermilk
- 2 eggs
- 1 teaspoon vanilla
- 1 teaspoon baking soda
- Pinch salt
- 2 cups sugar
- 2 cups flour
- Frosting (recipe follows)

Combine in saucepan butter, oil, cocoa, water and buttermilk; cook for 2 minutes. Add cocoa mixture to eggs, vanilla, baking soda, salt, sugar and flour. Bake in jelly roll pan at 350 degrees for 20 minutes.

Frosting

- 1 stick butter
- 6 tablespoons milk
- 2 tablespoons cocoa
- 1 pound confectioners' sugar

Place butter, milk and cocoa in saucepan and cook for 1 minute. Add confectioners' sugar; stir well. Frost warm cake.

Autumn Apple Cake

- 3 cups flour
- 2 teaspoons baking soda
- 1 teaspoon salt
- 1 teaspoon cinnamon
- ½ teaspoon nutmeg
- 1½ cups oil
- 1 cup sugar
- 1 cup brown sugar
- 4 eggs
- 1 teaspoon vanilla
- 3 cups apples, diced
- ¾ cup nuts, chopped

Sift together flour, baking soda, salt, cinnamon and nutmeg. In large bowl with mixer, beat oil and sugars about 6 minutes. Add eggs, one at a time, beating well. Beat in vanilla; add flour mixture. Fold in nuts and apples. Bake in greased 9-inch tube pan for 1½ hours at 350 degrees.

Applesauce Chocolate Cake

- ½ cup shortening
- ¾ cup sugar
- 1 egg *plus* 1 egg yolk
- 2 cups sifted flour
- ½ teaspoon baking soda
- 3 teaspoons baking powder
- 1 teaspoon salt
- ½ cup unsweetened cocoa powder
- 1 teaspoon cinnamon
- 1¼ cups sweetened applesauce
  Mint Beaten Frosting (recipe follows)

Cream shortening and sugar until light. Beat in the whole egg and the egg yolk until well-blended and light. Sift dry ingredients and alternately add with the applesauce. Bake in 2 greased and floured 8-inch layer cake pans at 350 degrees for 30–35 minutes. Cool and frost with Mint Beaten Frosting.

Mint Beaten Frosting

- 2 egg whites
- 1⅔ cups sugar
- 6 tablespoons cold water
- ⅛ teaspoon cream of tartar
- 8 teaspoons créme de menthe syrup
  Green maraschino cherries

Place all the ingredients, except syrup and cherries, in the top of a double boiler over boiling water. Beat continuously with an electric mixer until mixture will stand in soft peaks. Remove from heat and beat in creme de menthe syrup. Fill and frost cake. Decorate top of frosted cake with green cherries cut in half. The peppermint flavor of the créme de menthe syrup adds a special touch.

Sour Cream Pound Cake

- ½ cup butter
- 3 eggs
- ½ cup sour cream
- 1½ cups flour
- ¼ teaspoon baking powder
- ⅓ teaspoon baking soda
- 1 cup sugar
- ½ teaspoon vanilla
- ½ cup blueberries (optional)
  Confectioners' sugar

It is important that first 3 ingredients be at room temperature before you begin.

Heat oven to 325 degrees. Grease and flour an 8 x 4-inch or 9 x 5-inch pan. In large bowl beat butter on medium speed for 30 seconds. Add sugar, 2 teaspoons at a time, and beat on medium speed. Add vanilla. Add eggs, 1 at a time. Beat on low for *only 1 minute*. Sift together flour, baking powder and baking soda. Add flour mixture and sour cream alternately. Beat on low speed just to combine. Add blueberries, if desired. Bake for 1–1¼ hours. Remove from oven and dust with confectioners' sugar.

Cupid Cakes

- 1 (12-ounce) package pound cake
  Heart-shaped cookie cutter (3-inch)
  Raspberry *or* strawberry preserves
- 3 (16-ounce) cans frosting (vanilla, chocolate and strawberry)
  Assorted valentine candies

Using a serrated knife, slice pound cake horizontally into 3 equal layers (trim off rounded top). Separate layers. With cookie cutter, cut out 2 heart shapes from each layer. Spread preserves on top of 3 hearts. Cover with remaining 3 hearts. Decorate with frosting and candies. If desired, pipe your favorite frosting onto cakes. Makes 3 cakes.

Apple Nut Cake

- 1½ cups oil
- 2 eggs
- 2 cups sugar
- 1 teaspoon vanilla
- 2½ cups flour
- 1 teaspoon baking powder
- ½ teaspoon salt
- 1 teaspoon baking soda
- 3 cups apples, chopped
- 1 cup nuts, chopped
- 1 cup brown sugar
- 1 tablespoon cinnamon

Mix together oil, eggs, sugar and vanilla. Add flour, baking powder, salt and baking soda; stir in apples and nuts. Mixture will be stiff. Pour in 9 x 13 x 2-inch pan. Top with brown sugar and cinnamon. Bake for 55 minutes at 350 degrees.

Susannah's Twinkle Cake

- 1 white cake mix with pudding
- 1 cup milk
- 5 tablespoons flour
- 1 cup sugar
- ½ cup shortening
- ½ cup margarine
- 1 teaspoon vanilla
  Dash of salt
  Icing (recipe follows)

Prepare and bake cake according to directions on package. Cool; slice in half. Meanwhile, cook milk and 5 tablespoons flour over low heat, stirring constantly; cool. Combine 1 cup sugar, shortening, margarine, vanilla and salt; mix well. Beat together milk mixture and sugar mixture until fluffy and light. Spread between cut cake layers and on top layer.

Delicious Easy Icing

- 1 egg white
  Pinch of salt
- 1 cup corn syrup
- 1 teaspoon vanilla

Bring corn syrup to a boil; remove from burner. In separate bowl, beat egg white with salt, slowly pouring in corn syrup while beating. Add vanilla. Fold until cool. Frost cooled cake.

Fresh Apple Cake

- 1⅓ cups oil
- 3 eggs
- 2 cups sugar
- 2 teaspoons vanilla
- 1 teaspoon salt
- 1 teaspoon baking soda
- 2 teaspoons baking powder
- 2½ cups flour
- ½ cup dates, chopped
- 1 cup black walnuts, chopped
- 3 cups apples, peeled and diced
  Non-dairy whipped topping (optional)

Cream together oil, eggs, sugar and vanilla. Add salt, baking soda, baking powder and flour; mix well. Stir in dates, walnuts and apples; mix well. Place in 9 x 13-inch greased pan. Bake at 325–350 degrees for 1–1½ hours or until toothpick comes out clean. Let cool 20 minutes in pan before removing.

Strawberry Crunch Cake

2 (10-ounce) packages frozen, sliced strawberries, thawed
1 cup butter *or* margarine, softened
1¼ cups sugar
2 eggs
1 cup dairy sour cream
2 cups flour
1 teaspoon baking powder
½ teaspoon baking soda
½ teaspoon salt
½ cup chopped walnuts
½ cup packed brown sugar
2 tablespoons sugar
1 teaspoon cinnamon
4 teaspoons cornstarch
1 (9-ounce) container whipped topping

Preheat oven to 350 degrees. Drain strawberries, reserving juice; set aside. Cream together butter or margarine and 1¼ cups sugar until light and fluffy. Add eggs; beat well. Blend in sour cream. Stir together flour, baking powder, baking soda and salt. Add to creamed mixture, mixing well.

Spread half of batter into a greased 13 x 9-inch baking pan. Spoon drained strawberries over batter. Combine walnuts, brown sugar, 2 tablespoons sugar and cinnamon. Sprinkle half of nut mixture on top of strawberries. Spread remaining batter over all. Sprinkle with remaining nut mixture. Bake for 30–35 minutes, or until cake tests done. In a small saucepan, combine cornstarch and reserved syrup. Heat and stir until thickened and bubbly; cool. To serve, top each piece with whipped topping and then drizzle thickened syrup over top. Serves 12.

Orange Cake Delight

¾ cup shortening
1½ cups sugar
3 egg yolks, beaten
2¼ cups cake flour
½ teaspoon salt
3½ teaspoons baking powder
¾ cup cold water
¼ cup orange juice
1 tablespoon grated orange rind

3 egg whites, stiffly beaten
Orange Filling (recipe follows)
Orange Frosting (recipe follows)

Preheat oven to 350 degrees. Cream shortening and sugar; add egg yolks; beat well. Add sifted dry ingredients alternately with water, orange juice and rind. Fold in egg whites. Bake in 2 greased and floured 9-inch layer cake pans for 30–35 minutes. Place Orange Filling between layers and frost with Orange Frosting. Sprinkle grated orange rind in center. Feathery-light, this cake stays moist and has a grand orange flavor.

Orange Filling

2 tablespoons butter
¼ cup cornstarch
1 cup sugar
½ teaspoon salt
2 tablespoons grated orange rind
1 cup orange juice with pulp
1½ tablespoons lemon juice

Melt butter; add cornstarch; blend. Add sugar, salt, grated orange rind and orange juice; mix well. Cook in double boiler until thick. Remove from heat; add lemon juice.

Orange Frosting

¾ cup sugar
¼ cup water
2 egg whites, stiffly beaten
½ tablespoon orange juice
Grated orange rind

Cook sugar and water to thread stage (234 degrees). Pour over egg whites. Add orange juice; beat until thick.

Apple Cake

2 cups sugar
½ cup margarine
2 eggs
2 teaspoons baking soda
1 teaspoon cinnamon
2 cups flour
4 cups apples, sliced

Cream sugar and margarine; add eggs. Stir in baking soda, cinnamon and flour. Add sliced apples. Bake in 13 x 9-inch pan at 350 degrees for 55–60 minutes or until done.

Raisin Pudding Cake

1 cup all-purpose flour
1 cup sugar
2 teaspoons baking powder
¼ teaspoon salt
½ cup milk
3 eggs
1 cup raisins
½ cup chopped walnuts
1 cup brown sugar
1 teaspoon butter
1 cup boiling water

Preheat oven to 350 degrees. Grease 9-inch square baking pan. Sift together flour, sugar, baking powder and salt. Add milk, eggs, raisins and walnuts. Mix well. Spread in pan. Combine sugar, butter and water; stir well. Pour sugar mixture over batter but *do not mix together.* Bake for 35 minutes.

Mississippi Mud Cake

⅓ cup cocoa
2 sticks margarine
4 eggs
2 cups sugar
1½ cups flour
Pinch of salt
1½ cups nuts, chopped
Marshmallows
Frosting (recipe follows)

Melt cocoa and butter in pan over low heat. Pour into bowl and add eggs, sugar, flour and salt; mix thoroughly.

Stir in nuts. Bake at 350 degrees for 30 minutes or until done. Place on greased cookie sheet. Spread marshmallows over top when cake is done and just removed from oven. Place in oven for a couple minutes just until marshmallows are melted. Cool. Frost.

Frosting

½ stick butter
⅓ cup cocoa
1 teaspoon vanilla
4 cups confectioners' sugar
⅓ cup milk

Mix together butter, cocoa, vanilla, sugar and milk until smooth; frost cake.

Vanilla Wafer Cake

2 sticks butter
6 eggs
½ cup milk
3 cups vanilla wafer crumbs
2½ cups coconut
2 cups sugar
1 teaspoon vanilla
1 cup chopped walnuts
Confectioners' sugar

Cream butter until fluffy. Add sugar and beat until creamy. Add eggs, 1 at a time, beating well. Fold in vanilla crumbs, coconut and nuts, alternately with milk. Add vanilla. Butter and flour tube pan. Pour in batter and top with *brown paper.* Bake in a 350-degree oven for 1 hour. Top with confectioners' sugar while still warm.

Pudding Cake

2 cups flour
½ teaspoon salt
1½ cups sugar
4 teaspoons baking powder
1 cup milk
4 teaspoons butter, melted
2 teaspoons vanilla
1 cup nuts, chopped (optional)
1 cup sugar
1 cup brown sugar
10 teaspoons cocoa
2½ cups water

In large bowl, combine flour, salt, sugar and baking powder. Beat in milk, butter and vanilla; add nuts and stir. Pour into baking dish. Meanwhile, combine sugar, brown sugar and cocoa; add water and heat until sugar is dissolved. Pour cocoa mixture over cake batter. Bake at 350 degrees for 30–40 minutes.

Pineapple Fluff Cake

6 egg whites
¼ teaspoon salt
1½ cups sugar, divided
6 egg yolks
1 tablespoon lemon juice
½ cup unsweetened pineapple juice

1½ cups cake flour
1 teaspoon baking powder
Whipped cream
Maraschino cherries

Heat oven to 325 degrees. Beat egg whites with salt to form moist, glossy peaks. Gradually beat in ¾ cup sugar. Beat egg yolks and ¾ cup sugar until thick; add lemon and pineapple juices; beat until sugar dissolves. Add flour sifted with baking powder. Fold in egg whites. Bake in a 10-inch *ungreased* angel food cake pan for 1 hour. Invert to cool. Frost with whipped cream; decorate with maraschino cherries.

Delicious Apple Cake

1½ cups oil
2 cups sugar
2 teaspoons vanilla
2 eggs
3 cups flour
½ teaspoon salt
1 teaspoon baking soda
1 teaspoon cinnamon
3 cups apples, diced
1 cup pecans, chopped

Combine oil, sugar, vanilla and eggs. Stir in flour, salt, baking soda and cinnamon; add apples and pecans. Spread into a greased and floured 9 x 13-inch pan. Bake at 350 degrees for 45 minutes. Serve warm or cold.

Lemon-Frosted Angel Food Cake

9- or 10-inch angel food cake, prepared and baked
1 (21-ounce) can lemon pie filling *or* lemon topping
1 (8-ounce) carton lemon yogurt
1 (8-ounce) container non-dairy whipped topping
Lemon slices *or* lemon jelly candies (for garnish)

Cut cake into 4 layers. In medium bowl mix together lemon filling and yogurt. Spread filling between each layer, but not on top of cake. Frost sides and top of cake with whipped topping; garnish with lemon slices.

Cherry Upside-Down Cake

2 No. 2 cans pitted cherries
1½ cups sugar
2 teaspoons cinnamon
1 (2-layer) package cherry cake mix

Drain cherries, reserving liquid. Mix cherries, sugar and cinnamon in bowl. Line bottom of 12 x 9 x 2-inch pan with waxed paper; grease sides. Spread cherry mixture in pan. Prepare cake mix according to package directions, using cherry liquid as part of required liquid. Pour over cherry mixture. Bake at 350 degrees for 40 minutes. Invert immediately onto large platter.

Crumb Cake

2 cups brown sugar
2 cups flour
½ cup lard
1 cup sour milk
Pinch salt
1 egg
1 teaspoon baking soda
Nuts, chopped

Cream sugar and lard; add flour and make as pie dough. Save ¾ cup crumbs for topping. Stir in egg, sour milk, salt and baking soda; add nuts. Pour into a 13 x 9-inch pan and sprinkle reserved crumbs on top. Bake at 350 degrees for 45–50 minutes.

Sugar Cream Cake

1 box yellow cake mix
2 eggs
½ cup margarine, softened
1 pound confectioners' sugar
1 (8-ounce) package cream cheese
2 eggs

Preheat oven to 350 degrees. Beat cake mix, 2 eggs and margarine together. Batter will be rubbery. Spread in lightly greased 9 x 13 x 2-inch pan. Combine and beat sugar, cheese and eggs. Spread on top of cake batter. Bake for 30 minutes, or until toothpick inserted in center comes out clean. Store cake in refrigerator.

Cupcake Cones

1 (2-layer) package chocolate cake mix
24 (2- to 3-inch-high) flat-bottom ice cream cones
2 (16½-ounce) cans prepared chocolate frosting
   M & M chocolate candies
   Sprinkles
   Gumdrops
   Toasted coconut
   Chopped nuts

Preheat oven to 350 degrees. Prepare cake mix batter according to package directions. Spoon 3 tablespoons into each cone. Place 3 inches apart on ungreased baking sheet.

Bake for 30–35 minutes or until toothpick inserted in center comes out clean. Cool on wire rack. Frost and decorate with candies, coconut or nuts. Makes 2 dozen.

Orange Ring Cake

3 eggs, separated
1 cup butter *or* margarine
1 cup sugar
1 cup sour cream
   Grated rind of 1 orange
1 teaspoon baking powder
2 cups sifted cake flour *or* 1¾ cups sifted all-purpose flour
1 teaspoon baking soda
   Orange Glaze (recipe follows)

Preheat oven to 325 degrees. Grease and flour a 9-inch tube pan. Beat egg whites until stiff, but not dry; set aside. Cream butter and sugar. Add egg yolks, sour cream and orange rind; beat until light and fluffy. Sift together flour, baking powder and baking soda. Stir into butter mixture. Fold in egg whites. Turn into prepared pan. Bake for 1 hour. Remove from oven and let stand about 10 minutes. Loosen carefully around the edge and turn out on a plate with rim. Glaze.

Orange Glaze

   Juice of 2 oranges
   Juice of 1 lemon
   Pinch of salt
¾ cup sugar

Combine ingredients in a saucepan and boil gently for 3–4 minutes, stirring thoroughly. Slowly pour hot syrup over cake. Serves 10–12.

1-2-3-4 Cake

1 cup shortening
2 cups white sugar
3 cups flour
4 eggs
1 cup milk
3 teaspoons baking powder
2 teaspoons vanilla

Heat oven to 350 degrees. Sift together flour and baking powder; set aside. Cream together sugar and shortening. Add eggs, 1 at a time, alternating with small amounts of sifted mixture and milk. Beat well after each addition. Add vanilla; blend well. Grease 2 layer pans and fill with batter; bake for about 30 minutes or until done. Test with toothpick in middle of cake after 20 minutes.

Apple Cider Spice Cake

1 package spice cake mix
½ cup cornstarch
4 large eggs
1 cup apple cider
½ cup mayonnaise
2 cups nuts, finely chopped
   Confectioners' sugar

Combine cake mix and cornstarch. Stir until well blended. Add eggs, apple cider and mayonnaise; beat until blended—2 minutes, scraping bowl. Stir in nuts. Pour into greased and floured tube or bundt pan. Bake at 350 degrees for 20–30 minutes or until done. Before serving, sprinkle cake with confectioners' sugar.

Easy Apple Cake

1 cup oil
1 teaspoon vanilla
2 eggs
2 cups sugar
¼ teaspoon salt
2 cups flour
1 teaspoon baking soda
1 teaspoon cinnamon
3 cups apples, diced

Beat together oil, vanilla, eggs and sugar. Sift together salt, flour, baking soda and cinnamon; add to oil mixture. Fold in apples. Bake 1 hour at 325 degrees in 10 x 14-inch pan.

Aunt Kathy's Apple Cake

1½ cups oil
2 eggs
2 cups sugar
2½ cups flour
1 teaspoon salt
1 teaspoon baking soda
2 teaspoons baking powder
1 teaspoon vanilla
1 cup nuts, chopped
3 cups apples, finely chopped

Beat together oil, eggs and sugar until creamy. Add flour, salt, baking soda, baking powder and vanilla; mix well. Stir in nuts and apples. Pour into well-greased pan. Bake at 350 degrees for 1 hour.

Banana Cake

1¼ cup flour
⅔ cup sugar
¼ cup cornstarch
1 teaspoon baking soda
½ teaspoon salt
1 cup bananas, mashed
⅓ cup oil
1 egg, slightly beaten
1 teaspoon vinegar
1 teaspoon vanilla

Mix together flour, sugar, cornstarch, baking soda and salt; set aside. Combine bananas, oil, egg, vinegar and vanilla; stir into flour mixture. Bake at 350 degrees in a 13 x 9-inch pan for 55–60 minutes.

Washington's Surprise

1 (19-ounce) white cake mix
1 (21-ounce) can cherry pie filling
2 eggs, beaten
1 tablespoon vanilla
⅔ cup vegetable oil
¾ cup nuts

Stir cake mix and pie filling together. This will be very thick. Combine eggs, vanilla, oil and nuts; add to cake mix. Blend well. Place in a greased 9 x 13-inch pan. Bake at 350 degrees for 40–50 minutes. Cool and serve. Serves 15–20.

Cookies
& BARS

Gingerbread People

1 cup sugar
1 tablespoon ginger
2 teaspoons cinnamon
1 teaspoon cloves
½ cup water
½ cup corn syrup
1 cup (2 sticks) butter
4 cups all-purpose flour
1½ teaspoons baking soda
¼ teaspoon salt
Colored icing

Combine sugar, spices, water and corn syrup in small saucepan. Bring to boiling, stirring constantly. Remove from heat and pour over butter in large mixer bowl. Stir until butter melts; cool to lukewarm. Combine flour, baking soda and salt. Add to butter mixture; mix well. Cover and refrigerate dough overnight.

Preheat oven to 375 degrees. Roll dough on lightly floured surface to ⅛-inch-thickness. Cut with floured gingerbread people cutters. Bake on unbuttered cookie sheets 12–15 minutes, or until golden. Cool completely on wire racks; decorate as desired with icing. Makes 3 dozen.

Raspberry Meringue Bars

1 cup (2 sticks) butter
½ cup firmly packed brown sugar
1 egg
2 cups all-purpose flour
1 (12-ounce) jar raspberry preserves

½ cup seedless raisins
½ teaspoon almond extract
2 egg whites
¾ cup sugar
½ cup flaked coconut
½ cup sliced almonds

Preheat oven to 325 degrees. Cream butter and brown sugar in large mixer bowl until light and fluffy. Blend in egg. Add flour; mix well. Spread dough in buttered 13 x 9-inch baking pan. Bake 25 minutes.

Meanwhile, combine preserves, raisins and extract. Spread over baked cookie base. Beat egg whites until foamy. Gradually beat in sugar. Continue beating until stiff peaks form. Gently fold in coconut and almonds. Spread over raspberry mixture.

Return to oven and bake until meringue is lightly browned, about 20 minutes. Cool completely in pan on wire rack. Cut into bars. Makes 4 dozen.

Oatmeal Shortbread

1 cup butter *or* margarine, softened
½ cup firmly packed brown sugar
1 teaspoon vanilla
1 cup flour
½ teaspoon baking soda
2 cups oats

Cream together butter, brown sugar and vanilla until fluffy. Stir in flour, baking soda and oats. Chill 1–2 hours. Roll dough ¼-inch thick. Cut with 1½-inch cookie cutters. Bake on ungreased cookie sheet at 350 degrees for 10–12 minutes. Makes 3–4 dozen cookies.

Children's Delight

1 cup shortening
1 cup sugar
1 cup brown sugar
2 eggs
1 teaspoon vanilla
½ teaspoon salt
1 teaspoon baking soda
1 teaspoon baking powder
1 cup chocolate *or* butterscotch chips
2 cups oatmeal
2 cups flour

Cream shortening and sugars. Beat in eggs and vanilla. Stir together salt, baking soda, baking powder, oatmeal and flour. Combine creamed mixture with flour mixture. Stir in chips. Drop by spoonfuls onto lightly greased cookie sheets. Bake at 350 degrees for 8–10 minutes.

Angel Cookies

½ cup brown sugar
½ cup white sugar
1 cup shortening
1 egg
2 cups flour
1 teaspoon baking soda
½ teaspoon cream of tartar
¼ teaspoon salt

Cream sugars in shortening. Add egg and then sifted flour, baking soda, cream of tartar and salt. Roll into small balls. Cover bottom of glass with cloth. Moisten and dip in sugar and press. Bake at 325 degrees until lightly browned. Makes 6 dozen.

Candy Cane & Wreath Cookies

1¼ cups (2½ sticks) butter
1 cup confectioners' sugar
1 egg
1 teaspoon vanilla extract
½ teaspoon almond extract
3½ cups all-purpose flour
¼ teaspoon salt
   Red and green food color
1 egg white
   Red and green decorating sugar
   Cinnamon candies

Cream butter in large mixer bowl. Gradually add sugar and beat until light and fluffy. Beat in egg and extracts. Combine flour and salt. Gradually add to creamed mixture; mix well.

Set aside half of dough. Divide other half in 2 parts. Tint 1 part light green and the other light red with food color. Wrap all dough in plastic wrap. Refrigerate 30 minutes to 1 hour. Work with small amounts of dough. Keep remaining dough chilled for ease in handling.

Preheat oven to 350 degrees. For candy canes, roll, with hands, 1 teaspoonful of white dough and 1 teaspoonful of red dough into strips about 4 inches long. Place strips side by side and twist together gently. Carefully place on unbuttered cookie sheets and curve the top down to form a cane. Brush with egg white and sprinkle with red sugar. Bake 10–12 minutes.

For wreaths, roll 1 teaspoonful of white dough and 1 of green into strips about 4 inches long. Twist strips together; form into a circle on cookie sheet. Brush with egg white and sprinkle with green sugar. Use cinnamon candies for garnish and bake as for candy canes. Makes 4–5 dozen.

English Toffee Bars

1 cup (2 sticks) butter
1 cup sugar
1 egg yolk
1¾ cups all-purpose flour
1 teaspoon cinnamon

1 egg white, slightly beaten
1 cup chopped pecans
3 tablespoons milk
2 (1-ounce) squares semisweet chocolate

Preheat oven to 275 degrees. Cream butter in large mixer bowl. Gradually add sugar and beat until light and fluffy. Beat in egg yolk. Combine flour and cinnamon. Gradually add to creamed mixture. Press evenly into buttered 13 x 9-inch pan. Brush top with egg white. Sprinkle with pecans; press lightly into dough. Bake 1 hour.

Meanwhile, heat milk and chocolate together over low heat until chocolate is melted. Remove pan from oven; cool slightly. Cut into 1½-inch squares or diamonds; drizzle with melted chocolate. Cool completely in pan on wire rack. Makes 5–6 dozen.

Topped with colored sugar or tinted frosting or just served plain, these delicate spritz cookies are simple to make and taste delicious.

Surprise Packages

1 cup (2 sticks) butter
1 cup granulated sugar
½ cup firmly packed brown sugar
2 eggs
1 teaspoon vanilla extract
3 cups all-purpose flour
1 teaspoon baking soda
¼ teaspoon salt
48 thin-layered chocolate mint wafers
   Red and green decorator icing

Cream butter and sugars in large mixer bowl until light and fluffy. Beat in eggs and vanilla. Combine dry ingredients. Gradually add to creamed mixture; mix well. Divide dough in half; wrap each in plastic wrap and refrigerate 1–2 hours for ease in handling.

Preheat oven to 375 degrees. Work with half of dough at a time, leaving remaining half refrigerated. Using 1 scant tablespoon dough, cover each mint, forming rectangular-shaped cookie. Place about 2 inches apart on lightly buttered cookie sheets. Bake 10–12 minutes. Cool completely on wire racks; decorate with decorator icing to look like a wrapped package. Makes 4 dozen.

Coffee Pecan Crescents

1 cup (2 sticks) butter
⅓ cup sugar
1½ teaspoons instant coffee*
1½ teaspoons water*
½ teaspoon vanilla extract
2 cups all-purpose flour
2 cups finely chopped pecans
¼ teaspoon salt
   Confectioners' sugar
   Granulated sugar

Cream butter in large mixer bowl. Gradually add sugar and beat until light and fluffy. Dissolve coffee in water. Add to creamed mixture with vanilla. Combine flour, nuts and salt. Gradually stir into creamed mixture. Press dough into a ball. Wrap in plastic wrap and refrigerate at least 1 hour for ease in handling.

Preheat oven to 325 degrees. Shape teaspoonfuls of dough into crescents. Place 1 inch apart on unbuttered cookie sheets. Bake about 20 minutes, or until set, but not brown. While still warm, roll cookies first in confectioners' sugar, then in granulated sugar and again in confectioners' sugar. Cool completely on wire racks. Makes 5 dozen.

*Coffee and water may be deleted and dough shaped into 1-inch balls and flattened slightly; bake as above.

Chewy Cocoa Brownies

2 cups flour
1¼ cups cocoa
1 teaspoon salt
4 cups sugar
1 cup plus 2 tablespoons shortening
8 eggs
2 tablespoons vanilla
   Nuts
   Confectioners' sugar

Combine flour, cocoa, salt and sugar. Cream shortening with eggs; add vanilla. Mix together flour mixture with shortening mixture. Stir in nuts. Bake at 325–350 degrees for 40 minutes. Cut into squares when done. Roll in confectioners' sugar after cooled.

The Best Butter Cookies

2 cups (4 sticks) butter
1½ cups sugar
2 eggs
1 teaspoon vanilla extract
5 cups all-purpose flour
2 teaspoons baking powder
¼ teaspoon salt

Cream butter in large mixer bowl. Gradually add sugar and beat until light and fluffy. Blend in eggs and vanilla. Combine flour, baking powder and salt. Gradually add to creamed mixture; mix well. Divide dough into 4 equal portions. Mix and shape dough for each variety as follows:

Cutouts

Preheat oven to 375 degrees. Roll ¼ portion of dough on lightly floured surface to ⅛-inch thickness. Cut into desired shapes with floured cookie cutters. Place on unbuttered cookie sheets. Bake 6–8 minutes. Cool completely on wire racks; decorate as desired. Makes 2 dozen.

Peppermint Balls

Preheat oven to 375 degrees. Beat ¼ cup crushed peppermint candy and ¼ teaspoon peppermint extract into ¼ portion of dough. Shape into 1-inch balls. Place on unbuttered cookie sheet. Sprinkle with red colored sugar. Bake 8–10 minutes. Cool completely on wire racks. Makes 2 dozen.

Spicy Fruit Balls

Preheat oven to 375 degrees. Beat ½ cup each currants and chopped mixed candied fruit and ½ teaspoon cinnamon into ¼ portion of dough. Shape into 1-inch balls. Place on unbuttered cookie sheets. Bake 8–10 minutes. While still warm roll in confectioners' sugar. Cool completely on wire racks.

Chocolate Slices

Beat 1 ounce (1 square) melted unsweetened chocolate into ¼ portion of dough. Shape into log approximately 1½ inches in diameter. Roll in chopped nuts. Wrap in plastic wrap and refrigerate several hours or overnight. Preheat oven to 375 degrees. Cut dough into ⅛-inc-thick slices. Place on unbuttered cookie sheets. Bake 6–8 minutes. Cool completely on wire racks.

Chocolate Pixies

¼ cup (½ stick) butter
2 (1-ounce) squares unsweetened chocolate
2 eggs
1 cup sugar
1½ cups all-purpose flour
1 teaspoon baking powder
¼ teaspoon salt
¼ cup chopped walnuts
Confectioners' sugar

Melt butter and chocolate in a heavy saucepan over low heat. Beat eggs and sugar in large mixer bowl. Gradually mix in chocolate mixture. Combine flour, baking powder and salt; gradually add to chocolate mixture. Stir in walnuts. Chill dough at least 1 hour.

Preheat oven to 300 degrees. Shape dough into 1-inch balls. Roll in confectioners' sugar. Place on buttered cookie sheets. Bake 15–18 minutes. Cool completely on wire racks. Makes 3 dozen.

Buttermilk Sugar Cookies

1 cup shortening
2 cups sugar
2 large eggs
1 cup buttermilk
1 teaspoon baking soda
4 teaspoons baking powder
4 cups flour
Pinch salt
Confectioners' Sugar Frosting (recipe follows)

Cream shortening and sugar; add eggs. Stir in buttermilk, baking soda, baking powder, flour and salt. Chill dough several hours. Roll out ¼ of dough at a time on floured surface. Cut into desired shapes. Bake at 350 degrees for 10 minutes. Do not overbake. Ice with Confectioners' Sugar Frosting.

Confectioners' Sugar Frosting

½ cups confectioners' sugar
½ cup shortening
1 teaspoon vanilla
½ teaspoon almond extract
5 tablespoons milk

Mix together sugar, shortening, vanilla, almond extract and enough milk to make smooth. Frost cookies.

Breakstick Cookies

½ cup raisins
3 cups brown sugar
1½ cups margarine or butter
¼ teaspoon salt
1 cup corn syrup
3 eggs
2 teaspoon vanilla
4½ teaspoons baking soda
½ cup nuts, chopped
6½ cups flour

Cover raisins with water and simmer until liquid is almost absorbed. Let stand until cool. Cream brown sugar and margarine. Add salt, corn syrup, eggs, vanilla, baking soda, flour, nuts and raisins; mix well. Make dough in long rolls the size of a breakstick handle or smaller. This will make about 12 rolls. Place 3 rolls on a cookie sheet as they will spread.

Bake for 15–20 minutes at 350–375 degrees. Make a spread of confectioners' sugar and water. Dribble over the hot baked cookies back and forth. Cut at once diagonally about ½ inch apart. Remove from cookie sheet. Freezes well. Makes 80–100 cookies.

Cream Cheese Spritz

1 cup (2 sticks) butter
1 (3-ounce) package cream cheese, softened
1 cup sugar
1 egg yolk
1 teaspoon vanilla extract
2 cups all-purpose flour
½ teaspoon salt
¼ teaspoon baking powder

Preheat oven to 350 degrees. Cream butter and cream cheese in large mixer bowl. Gradually add sugar and beat until blended. Beat in egg yolk and vanilla. Combine flour, salt and baking powder. Gradually add to creamed mixture. Fill cookie press. Use attachments to form cookie designs on unbuttered cookie sheets. Bake 12–15 minutes. Cool completely on wire racks. Makes 7 dozen.

Note: Before baking, dough may be tinted or sprinkled with colored sugar or a cinnamon-sugar mixture; or decorate cookies with a tinted frosting after baking.

Orange Filled Cookies

1 cup butter
½ cup sugar
½ cup firmly packed brown sugar
1 egg
3 cups flour
¼ teaspoon baking soda
½ teaspoon salt
1 tablespoon grated orange peel
¼ cup orange juice
1 teaspoon vanilla
Orange Filling (recipe follows)

Cream together butter, sugars and egg until fluffy. Stir in flour, baking soda, salt, orange peel, orange juice and vanilla. Shape into 2 (6½-inch) rolls; chill. Cut into ⅛-inch slices. Bake on ungreased cookie sheets at 375 degrees for 12–15 minutes. Cool; spoon 1 teaspoon of Orange Filling on a cookie and top with another cookie.

Orange Filling

2 cups confectioners' sugar
¼ cup butter, softened
2–3 tablespoons orange juice concentrate (thawed)

Mix together sugar, butter and orange juice concentrate.

Amish Cookies

2 cups oil
3 cups sugar
4 eggs
6 cups flour
1 teaspoon baking soda
2 tablespoons baking powder
2 cups buttermilk
1½ teaspoons vanilla
½ teaspoon salt
1 teaspoon cinnamon
½ teaspoon nutmeg
Cinnamon
Sugar

Combine oil, sugar and eggs. Stir in flour, baking soda, baking powder, buttermilk, vanilla, salt, cinnamon and nutmeg. Drop 4 or 5 cookies on ungreased cookie sheet, each cookie measuring ¼ cup. Sprinkle with cinnamon and sugar. Bake 7–8 minutes at 375 degrees.

Soft Sugar Cookies

2 cups sugar
1 cup shortening
2 eggs
1 teaspoon vanilla
1 cup sour milk
1 teaspoon baking soda
2 teaspoons baking powder
5 cups flour
1 teaspoon salt
Sugar

Cream together sugar and shortening; add eggs and vanilla. Blend baking soda and milk; set aside. Combine baking powder, flour and salt. Alternately add flour and milk mixtures to creamed mixture. Chill for 1 hour. Roll; cut with cookie cutters. Sprinkle with sugar. Bake at 350 degrees for 10–12 minutes or until done, but not brown.

Gelatin Cookies

½ cup sugar
1 (3-ounce) box gelatin, any flavor
½ cup butter
½ teaspoon salt
2 eggs
½ teaspoon almond flavoring
1 teaspoon vanilla
½ cup milk
2¾ cups flour
1 teaspoon baking soda
Confectioners' sugar
gelatin, any flavor

Cream sugar and gelatin; add butter, salt and eggs. Stir in almond flavoring, vanilla and milk. Add flour and baking soda. Drop onto ungreased cookie sheets. Bake at 350 degrees for 8–10 minutes or until done. Frost with the same kind of gelatin used in cookie mix. Add confectioners' sugar and water to make spreading consistency.

Chewy Date Drops

2 cups chopped dates
½ cup sugar
½ cup water
4 cups flour
1 teaspoon baking soda

1 cup margarine
1 cup sugar
1 cup brown sugar
3 eggs, beaten
1 teaspoon vanilla
1 cup chopped nuts (optional)

Combine dates, ½ cup sugar and ½ cup water; cook until thickened; cool. sift together flour and baking soda. Cream margarine; gradually add sugar; mix well. Blend eggs into sugar mixture; add vanilla. Stir in flour mixture. Mix thoroughly. Add nuts and stir. Drop dough by rounded teaspoonfuls onto greased cookie sheets and bake at 350 degrees for 12–15 minutes until golden brown.

Rolled Sugar Cookies

1 cup sugar
½ cup butter, softened
1 egg
¼ cup milk
½ teaspoon vanilla
2¼ cups flour
2 teaspoons baking powder
½ teaspoon salt

Cream together sugar and butter; add egg, milk and vanilla. Beat well. Sift together flour, baking powder and salt. Cover. Chill 1 hour. Divide dough in half. Roll to ⅛-inch thickness; cut with cookie cutters. Bake at 375 degrees for 7–8 minutes.

Chocolate Cookies

1 cup brown sugar
½ cup butter
2 eggs, well beaten
1¾ cups flour
½ teaspoon baking soda
½ cup milk
4 tablespoons cocoa
1 cup nuts, chopped

Cream brown sugar and butter. Add eggs; beat well. Stir in flour, baking soda, milk and cocoa. Add nuts; stir. Drop by spoonfuls onto cookie sheets. Bake at 350 degrees for 8–10 minutes.

Oatmeal Crispies

1 cup shortening
1 cup brown sugar
1 cup sugar
2 eggs
1 teaspoon vanilla
1½ cups flour
1 teaspoon salt
1 teaspoon baking soda
3 cups oatmeal
½ cup nuts, chopped
¾ cup chocolate chips

Cream together shortening and sugars; add eggs and vanilla; mix. Stir together flour, salt, baking soda, oatmeal, nuts and chocolate chips. Stir into sugar mixture; mix well. Drop by spoonfuls onto ungreased cookie sheets. Bake at 350 degrees for 8–10 minutes.

Gingerbread Men

1 cup dark molasses
½ cup light brown sugar
½ cup sugar
4 teaspoons ground ginger
4 teaspoons cinnamon
½ teaspoon allspice
¾ tablespoons baking soda
1 cup butter
2 eggs
6 cups flour, sifted

Heat molasses, sugars and spices in double boiler. When sugar has melted, add baking soda and stir until mixture bubbles; remove from heat. Add butter to molasses mixture and let cool to room temperature. Stir in eggs; gradually add flour. Roll dough and cut into desired shapes. Bake on parchment paper at 325 degrees for 15–20 minutes.

Monster Cookies

12 eggs
4 cups brown sugar
4 cups sugar
1 tablespoon vanilla
3 pounds peanut butter
1 pound butter *or* margarine
1 tablespoon corn syrup
8 teaspoons baking soda
18 cups oatmeal
1 pound chocolate chips
1 pound M&Ms

Combine eggs with sugars; add butter, peanut butter, vanilla and corn syrup; mix well. Stir in baking soda, oatmeal, chocolate chips and M&Ms. Drop by spoonfuls onto greased cookie sheets. Bake at 350 degrees for 12 minutes or until done. Do not overbake.

Browned Butter Cookies

2½ cups flour
1 teaspoon baking soda
½ teaspoon baking powder
¼ teaspoon salt
1½ cups firmly packed brown sugar
½ cup margarine
2 eggs
1 teaspoon vanilla
1 cup sour cream
1 cup coarsely chopped walnuts
Browned Butter Icing (recipe follows)

Mix together flour, baking soda, baking powder and salt; set aside. Combine brown sugar and margarine; beat on medium speed with an electric mixer until well combined. Beat in eggs and vanilla until fluffy. Add dry ingredients to margarine mixture; stir in sour cream; mix well. Add nuts, Drop by teaspoonfuls onto greased cookie sheet and bake at 350 degrees for 10 minutes; cool; frost. Makes 56 cookies.

Browned Butter Icing

¼ cup butter
2 cups sifted confectioners' sugar
Boiling water

Heat butter until light brown in color; remove from heat. Stir in sugar and enough boiling water to make icing smooth. Frost cookies immediately.

Pineapple Cookies

1 cup brown sugar
1 cup sugar
1 cup lard
2 eggs
Pinch of salt
1 (15-ounce) can crushed pineapple, drained
1½ teaspoons vanilla
3 teaspoons baking powder
1½ teaspoons baking soda
4 cups flour

Cream together sugars and lard. Add eggs, pinch of salt; beat well. Fold in drained pineapple and vanilla. Stir together baking powder, baking soda and flour. Stir into sugar mixture. Drop by spoonfuls onto cookie sheets. Bake at 350 degrees for 8–10 minutes.

Old-Fashioned Sugar Cookies

2 cups vegetable oil
3 cups sugar
4 eggs
2 cups buttermilk
6 cups flour
6 teaspoons baking powder
3 teaspoons vanilla

Mix together oil, sugar and eggs. Add buttermilk, flour, baking powder and vanilla. Drop on ungreased cookie sheet; sprinkle with sugar. Bake at 400 degrees for 5–7 minutes. Makes 3 dozen.

Apple Pie Bars

2½ cups flour
1 cup shortening
¾ teaspoon salt
1 egg, separated
Milk
6 cups apples, peeled and sliced
1⅓ cups sugar
½ teaspoon cinnamon
2 tablespoons flour
4 tablespoons tapioca

Mix together flour, shortening and salt. Add enough milk to egg yolk to make ⅔ cup liquid; add to flour mixture. Roll out half of the dough to cover a large oblong cookie sheet; place in bottom of pan.

Cover with apples. Sprinkle with mixture of sugar, cinnamon, 2 tablespoons flour and tapioca.

Roll out the rest of the dough and put on top of the apples, sealing edges together. Beat egg white until foamy and brush over top of dough. Bake at 425 degrees for 10 minutes, reduce heat to 375 degrees and cook an additional 20–25 minutes. Cut into bars.

Old Fashioned Oatmeal Cookies

- 2 cups raisins
- 1 cup sugar
- 1 cup shortening
- 2 eggs
- 1 teaspoon vanilla
- 2 cups flour, sifted
- 1 teaspoon baking soda
- ½ teaspoon salt
- 1 teaspoon cinnamon
- ½ teaspoon nutmeg
- ½ teaspoon cloves
- 2 cups quick-cooking oats

Cover raisins with water, barely covering. Simmer for 10 minutes. Save ⅓ cup of raisin water, drain off the rest. Cream sugar and shortening. Blend in eggs and vanilla; beat well. Stir in raisins and the ⅓ cup reserved raisin water. In another bowl combine flour, baking soda, salt, cinnamon, nutmeg, cloves and oats. Stir into creamed mixture. Drop by teaspoonfuls onto lightly greased cookie sheets. Bake at 350 degrees for 10–12 minutes.

Liqueur Gingerbread People

- ½ cup shortening
- ¼ cup butter
- ¼ cup firmly packed light brown sugar
- ½ cup sugar
- 1 large egg
- ¼ cup light molasses
- 2 tablespoons coffee liqueur
- 2¼ cups flour
- 1 tablespoon baking soda
- 1 teaspoon salt
- 1 teaspoon ginger
- ½ teaspoon cinnamon
- ½ teaspoon nutmeg
  Coffee Liqueur Icing (recipe follows)

Cream together shortening, butter and sugars; add egg; beat until fluffy. Stir in molasses and coffee liqueur. Add flour, baking soda, salt, ginger, cinnamon and nutmeg; blend well. Refrigerate at least 2 hours until dough is firm.

Divide dough and roll each ⅜ inch thick. Cut with cookie cutters. Bake on greased cookie sheet at 350 degrees for 6–8 minutes. Let stand 1 minute to firm. Decorate with Coffee Liqueur Icing.

Coffee Liqueur Icing

- 1 pound confectioners' sugar
- 4–6 tablespoons coffee liqueur
- 3 tablespoons shortening
- 3 tablespoons butter
- 2 teaspoons light corn syrup

Combine sugar with coffee liqueur, shortening, butter and corn syrup. Spread on cookies. Makes 2–3 dozen cookies.

Cream Puffs

- ½ cup water
- ¼ cup butter
  Pinch salt
- ½ cup flour
- 2 medium eggs
- 4 cups prepared pudding (any flavor)
- 2 cups melted chocolate

Bring water, butter and salt to a boil. Add flour, all at once. Stir continually until dough pulls from sides of pan and forms ball. Cool. Beat in eggs, 1 at a time. Drop by teaspoonfuls onto a greased cookie sheet. Bake at 350 degrees for 15–20 minutes or until hollow sounding when tapped.

Cool completely and freeze. To freeze, wrap in plastic, then in aluminum foil. When thawing, leave wrapped until completely thawed. Fill cream puffs with assorted pudding flavors and dip the tops of cream puffs in different colors of chocolate. Example; chocolate pudding–dark chocolate coating; pistachio pudding–green chocolate coating, etc.

Mexican Wedding Rings

- 1 cup butter
- 4 tablespoons sugar
- 2 teaspoons vanilla
- 2 cups pecans
- 2 cups flour
  Confectioners' sugar

Cream together butter and sugar; add vanilla. Stir in pecans and flour. Roll into balls. Bake at 350 degrees 10–12 minutes. Roll in confectioners' sugar.

Molasses Cookies

- 1 cup sugar
- ½ cup shortening
- 1 cup dark molasses
- ½ cup water
- 4 cups flour
- 1½ teaspoons salt
- 1 teaspoon baking soda
- 1½ teaspoons ground ginger
- ½ teaspoon ground cloves
- ½ teaspoon ground nutmeg
- ¼ teaspoon ground allspice
  Sugar

Cream together sugar, shortening and molasses. Stir in water. Add flour, salt, baking soda, ginger, cloves, nutmeg and allspice. Refrigerate at least 2 hours.

Roll dough ¼-inch thick; cut into 3-inch circles. Sprinkle with sugar; place about 1½ inches apart on ungreased cookie sheet. Bake at 375 degrees for 10–12 minutes. Let cool 2 minutes before removing from cookie sheet. Makes 3 dozen cookies.

Roll Out Cookies

- 1 cup brown sugar
- ½ cup butter, softened
- 2 eggs
- ½ cup milk
- 1½ teaspoons salt
- 2½ cups flour
- 4 teaspoons baking powder
- 1 teaspoon vanilla

Cream together sugar, butter and eggs; add milk. Stir in salt, flour, baking powder and vanilla. Roll and cut with cookie cutters. Bake at 350 degrees for 6–8 minutes until lightly browned.

Scotch Shortbread

- ¾ cup margarine or butter, softened
- ¼ cup sugar
- 2 cups flour

Cream margarine with sugar; mix in flour. Add 1–2 tablespoons margarine if dough is crumbly. Roll dough ½ inch thick. Cut with cookie cutters. Bake at 350 degrees on ungreased cookie sheet for 20 minutes. Makes 2 dozen cookies.

Peanut Cookies

1 cup butter
1 cup sugar
1 egg
2 teaspoons vanilla
3 cups flour
½ teaspoon salt
½ teaspoon baking soda
1 cup salted peanuts, finely chopped
Vanilla Filling (recipe follows)
Chocolate Frosting (recipe follows)

Cream together butter, sugar, egg and vanilla. Stir in flour, salt and baking soda. Add peanuts. Chill. Roll out to ⅛-inch thickness. Cut with 2-inch cookie cutters. Bake on ungreased cookie sheets at 400 degrees for 7–10 minutes. Stack 3 cookies together with filling. Top with frosting.

Vanilla Filling

6 tablespoons butter
1 pound confectioners' sugar
¼ cup milk
1½ teaspoons vanilla

Combine butter, sugar, milk and vanilla; mix until smooth. Fill cookies; save about ⅓ for Chocolate Frosting.

Chocolate Frosting

1 cup semi-sweet chocolate chips, melted
Reserved filling

Add chocolate chips to reserved filling. Frost cookies. Makes 3–4 dozen cookies.

Golden Apple Bars

⅔ cup shortening
2 cups brown sugar
2 eggs
1 teaspoon vanilla
½ teaspoon salt
2 cups sifted flour
2 teaspoons baking powder
1½ cups apples, shredded
½ cups nuts, chopped

Cream together shortening and brown sugar; add eggs, vanilla and salt. Beat well. Add flour and baking powder. Stir in apples and nuts. Bake in 12 x 8-inch pan at 350 degrees for 35–40 minutes. Cool. Cut into bars. Serve warm with whipped cream or ice cream. Makes 24 squares.

Big Soft Ginger Cookies

2¼ cups flour
2 teaspoons ground ginger
1 teaspoon baking soda
¾ teaspoon ground cinnamon
½ teapsoon ground cloves
¼ teaspoon salt
¾ cup margarine
1 cup sugar
1 egg
¼ cup molasses
2 tablespoons sugar

Mix together flour, ginger, baking soda, cinnamon, cloves and salt; set aside. Beat margarine with an electric mixer on low speed for 30 seconds to soften. Gradually add 1 cup sugar; beat until fluffy. Add egg and molasses; beat well. Stir dry ingredients into beaten mixture.

Shape into 1½-inch balls. Roll in sugar. Bake on ungreased cookie sheet at 350 degrees for 10 minutes or until light brown. Let stand on cookie sheet 2 minutes before removing. Makes 24 cookies.

Twin Cinnamon Whirls

½ cup butter
¼ cup sugar
1 egg
1 teaspoon vanilla
1 cup creamed cottage cheese
2¼ cups flour
2 teaspoons baking powder
1 teaspoon salt
¾ cup sugar
2–3 teaspoons cinnamon
3 tablespoons jelly

Cream together butter and ¼ cup sugar; add egg and vanilla. Stir in cottage cheese; blend well. Add flour, baking powder and salt. Divide dough into thirds; flatten and wrap in waxed paper. Chill at least 2 hours. Combine ¾ cup sugar and cinnamon. Roll 1 dough portion into a 12-inch circle. Sprinkle with ⅓ cinnamon/sugar mixture. Turn dough over several times to absorb cinnamon/sugar mixture. Brush with 1 tablespoon jelly.

Cut into 16 wedges. Roll up, starting with wide end and roll to a point. Cut ¾ of the way through center of wedges. Spread apart; place, cut side down, on greased cookie sheet. Repeat with remaining dough. Bake at 350 degrees for 20–25 minutes. Makes 4 dozen cookies.

Chocolate Pinwheel Cookies

1 cup margarine
1 cup peanut butter
1 cup sugar
1 cup brown sugar
2 eggs
2½ cups flour
1 teaspoon baking powder
1½ teaspoons baking soda
½ teaspoon salt
6 ounces Chocolate chips

Mix together margarine, peanut butter, sugars and eggs; stir in flour, baking powder, baking soda and salt. Melt chocolate chips in pan in oven. Roll out dough; spread chocolate over dough. Roll up like a jelly roll. Refrigerate; slice. Bake at 350–375 degrees for 9 minutes.

Cherry Winks

2¼ cups sifted flour
1 teaspoon baking powder
½ teaspoon baking soda
½ teaspoon salt
¾ cup shortening
1 cup sugar
2 eggs
2 tablespoons milk
1 teaspoon vanilla
1 cup chopped pecans
1 cup chopped dates
⅓ cup maraschino cherries
1 cup crushed cornflakes

Sift together flour, baking powder, baking soda and salt; set aside. Cream shortening and sugar; add eggs. Mix in milk and vanilla; blend in dry ingredients; mix well. Add pecans and dates. Shape into balls; roll in cornflakes; top with cherry. Bake at 375 degrees for 12–15 minutes.

Orange Cream Cookies

2¼ cups flour
½ teaspoon salt
1 cup shortening
1 cup sugar
1 (3-ounce) package cream cheese, softened
2 eggs
2 teaspoons orange juice
1 teaspoon grated orange rind
1 (6-ounce) package semisweet chocolate chips
Orange Icing (recipe follows)

Mix together flour and salt. Beat shortening, sugar and cream cheese. Beat in eggs 1 at a time. Add juice and rind. Blend in flour mixture, then chocolate pieces. Drop dough by rounded teaspoons 2-inches apart on greased sheets. Bake at 350 degrees for 12 minutes or until lightly browned around edges.

Spread with orange icing. Makes 3 dozen cookies.

Orange Icing

2 cups confectioners' sugar
1 (3-ounce) package cream cheese, softened
2 teaspoons orange juice
1 teaspoon grated orange rind

Beat confectioners' sugar into cream cheese until well blended. Stir in orange juice and rind.

Sugar Drop Cookies

1 cup shortening
2 cups sugar
2 eggs
1 teaspoon salt
1 teaspoon vanilla
1 teaspoon baking soda
1 teaspoon baking powder
1 cup milk
5¾ cups flour

Cream shortening and sugar; add eggs one at a time. Stir in salt, vanilla, baking soda and baking powder. Alternately mix in flour and milk. Refrigerate for at least 2 hours. Drop by teaspoonfuls on an ungreased cookie sheet. Bake at 375 degrees around 12 minutes.

Oatmeal Cookies

¾ cup flour
1 teaspoon baking powder
½ teaspoon salt
¾ cup oatmeal
½ teaspoon cinnamon
½ cup sugar
¼ cup shortening
½ cup raisins
1 egg
3 tablespoons milk

Sift together flour, baking powder, salt and cinnamon. Cream shortening and sugar together until smooth; add egg. Beat until well blended. Stir in oatmeal, raisins and milk. Add flour mixture. Drop by teaspoonful onto greased cookie sheets. Bake at 350 degrees for 12 minutes.

Raw Apple Cookies

1½ cups flour
½ teaspoon salt
½ teaspoon baking powder
½ teaspoon baking soda
½ teaspoon cinnamon
1 cup brown sugar, packed
½ cup shortening
1 cup quick oats
1¾ cups apples, chopped
2 eggs

Stir together flour, salt, baking soda, baking powder and cinnamon; set aside. In a large bowl, beat shortening and sugar until creamy. Beat in eggs until well-blended. Stir in flour mixture, then add oats and apples. Drop by well-rounded teaspoonfuls 2 inches apart on greased baking sheet. Bake at 350 degrees for 12–15 minutes. Makes 60 cookies.

Nutty Sandwich Cookies

¾ cup butter
1 cup sugar
½ teaspoon salt
¾ cup chopped pecans
1¾ cups flour
Creamy Filling (recipe follows)
Orange Glaze (recipe follows)

Cream together butter, sugar and salt. Stir in pecans and enough flour to form a stiff dough. Shape into balls; flatten with fork dipped in flour. Bake at 350 degrees on ungreased cookie sheet for 12–15 minutes. Place 2 cookies together with filling. Top with glaze.

Creamy Filling

1½ cups confectioners' sugar
⅓ cup cream cheese
1 tablespoon butter, softened
1 teaspoon grated orange rind

Combine sugar, cream cheese, butter and orange rind. Beat until smooth.

Orange Glaze

¼ cup confectioners' sugar
1 teaspoon grated orange rind
4 teaspoons orange juice
2 drops yellow food coloring

Mix together sugar, orange rind, orange juice and food coloring until smooth.

Chocolate Drop Cookies

1 cup sugar
⅔ cup margarine, softened
1 egg
½ cup cocoa
⅓ cup buttermilk
1 teaspoon vanilla
1¾ cups flour
½ teaspoon baking soda
½ teaspoon salt
1 cup chopped nuts
Light Brown Frosting (recipe follows)

Cream sugar, margarine and egg. Stir in cocoa, buttermilk and vanilla. Combine flour, baking soda, salt and nuts; mix together with creamed mixture. Drop by rounded teaspoonfuls 2 inches apart onto ungreased cookie sheet. Bake at 400 degrees for 8–10 minutes. Frost with Light Brown Frosting.

Light Brown Frosting

¼ cup margarine, melted
2 cups confectioners' sugar
1 teaspoon vanilla
1–2 tablespoons half-and-half

Heat margarine over low heat until golden brown; beat in confectioners' sugar, vanilla and half-and-half.

Crunchy Double Peanut Butter Cookies

1½ cups flour
¼ teaspoon salt
1 teaspoon baking powder
½ cup margarine
½ cup peanut butter
1 cup sugar
2 eggs
½ teaspoon vanilla
4 cups crunchy honey and nut flavored cereal crushed to 2 cups
1 cup peanut butter chips

Stir together flour, salt and baking powder. Beat margarine, peanut butter and sugar. Add eggs and vanilla, beating well. Stir in dry ingredients, cereal and peanut butter chips. Drop onto cookie sheets. Bake at 350 degrees for 12 minutes or until golden brown. Cool.

Cowboy Cookies

1 cup butter
½ cup sugar
1½ cups brown sugar
2 eggs
1½ teaspoons vanilla
2 cups flour
1 teaspoon baking soda
½ teaspoon salt
2 cups rolled oats
1 cup coconut
12 ounces chocolate chips

Cream together butter, sugars, eggs and vanilla; beat well. Stir in flour, baking soda, salt, oats, coconut and chocolate chips. Drop by teaspoonfuls onto greased cookie sheet. Bake at 350 degrees for 10–15 minutes.

Creative Candy Cookies

¼ cup butter, softened
¾ cup firmly packed brown sugar
1 egg
½ cup chopped nuts
2 (1½-ounce) bars chocolate-covered coconut or almond candy, cut up

1½ cups biscuit baking mix

Cream together butter, sugar and egg. Add nuts, candy and baking mix. Drop by teaspoonfuls on lightly greased baking sheet. Bake at 375 degrees for 10 minutes or until light brown. Leave cookies on baking sheet a few minutes before removing. Makes 3 dozen cookies.

Sour Cream Apple Squares

2 cups flour
2 cups brown sugar
½ cup margarine
1 cup nuts, chopped
1½ teaspoons cinnamon
1 teaspoon baking soda
½ teaspoon salt
1 cup sour cream
1 teaspoon vanilla
1 egg
2 cups apples, chopped

Combine flour, sugar and margarine. Blend until crumbly. Stir in nuts. Press 2¾ cups of crumbs in an ungreased 9 x 12-inch pan. Add the rest of the ingredients to remaining crumbs, adding apples last. Spread evenly over base and bake 25–30 minutes at 350 degrees. Cut in squares and serve with whipped topping, if desired.

Candy Cane Cookies

½ cup shortening
½ cup confectioners' sugar
2 tablespoons egg, slightly beaten
1¼ cups flour
½ teaspoon salt
½ teaspoon almond extract
½ teaspoon vanilla
¼ teaspoon red food coloring

Blend shortening, sugar and egg thoroughly. Stir in flour, salt, almond extract and vanilla. Divide dough in half. Tint 1 part of dough with red food coloring. Leave other part plain. Roll 6 small pieces of plain dough between palms. Repeat with tinted piece of dough. Twist the 2 together and shape to resemble a candy cane. Bake at 375 degrees for 8–10 minutes.

Fruit & Honey Cookies

¼ cup brown sugar
½ cup honey
½ cup butter
2 eggs
1½ cups flour
½ teaspoon salt
½ teaspoon baking soda
1 teaspoon cinnamon
½ cup milk
1/2 cup raisins
½ cup finely ground nuts
¼ cup coconut

Cream brown sugar, honey, butter and eggs. Sift together flour, salt, baking soda and cinnamon. Alternately add with milk to creamed mixture. Mix well. Stir in raisins, nuts and coconut. Drop by teaspoonfuls onto greased cookie sheets. Bake at 400 degrees for 6–8 minutes.

Low-Calorie Applesauce Nut Squares

2 cups unsweetened applesauce
4 envelopes unflavored gelatin
½–1 cup nuts, finely chopped
¼ teaspoon cinnamon
⅛ teaspoon nutmeg
2 teaspoons vanilla
¾ cup boiling water

Lightly toast nuts; set aside. Blend gelatin into ½ cup of applesauce. Add boiling water and stir until gelatin is dissolved. Add remaining applesauce and cinnamon, nutmeg and vanilla. Pour into 9-inch square pan and top with nuts. Chill. Cut into squares.

Caramel Cookies

6 cups oatmeal
3 cups brown sugar
3 cups margarine
3 cups flour
3 teaspoons baking soda

Mix together thoroughly oatmeal, brown sugar, margarine, flour and baking soda. Drop on ungreased cookie sheets. Bake at 350 degrees for 10 minutes.

Gingerbread Cookies

3¼ cups flour
1 teaspoon cinnamon
¼ teaspoon baking soda
¼ teaspoon ginger
¼ teaspoon cloves
1 cup firmly packed brown sugar
½ cup honey
¼ cup applesauce
¼ cup shortening
1 egg
½ cup ground almonds
   Raisins
   Cinnamon candy

Combine flour, cinnamon, baking soda, ginger and cloves; set aside. In medium saucepan combine brown sugar, honey, applesauce and shortening. Bring to a boil; simmer 5 minutes. Cool to luke-warm. Add egg, almonds and dry ingredients. Mix well. Chill overnight.

Make head, body, legs and arms. Place on greased cookie sheet. Make eyes and nose from raisins and cinnamon candies Bake at 325 degrees for 12–15 minutes. Do not brown.

Cloud Nine Cookies

2 egg whites
⅔ cup sugar
⅛ teaspoon salt
1 cup chopped almonds
1 cup miniature chocolate chips

Preheat oven to 350 degrees for 15 minutes. Turn off when putting cookies in oven. Beat egg whites until stiff. Fold in sugar, salt, nuts and chips. Drop by tea-spoonfuls onto well greased cookie sheet. Leave in oven for 2½ hours or overnight, but do not open door until time has expired.

Honey Oatmeal Cookies

2 tablespoons butter, room temperature
1 tablespoon oil
½ cup brown sugar
¼ cup honey
1 egg

1 tablespoon water
½ cup flour
½ teaspoon salt
¼ teaspoon baking soda
1½ cups quick rolled oats
   Raisins, nuts or chocolate chips (optional)

Blend butter, oil, brown sugar, honey, egg and water; set aside. Mix together flour, salt, baking soda and oats. Blend with butter mixture. Stir in raisins, nuts or chocolate chips. Drop by teaspoon-fuls onto cookie sheets. Bake at 350 degrees for 10–12 minutes.

Cutout Cookies

1 cup lard
2 cups brown sugar
   Salt
2 eggs
1 cup sour milk
1 teaspoon baking soda
6 cups flour
1 teaspoon baking powder
1 teaspoon vanilla

Cream lard with brown sugar; add salt, eggs and milk. Stir in baking soda, flour, baking powder and vanilla; mix well. Roll out on floured board. Cut with cookie cutters. Bake at 350 degrees for 10–12 minutes or until lightly browned.

Buttermilk Oatmeal Cookies

2 cups firmly packed brown sugar
1 cup shortening
½ cup buttermilk
1 teaspoon vanilla
4 cups quick-cooking oats
1¾ cups flour
1 teaspoon baking soda
¾ teaspoon salt

Cream brown sugar with shortening; stir in buttermilk and vanilla. Add oats, flour, baking soda and salt. Shape dough into 1-inch balls. Place 3 inches apart on ungreased cookie sheet. Flatten with glass bottom dipped in water. Bake at 375 degrees for 8–10 minutes until gold-en brown.

Chocolate Chip Cookies

½ cup sugar
½ cup firmly packed brown sugar
⅓ cup margarine, softened
⅓ cup shortening
1 egg
1 teaspoon vanilla
1½ cups flour
½ teaspoon baking soda
½ teaspoon salt
½ cup chopped nuts
1 (6-ounce) package semisweet chocolate chips

Cream sugars, margarine, shortening, egg and vanilla. Stir in flour, baking soda and salt. Blend in nuts and chips. Drop by rounded teaspoonfuls about 2 inches apart onto ungreased cookie sheet. Bake at 375 degrees for 8–10 minutes. Cool slightly before remov-ing from cookie sheet. Makes 3–4 dozen cookies.

Walnut Oatmeal Cookies

1 cup lard
1 cup sugar
1 cup brown sugar
2 eggs, beaten
1 teaspoon vanilla
1½ cups flour
1 teaspoon baking soda
1 teaspoon salt
3 cups oatmeal
½ cup nuts, chopped

Cream together lard and sugars; add eggs and vanilla. Beat well. Mix in flour, baking soda, salt, oatmeal and nuts. Form long roll and chill. Slice ¼ inch thick. Bake at 350 degrees for 10–12 minutes or until done.

Meringue Cookies

1 egg white
¼ teaspoon salt
1 cup brown sugar
1 cup chopped nuts

Beat egg with salt. Gradually add brown sugar and nuts. Drop by ½ teaspoonfuls on baking sheet. Bake at 325 degrees for 6–8 minutes or until slightly brown.

Buttermilk Raisin Spice Cookies

½ cup shortening
1 cup firmly packed brown sugar
½ cup molasses
½ cup buttermilk
1 teaspoon vinegar
2½ cups flour
1 teaspoon baking soda
½ teaspoon salt
½ teaspoon ginger
½ teaspoon cinnamon
  Raisins

Cream shortening with sugar; stir in molasses, buttermilk and vinegar. Blend in flour, baking soda, salt, ginger and cinnamon. Drop dough by rounded teaspoonfuls about 2½ inches apart onto ungreased baking sheet. Press raisins on each cookie. Bake for 10–12 minutes at 400 degrees. Cool 1 minute before removing from baking sheet. Makes 4 dozen cookies.

Cutout Butter Cookies

1½ cups sugar
1 cup margarine
1 (8-ounce) package cream cheese
1 egg
1 teaspoon vanilla
3½ cups flour
1 teaspoon baking powder

Cream sugar, margarine and cream cheese together until fluffy. Stir in egg and vanilla. Combine flour and baking powder; add to creamed mixture. Refrigerate 2 hours. Roll out; cut with cutters. Bake at 400 degrees for 8–10 minutes.

Chocolate Mint Cookies

½ cup semisweet chocolate chips
¼ teaspoon peppermint extract
1¼ cups flour
¾ teaspoon baking soda
½ teaspoon salt
½ cup sugar
½ cup firmly packed brown sugar
1 egg
½ cup shortening

½ cup peanut butter

Melt chocolate chips; stir in peppermint extract. Combine flour, baking soda and salt; set aside. Cream sugar, brown sugar and egg; stir in shortening and peanut butter until well blended. Mix in dry ingredients. Fold in chocolate.

Shape into teaspoon-size balls. Place balls on greased cookie sheet. Flatten with glass bottom which has been dripped in sugar. Bake at 375 degrees for 8–10 minutes until delicately browned.

Toll House Chocolate Chip Cookies

1 cup shortening
¾ cup brown sugar
¾ cup white sugar
2 eggs, beaten
1 teaspoon hot water
1 teaspoon vanilla
1½ cups flour
1 teaspoon baking soda
1 teaspoon salt
2 cups oatmeal
  Chocolate chips

Mix together shortening, brown sugar, sugar, eggs, water and vanilla. Add flour, baking soda and salt. Stir in oatmeal and chocolate chips. Drop by teaspoonfuls on cookie sheet. Bake for 10–15 minutes at 350 degrees.

Classic Chocolate Chip Cookies

2¼ cups flour
1 teaspoon baking soda
1 cup butter
1 cup brown sugar
1 teaspoon vanilla
2 eggs
1 (12-ounce) package chocolate chips
1 cup chopped nuts
1 (3-ounce) package instant vanilla pudding mix

Combine flour and baking soda; set aside. Mix together butter, sugar, vanilla and pudding mix until smooth. Beat in eggs. Gradually add flour mixture, beating well. Stir in chocolate chips and nuts. Drop by spoonfuls onto ungreased cookie sheets. Bake at 350 degrees for 10–12 minutes.

Apple Almond Squares

1 cup sifted flour
¼ cup sugar
6 tablespoons butter *or* margarine
2 eggs
1 cup brown sugar
½ teaspoon vanilla
2 cups tart apples, pared and diced
¼ cup almonds, blanched and chopped
½ cup sifted flour
1 teaspoon baking powder
¼ teaspoon salt

Combine 1 cup flour and sugar; cut in butter until crumbly. Press on bottom of 8 x 8 x 2-inch baking pan. Bake at 350 degrees for 20 minutes or until lightly browned. Meanwhile beat eggs until thick and lemon-colored; stir in brown sugar, vanilla, apples and almonds. Sift together remaining ingredients; stir into egg mixture. Spread over baked layer. Bake for 35 minutes or until done. Cut in 9 squares.

Congo Bars

⅔ cup butter *or* margarine
2¼ cups brown sugar
3 eggs, slightly beaten
2¾ cups flour
3 tablespoons baking powder
¾ teaspoon salt
1 cup chocolate chips
1 cup nuts, optional

Melt butter until soft; add brown sugar and eggs. Add flour, baking powder, salt, chocolate chips and nuts. Bake in a 9 x 13-inch pan for 40 minutes at 350 degrees. When cool, cut bars.

Quick Peanut Butter Cookies

1 cup peanut butter
1 cup sugar
1 egg
1 teaspoon vanilla

Mix peanut butter and sugar; stir in egg and vanilla. Shape in 1-inch balls and place on ungreased cookie sheet. Press with fork to flatten slightly. Bake at 350 degrees for 12–15 minutes.

Butterfinger Cookies

2²/₃ cups flour
  1 teaspoon baking soda
²/₃ cup shortening
½ teaspoon salt
1½ cups sugar
  2 eggs
  4 Butterfinger candy bars, chopped

Cream together shortening and sugar; beat in eggs. Sift together flour, baking soda and salt; stir in candy pieces. Combine creamed mixture with flour mixture. Shape dough into rolls. Cover and chill several hours or overnight. Cut into thin slices and place onto greased cookie sheets. Bake at 350 degrees for 12 minutes. Remove from pan immediately.

Potato Chip Cookies

1 cup shortening
1 cup white sugar
1 cup brown sugar
2 eggs
2 cups flour
1 teaspoon salt
1 teaspoon baking soda
2 cups crushed potato chips

Cream shortening and sugars; stir in eggs and mix well. Combine together flour, salt, baking soda and chips and add to creamed mixture. Shape into little balls and place on ungreased cookie sheet. Press down with floured fork. Bake at 350 degrees for 10–12 minutes.

Coconut Macaroons

2 cups coconut
⅓ cup sweetened condensed milk
½ teaspoon vanilla
1 egg white

Blend coconut, milk and vanilla thoroughly. Beat egg white until stiffly beaten; fold into coconut mixture. Drop by teaspoonfuls onto greased cookie sheet. Bake at 250 degrees for 15 minutes.

Great Chocolate Chip Cookies

  1 cup butter, softened
¾ cup sugar
¾ cup firmly packed brown sugar
  1 teaspoon vanilla
  2 eggs
2¼ cups flour
  1 teaspoon baking soda
½ teaspoon salt
  2 cups semisweet chocolate chips
  1 cup chopped nuts

Cream together butter, sugar, brown sugar, vanilla and eggs; beat well. Combine flour, baking soda and salt; gradually add to creamed mixture. Beat well. Stir in chips and nuts. Drop by teaspoonfuls onto ungreased cookie sheet. Bake at 375 degrees for 8–10 minutes or until lightly browned. Makes 6 dozen cookies.

Sugar Cookies

3 cups sugar
1 cup margarine
4 eggs
1 cup thinned cream
1 cup milk
1 tablespoon vanilla
4 teaspoons baking powder
1 teaspoon baking soda
1 teaspoon salt
¾ cup salad dressing
6 cups flour

Cream together sugar, margarine; add eggs. Stir in cream, milk and vanilla. Mix together baking powder, baking soda, salt, salad dressing and flour and add to creamed mixture. Drop by teaspoonfuls on greased cookie sheet. Bake at 400 degrees for 10–12 minutes or until lightly browned.

Coffee Cookies

1 cup shortening
2 cups brown sugar
3 eggs
1 cup cold strong coffee
2 teaspoons vanilla
5 cups flour
1 teaspoon baking soda

1 teaspoon baking powder
½ teaspoon salt
1 cup chopped nuts
1 cup raisins

Cream together shortening, sugar and eggs; add coffee and vanilla. Mix together flour, baking soda, baking powder and salt. Stir into creamed mixture. Blend in nuts. Add raisins that have been softened in simmering water. Drop by teaspoonfuls on greased cookie sheet. Bake 12 minutes in 425-degree oven.

Chocolate Drops

2½ cups cake flour
½ teaspoon baking soda
½ teaspoon salt
1½ squares baking chocolate
  1 cup shortening
1²/₃ cups brown sugar
  2 eggs
½ cup chopped nuts
½ cup flaked coconut

Combine flour, baking soda and salt. Melt chocolate over double boiler filled with hot water. Combine shortening, brown sugar and eggs; beat until smooth. Blend in chocolate mixture, then add flour mixture. Stir in coconut and nuts. Drop by rounded teaspoonfuls onto lightly greased cookie sheet. Bake at 350 degrees for 12–15 minutes.

Applesauce Fritters

1 cup flour
1 tablespoon sugar
1 teaspoon baking powder
¼ teaspoon salt
1 egg
¼ cup milk
2 tablespoons vegetable oil
1 cup applesauce
   Confectioners' sugar

Sift together flour, sugar, baking powder and salt. Combine egg, milk, vegetable oil and applesauce. Stir into the dry ingredients. Drop by spoonfuls into deep shortening heated to 365 degrees. Fry until golden brown (3–5 minutes). Drain on paper towels. Sprinkle with confectioners' sugar.

Cherry Nut Cookies

½ cup butter *or* margarine, softened
1 cup packed brown sugar
1 egg, slightly beaten
1 teaspoon vanilla
2 cups flour
½ teaspoon baking soda
¼ teaspoon salt
1 cup walnuts, chopped
⅓ cup Maraschino cherries, chopped

Cream together butter and sugar; add egg and vanilla. Blend in flour, baking soda and salt. Stir in walnuts and cherries. Shape dough into a roll about 14 inches long. Refrigerate overnight. Cut into ¼-inch slices. Bake on ungreased cookie sheets at 350 degrees for about 10 minutes or until just golden brown.

Maryann Cookies

2 cups brown sugar
2 cups sugar
2 cups butter
4 eggs
2 cups milk
3 teaspoons baking soda
2 tablespoons vinegar
6 teaspoons baking powder
8 cups flour

Cream together sugars and butter. Beat in eggs and milk. Dissolve baking soda in vinegar. Add to batter with baking powder and flour. Drop by spoonful onto lightly greased cookie sheet. Bake at 350 degrees for 8–12 minutes.

Forever Ambers

1 pound orange slice candy, chopped
1 cup chopped nuts
2 cans sweetened condensed milk
1 (7-ounce) can coconut, flaked
1 teaspoon vanilla
Confectioners' sugar

Combine candy, nuts, milk, coconut and vanilla. Spread on cookie sheet and bake at 350 degrees for 30 minutes. Let cool enough to handle and roll into balls. Roll balls in confectioners' sugar.

Christmas Cookie Slices

1 cup sugar
1 cup margarine *or* butter, softened
2 eggs
1½ teaspoons vanilla
3 cups flour
1 teaspoon salt
½ teaspoon baking soda

Cream together sugar, margarine, eggs and vanilla. Stir in flour, salt and baking soda. Divide dough into 3 equal parts. Shape each into a roll 1½ inches in diameter. Refrigerate at least 4 hours. Cut rolls into ⅛-inch slices. Place 1 inch apart on ungreased cookie sheet. Bake at 400 degrees for 8–10 minutes. Makes 7 dozen cookies.

Apple Puffs

2 cups flour
¼ cup sugar
1 tablespoon baking powder
1 teaspoon salt
½ teaspoon nutmeg
½ cup vegetable oil
¾ cup milk
1 egg
1 cup apples, peeled and chopped

Blend together flour, sugar, baking powder, salt and nutmeg. Add oil, milk and egg. Mix well with fork. Stir in apples. Drop by teaspoons into 375-degree fat. Fry about 3 minutes or until golden brown. Roll warm puffs in cinnamon-sugar mixture. Makes 2½ dozen puffs.

Easy Chocolate Balls

1 box yellow cake mix
½ cup cocoa
⅓ cup oil
2 eggs
¼ cup sour milk
Confectioners' sugar

Combine cake mix, cocoa, oil, eggs and milk. Shape into 1-inch balls. Roll in confectioners' sugar. Bake on ungreased cookie sheets at 350 degrees for 10–12 minutes. Do not overbake. Makes 4 dozen cookies.

Buttermilk Cookies

2 teaspoons baking soda
1½ cups buttermilk
3 eggs
2 cups sugar
1½ cups lard
3 teaspoons baking powder
1 tablespoon nutmeg
1 teaspoon salt
6 cups flour

Mix baking soda with buttermilk; set aside. Beat eggs, sugar and lard until creamy. Stir in baking powder, nutmeg, salt and flour. Combine buttermilk mixture with flour mixture, beating until smooth. Drop by teaspoonful on greased cookie sheet. Bake at 375 degrees for 8–10 minutes or until slightly browned.

Aunt Dolly's Cutout Cookies

1 cup butter
1½ cups sugar
2 eggs
1 teaspoon vanilla
3 cups flour, scant
½ teaspoon salt
½ teaspoon baking soda

Cream together butter and sugar; add eggs and vanilla. Sift flour, salt and baking soda; add to creamed mixture. Chill overnight or 4 hours. Roll to desired thickness and cut. Bake at 375 degrees for 6–8 minutes. These are better a little underbaked than overbaked.

Date Balls

1 cup sugar
1 cup chopped dates
1 stick butter
1 egg, beaten
1 teaspoon vanilla
2 cups crispy rice cereal
⅓ cup pecans
Coconut

Heat sugar, dates and butter to boiling. Add egg slowly and cook for 5 minutes. Set aside until partly cool. Add vanilla, cereal and pecans. Roll into balls; roll in coconut.

Coconut Cookies

1 cup lard
1 cup brown sugar
1 cup white sugar
1 teaspoon coconut flavoring
½ teaspoon vanilla
2 eggs
1 teaspoon salt
1 teaspoon baking soda
1½ cups flour
3 cups oatmeal

Cream lard with sugars, coconut flavoring, vanilla, and eggs. Add salt, baking soda, flour and oatmeal; mix well. Shape in a roll or a ball. Bake at 350 degrees for 12 minutes.

Caramel Apple Oatmeal Bars

1 cup brown sugar
¼ cup margarine
1 egg
2 cups apples, chopped
¾ cup flour
1 cup rolled oats
1 teaspoon baking soda
1 teaspoon cinnamon
½ teaspoon nutmeg
¼ teaspoon salt
1 cup raisins

Cream together sugar, margarine, and eggs. Stir in apples. Add flour, rolled oats, baking soda, cinnamon, nutmeg, salt and raisins. Spread in greased 9 x 9-inch pan. Bake at 350 degrees for 30 minutes. Cool in pan. Cut into bars.

Apple Treat Nut Squares

1 egg, beaten
¾ cup sugar
½ cup sifted flour
1 teaspoon baking powder
¼ teaspoon salt
1 cup apples, chopped
½ cup walnuts, chopped

Combine egg and sugar. Add sifted flour, baking powder and salt; mix well. Add apples and walnuts. Spread in 8 x 8 x 2-inch pan. Bake at 350 degrees for 30 minutes or until done.

Butterscotch Sugar Cookies

¾ cup shortening
1 cup brown sugar
2 eggs
1 teaspoon vanilla
2½ cups flour
1 teaspoon baking powder
1 teaspoon salt
1 cup chopped black walnuts

Cream together shortening and brown sugar; add eggs and vanilla. Blend in flour, baking powder and salt. Stir in walnuts. Cover dough; chill at least 1 hour. Roll dough ⅛-inch thick on lightly floured board. Cut with cookie cutters. Bake at 400 degrees on ungreased baking sheet for 6–8 minutes or until very light brown. Makes 4 dozen cookies.

Bon Bon Cookies

1 cup butter, softened
1½ cups confectioners' sugar
3 cups flour
2 tablespoons vanilla
¼ teaspoon salt
   Cream
   Maraschino cherries
   Pecan halves
   Chocolate kisses

Melt butter; add sugar, flour, vanilla, salt and enough cream as needed to make dough stick together. Wrap dough around maraschino cherries, pecan halves and chocolate kisses. Bake at 350 degrees for 8 minutes. Freeze when completely cooled.

Magic Pudding Cookies

1 cup biscuit baking mix
1 (4-serving size) box instant pudding mix, any flavor
¼ cup oil
1 egg
   Colored sugar sprinkles

Combine baking mix with instant pudding mix. Add oil and egg. When dough forms a ball, shape a teaspoonful into a ball and place on greased cookie sheet. Flatten balls slightly and sprinkle with colored sugar. Bake at 350 degrees for 5–8 minutes.

Cutout Cookies

3 cups flour
¼ teaspoon salt
½ teaspoon nutmeg
1 cup butter or margarine
½ cup milk
1 cup sugar
1 teaspoon baking soda

Combine flour, salt and nutmeg; cut butter into flour mixture. Heat milk, sugar and soda until foaming. Do not boil. Cool; add to flour mixture. Chill dough thoroughly. Roll; cut with cookie cutters. Bake on greased cookie sheet at 375 degrees for 3–5 minutes or until lightly browned.

Easy Peanut Butter Cookies

1 (14-ounce) can sweetened condensed milk
1 cup peanut butter
1 egg
1 teaspoon vanilla
2 cups biscuit baking mix
   Sugar

Beat together sweetened condensed milk, peanut butter, egg and vanilla until smooth. Stir in biscuit mix. Chill 1 hour. Shape into 1-inch balls. Roll in sugar. Place cookies on ungreased cookie sheet; flatten with fork. Bake at 350 degrees for 6–8 minutes.

Monster Oatmeal & Raisin Cookies

1 cup margarine
2¼ cups brown sugar
2 cups sugar
6 eggs
2½ cups peanut butter
2 tablespoons vanilla
4 teaspoons baking soda
9 cups oatmeal
9 ounces raisins

Cream together margarine, sugars, eggs and peanut butter; mix well. Add vanilla, baking soda, oatmeal and raisins. Drop on cookie sheet. Bake at 350 degrees for 10–12 minutes or until done.

Desserts
DELICIOUS

Baked Apples #1

4 cups apples
1 cup sugar
3/4 cup flour
1 stick butter
1/2 cup water
Pinch of salt
Dash of cinnamon

Place sliced apples in baking dish. Mix sugar, flour and butter until crumbly. Sprinkle over apples, add water, salt and cinnamon. Bake at 350 degrees, 30–40 degrees until lightly browned.

Baked Apples #2

1 cup water
1 cup brown sugar
2 tablespoons cornstarch
1 tablespoon butter
Apples, sliced
1/4 cup nuts, chopped
Marshmallows (optional)

Mix water, brown sugar, cornstarch and butter in a small saucepan; cook until thick syrup. Pour syrup over apples; sprinkle with nuts. Bake 30–40 minutes at 350 degrees. Marshmallows can be added during last 5 minutes of baking.

Baked Apples #3

6 medium apples
1/2 cup sugar
4 tablespoons cinnamon

Peel and slice apples in eighths. Cook with medium amount of water on medi-um heat. Bring to a boil; slowly add sugar and cinnamon. Apples are done when they are soft and light brown. Serve warm or cold with ice cream or whipped topping.

Baked Apples #4
In Memory of Marilyn Lehrman

12 small apples, peeled, cored and halved
1 cup sugar
1 cup water
2 tablespoons cornstarch
1 teaspoon vanilla
1 lump butter
1/2 cup red hots (optional)
Marshmallows

Place apples in 9 x 13-inch baking dish. Stir together sugar and cornstarch. Stir in water; bring to boil. Add vanilla, butter and red hots; stir. Pour over apples. Bake at 350 degrees until apples are soft. Top each apple half with a marshmallow; place back in oven until marshmallow melts and turns a delicate brown color.

Rhubarb Crunch

3 cups rhubarb, chopped
1 cup sugar
3 tablespoons flour
1 cup brown sugar
1 cup quick-cooking rolled oats
1 1/2 cups flour
1/2 cup margarine or butter

Combine rhubarb, sugar and flour; place in greased 9 x 13-inch loaf pan. Mix brown sugar, oats, flour and margarine until crumbly. Sprinkle crumbs over fruit. Bake at 375 degrees for 40 minutes.

Cinnamon Pudding

2 cups brown sugar
1 1/2 cups cold water
2 tablespoons butter
1 cup sugar
2 tablespoons butter
1 teaspoon cinnamon
2 teaspoons baking powder
1 cup milk
Flour
Nuts, chopped
Whipped cream

Mix together brown sugar, water and 2 tablespoons butter in saucepan; bring to boil. Combine sugar, 2 tablespoons butter, cinnamon, baking powder, milk and enough flour to make a batter. Pour batter in bottom of greased pan. Pour brown sugar mixture over batter and sprinkle with nuts. Bake at 350 degrees for 45 minutes. Serve with whipped cream.

Half Moon Pies

4 sticks margarine
5 cups flour
1/2 teaspoon salt
1/2 cup milk
2 quarts pie filling

Combine margarine, flour and salt; mix well. Add milk (more or less) to resemble pie dough. Roll out and cut small circles; make knife holes on 1/2 of circle. Place 1 teaspoon of favorite pie filling in center. Wet edges of dough with water and fold. Bake at 375 degrees for 15 minutes or until golden. Sprinkle with sugar.

Chou Paste

1 cup flour
8 tablespoons butter
1 teaspoon salt
1 cup water
4 eggs

Bring water, butter and salt to rolling boil. Turn heat to low, add flour all at once. Stir over heat until dough doesn't stick to sides of pan and forms a ball. Cool; beat in eggs 1 at a time. For techniques and baking times, follow the recipes below.

Cream Puffs

With a pastry bag or a teaspoon, make round mounds of chou paste on a greased cookie sheet. Bake at 400 degrees for 20 minutes or until lightly browned and firm. Prick with toothpick and return to oven to dry for a few minutes. Split to fill. Makes 15 (3-inch) cream puffs.

Fillings for Cream Puffs

Ice cream with hot fudge sauce; plain or vanilla pastry cream sprinkled with confectioners' sugar; any meat salad, including tuna, ham and chicken salad with cashews and red grapes; Hawaiian salad (bacon, pineapple, cheddar cheese and mayonnaise).

Flavored Cream Filling

1 cup whipping cream
1½ tablespoons confectioners' sugar
2 tablespoons liqueur (any flavor desired)

Whip cream until soft peaks are formed; add sugar and liqueur.

Hazelnut, Raspberry, Chocolate Filling

1 (10-ounce) package frozen raspberries
¼ cup sugar
1 (8-ounce) bar milk chocolate, chopped
1 (4-ounce) package chocolate chips
¼ cup butter
1½ cups chopped hazelnuts
3 tablespoons butter, melted
1 quart vanilla ice cream, softened

Cook berries with sugar until medium thick sauce is formed. Melt chocolates; add ¼ cup butter and cool to room temperature. Mix nuts with melted butter and softened ice cream. Fill puffs with ice cream mix; freeze until firm. Spoon raspberry sauce over ice cream. Put lids on puffs and drizzle with warm chocolate sauce.

Eclairs

Using a pastry bag, form 4-inch strips on greased cookie sheet. Bake at 400 degrees for 20 minutes. Fill with plain or flavored Pastry Creme (recipe following article) and ice with Chocolate Icing (recipe following article).

Carolines

Follow directions for cream puffs; mounds should be dime size. Bake at 400 degrees for 10–15 minutes. Poke a small hole in bottom of puff; cool. Using a pastry bag with a small round tip, fill from the bottom with pastry cream or sweetened whipped cream. Glaze with chocolate icing.

Croquembouche

These are small Carolines filled with flavored pastry cream. Dip each puff (after filling) in light brown caramel sugar (sugar cooked in skillet until liquid and light brown in color). Cool on greased pan, then arrange in a pyramid. Decorate pyramid as desired.

Paris Brest

A speciality in Paris. Chou paste is piped into a crown shape (circle), then sprinkled with almonds. Bake at 400 degrees until firm and hollow sounding. After it has been baked, cool and split across, then fill with praline butter cream. *Hint:* Use your favorite custard recipe and flavor with praline liqueur to desired taste.

Cheesecake

1 (3-ounce) package lemon gelatin
1 cup boiling water
1 (8-ounce) package cream cheese
1 cup confectioners' sugar
1 can Milnot
4 cups graham cracker crumbs
1½ sticks margarine

Dissolve gelatin in boiling water; chill until it starts to jell. Mix together cream cheese and confectioners' sugar until smooth. Whip Milnot until it peaks; slowly add cream cheese mixture and gelatin. Mix cracker crumbs with margarine, reserving ¼ cup. Line a cake pan with rest of crumbs. Pour in cream cheese mixture; sprinkle with rest of crumbs. Chill.

Raspberry Baked Alaska

1 (4½-ounce) package ladyfingers
⅓ cup orange-flavored liqueur
1 (10-ounce) package frozen raspberries, slightly thawed, crushed
3 pints vanilla ice cream, slightly softened
4 egg whites, at room temperature
¼ teaspoon salt
⅛ teaspoon cream of tartar
⅔ cup sugar

Line a 9-inch pie pan with ⅔ of ladyfingers, allowing rounded ends to extend slightly over rim; sprinkle with half of liqueur. Drop spoonfuls of raspberries onto ice cream; cut through with knife to create a ripple effect. Spoon half of ice cream mixture into pie pan. Layer remaining ladyfingers on top; sprinkle with remaining liqueur. Spoon remaining ice cream on top. Freeze until firm.

About 20 minutes before serving beat egg whites, salt and cream of tartar until soft peaks form. Beat in sugar, 2 tablespoons at a time, until stiff. Spread meringue over top of pie, sealing to edge; swirl meringue with back of spoon. Bake at 500 degrees for 3–4 minutes until meringue is lightly browned. Makes 12 servings.

Angel Pudding

1 cup milk
½ cup sugar
1 envelope unflavored gelatin
3 eggs, separated
½ cup sugar
Pinch of salt
1 pint whipping cream
1 (15-ounce) can crushed pineapple, drained
1½ packages graham crackers, crushed

In bowl, stir together milk, ½ cup sugar and gelatin. Let soak ½ hour. Stir in 3 egg yolks, ½ cup sugar and pinch of salt; cook 15 minutes over medium heat, stirring often; will thicken as it cooks. Cool. Beat whipping cream until stiff. Beat egg whites until stiff. Fold in whipped cream, egg whites and pineapple. In 9 x 13-inch pan, layer pudding and graham crackers. Cool.

Merry Berry Dessert

1 (16-ounce) package thawed frozen strawberries, reserve juice for Strawberry Sauce
2 cups flour
½ teaspoon salt
1 teaspoon baking soda
1¼ cups sugar
½ cup shortening
½ cup sour cream
3 eggs
1 teaspoon vanilla
Strawberry Sauce (recipe follows)

Sift together flour, salt, baking soda and sugar; add shortening, sour cream, eggs and vanilla. Beat for 3 minutes with electric mixer until well blended. Fold in strawberries. Pour into well-greased and floured 12 x 8 x 2-inch pan. Bake at 350 degrees for 40–45 minutes. Serve with Strawberry Sauce.

Strawberry Sauce
¾ cup reserved strawberry juice
¼ cup water
1 tablespoon cornstarch

Combine reserved strawberry juice, water and cornstarch; cook over low heat until thickened and clear, stirring constantly.

Apple Goodie

1½ cups sugar
2 tablespoons flour
Pinch salt
1 teaspoon cinnamon
½ quart sliced apples
1 cup oatmeal
1 cup brown sugar
1 cup flour
¼ teaspoon baking soda
⅓ teaspoon baking powder
⅔ cup butter

Mix together sugar, flour, salt and cinnamon; add to apples; mix. Place in the bottom of greased 9 x 13-inch pan. Combine oatmeal, brown sugar, flour, baking soda, baking powder and butter; sprinkle on top of apples; pat firm. Bake at 350 degrees for 30 minutes or until crusty and brown.

Baklava

4 cups finely chopped walnuts
½ cup sugar
1 teaspoon cinnamon
1 pound phyllo (strudel leaves)
1 cup butter, melted
1 (12-ounce) jar honey

Grease 13 x 9-inch pan 2–3 hours before serving. Mix together walnuts, sugar and cinnamon; blend well. Cut phyllo into 13 x 9-inch rectangles. Place 1 sheet phyllo in baking dish; brush with some butter. Repeat to make 5 more layers of phyllo; sprinkle with 1 cup walnut mixture.

Place 1 sheet phyllo in baking dish over walnut mixture; brush with butter. Repeat to make at least 6 layers, overlapping any small strips of phyllo to make rectangles if necessary. Sprinkle 1 cup walnut mixture over phyllo. Repeat layers 2 times.

Place remaining phyllo on top of last walnut layer; brush with butter or margarine. With sharp knife, cut just halfway through layers in triangle pattern to make 24 servings. Bake at 300 degrees for 1 hour and 25 minutes or until top is golden brown.

Heat honey over medium-low heat until hot but not boiling; spoon over hot Baklava. Cool in pan at least 1 hour; cover and leave at room temperature until serving. To serve, finish cutting through layers with sharp knife.

Pastry Creme

5 egg yolks
½ cup sugar, divided
1 teaspoon vanilla
2 cups milk, divided
6 tablespoons flour
Almond flavoring (optional)
Nuts (optional)

Beat egg with ¼ cup sugar until fluffy and pale yellow in color. Stir in vanilla and ½ cup milk; sift flour into egg mixture, blending well. Set aside. In saucepan, bring remaining sugar and milk to a boil. Remove from heat; slowly add egg mixture with wire whisk, blending well. Boil for 2 minutes or until thick, stirring constantly. May stir in flavoring and nuts, if desired. Pour into dish; use to fill pastry.

Cranberry & Apple Cobbler

2 cups fresh cranberries
5 cups peeled and sliced apples
1¼ cups sugar
2½ tablespoons quick-cooking tapioca
1 teaspoon vanilla extract
2 tablespoons butter
1 cup flour
½ teaspoon salt
⅓ cup plus 1 tablespoon shortening
2–3 tablespoons cold water

Toss gently together cranberries, apples, sugar, tapioca and vanilla. Spoon fruit mixture into a lightly greased 12 x 8 x 2-inch baking dish. Dot with butter; set aside.

Combine flour and salt; cut in shortening with a pastry blender until mixture is crumbly. Sprinkle with water; stir with fork. Shape into ball. Roll out pastry; cut strips; arrange lattice over fruit. Bake at 425 degrees for 15 minutes; reduce heat to 350 degrees and bake an additional 30 minutes.

Fig-Date-Nut Torte

3 eggs, separated
1 cup sugar
½ cup finely cut dates
½ cup finely cut figs
2 tablespoons flour
1 teaspoon baking powder
1 cup walnuts, chopped
Pinch salt
1 teaspoon vanilla
Whipped cream
Chopped nuts
Candied cherries

Beat egg yolks until light; gradually add sugar, beating until light and fluffy. Mix dates and figs with flour and baking powder mixture; add egg yolk mixture and walnuts. Beat egg whites with salt and vanilla until stiff; fold into egg yolk mixture. Pour into 2 greased and lightly floured round cake pans. Bake at 325 degrees for 30 minutes. Spread whipped cream between layers and over cake. Garnish with nuts and cherries.

Pumpkin Flan

½ cup sugar
8 eggs
⅔ sugar
¼ teaspoon salt
2 (13-ounce) cans evaporated milk
2 teaspoons vanilla
1 cup canned pumpkin
1 (8-ounce) can jellied cranberry sauce

Heat ½ cup sugar in saucepan over medium heat until caramelized, stirring constantly. Pour caramel into 9 x 5-inch loaf pan; set aside. Beat eggs, ⅔ cup sugar, salt, evaporated milk, vanilla and pumpkin until just blended. Carefully pour pumpkin mixture into pan over caramel layer.

Set pan inside large shallow baking pan. Place pans on oven rack and pour boiling water in outer pan to 1 inch. Bake at 350 degrees 1 hour or until knife inserted in center comes out clean. Cool on wire rack. Chill.

Just before serving, blend cranberry sauce until smooth. Loosen flan from sides of pan and invert onto serving plate. Cover top of flan with cranberry purée.

Cranberry Delight

1 cup graham cracker crumbs
¼ cup margarine, melted
1 cup cranberries
¾ cup sugar
½ cup water
¼ cup chopped nuts
2 tablespoons orange marmalade
1 (8-ounce) package cream cheese
⅓ cup confectioners' sugar
1 tablespoon milk
1 teaspoon vanilla
1 cup heavy cream, whipped

Combine graham cracker crumbs and margarine. Press into 8-inch square pan. In saucepan, combine cranberries, sugar and water; simmer 20 minutes. Stir in nuts and marmalade. Chill in refrigerator; set aside. Mix cream cheese, confectioners' sugar, milk and vanilla. Fold in whipped cream; spoon over crust. Top with cranberry mixture. Chill overnight.

Strawberry Sauce With Dumplings

2 (16-ounce) packages frozen whole strawberries, thawed
1 cup water
2 tablespoons sugar
2 tablespoons butter
⅛ teaspoon salt
1 cup flour
1½ teaspoons baking powder
Dash of salt
¼ cup sugar
2 tablespoons butter
⅓ cup milk
½ teaspoon vanilla extract
Ice cream

Combine strawberries, water, sugar, butter and salt in saucepan and bring to a boil. Combine flour, baking powder, salt and ¼ cup sugar; cut in butter until mixture is crumbly. Stir in milk and vanilla; mix well.

Drop mixture by teaspoonfuls into boiling strawberry mixture; cook, uncovered, 5 minutes. Cover, reduce heat, and simmer 15 minutes. Serve over ice cream.

Chocolate Chip Cheesecake

24 creme-filled chocolate sandwich cookies, finely crushed
¼ cup shortening, melted
3 (8-ounce) packages cream cheese, softened
1 (14-ounce) can sweetened condensed milk
3 eggs
2 teaspoons vanilla
1 cup miniature chocolate chips, divided
1 teaspoon flour

Combine crumbs and shortening; press firmly on bottom of 9-inch springform pan. Beat cream cheese until fluffy; gradually beat in sweetened condensed milk until smooth. Beat in eggs and vanilla.

Coat ½ cup chips with flour; stir into cream cheese mixture. Pour into pan. Sprinkle remaining chips over top. Bake at 350 degrees for 55 minutes or until center is set. Cool. Chill. Refrigerate leftovers.

Chocolate Cream Torte

8 egg whites
1 teaspoon almond extract
½ teaspoon cream of tartar
½ teaspoon salt
⅔ cup sugar
¾ cup flour
⅔ cup sugar
½ cup flaked coconut
1 (6-ounce) package semisweet chocolate chips
1 cup miniature marshmallows
⅔ cup evaporated milk
1 cup whipping cream, whipped

Beat together egg whites, almond extract, cream of tartar and salt; gradually add sugar. Continue beating until very stiff. Fold in flour, sugar and coconut. Spread meringue on greased and floured cookie sheets to make 3 (8-inch) circles and 1 (2-inch) circle. Bake at 300 degrees for 25–30 minutes, until lightly browned. Remove from sheet immediately. Cool.

Melt chocolate chips and marshmallows with milk; chill. Fold whipped cream into chocolate. Stack large layers, spreading filling between and on top. Top with small layer. Chill 6–8 hours. Makes 6–8 servings.

Chocolate Potato Torte

¾ cup cocoa
1 cup finely chopped nuts
1 cup boiled, grated cold potatoes
1 cup butter, softened
1¾ cups sugar
4 eggs
½ cup milk
1 teaspoon cinnamon
1 teaspoon vanilla
1 teaspoon baking powder
1¼ cups flour

Combine cocoa, nuts and potatoes. Cream butter and sugar until thoroughly blended; stir in cocoa mixture. Add eggs, milk, cinnamon, vanilla, baking powder and flour; mix well. Spoon into greased and floured springform pan. Bake at 350 degrees for 60 minutes. Frost with favorite chocolate fudge frosting. Makes 20 servings.

Chocolate Chestnut Torte

1 (15-ounce) can unsweetened chestnut purée
5 egg yolks
1 cup sugar, divided
2 teaspoons vanilla
½ cup cake flour, sifted
3 tablespoons cocoa
5 egg whites
Chestnut Filling (recipe follows)
Whipped Cream Frost (recipe follows)

Reserve half of chestnut puree for filling. Combine remaining chestnut puree, egg yolks, ¾ cup sugar and vanilla; beat on medium speed with an electric mixer until blended. Sift together flour and cocoa; add to egg yolk mixture; beat well; set aside.

Beat egg whites with an electric mixer on high until soft peaks form. Gradually add remaining ¼ cup sugar, beating until stiff peaks form. Fold ¼ of egg whites into chestnut mixture, then fold chestnut mixture into remaining egg whites.

Divide and spread batter evenly in 3 greased 8 x 1½-inch round cake pans lined with greased waxed paper. Bake at 350 degrees for 20 minutes until knife comes out clean. Let cool.

Spread half of Chestnut Filling on top of 1 cake layer; top with second cake layer and remaining filling; top with last cake layer. Spread with Whipped Cream Frosting. Serve immediately or chill up to 4 hours. Makes 10 servings.

Chestnut Filling

Remaining chestnut puree
1 cup confectioners' sugar
1 (3-ounce) package cream cheese, softened
1 tablespoon rum

Beat together chestnut puree, confectioners' sugar, cream cheese and rum until smooth.

Whipped Cream Frosting

1 cup whipping cream
2 tablespoons confectioners' sugar, sifted
2 teaspoons rum

Beat together whipping cream, confectioners' sugar and rum with mixer until soft peaks form.

Apple Torte

1½ cups flour
1 cup almonds, ground
⅓ cup sugar
¼ teaspoon cinnamon
½ cup margarine
1 egg, beaten
¼ cup margarine
6 cups apples, peeled, cored, sliced
1 tablespoon lemon juice
⅓ cup sugar
2 tablespoons flour
⅛ teaspoon nutmeg
½ cup raspberry preserves, melted

Mix together 1½ cups flour, almonds, ⅓ cup sugar and cinnamon; cut in ½ cup margarine until crumbly. Add egg, stirring to blend well. Reserve ¼ of crust. Press remaining crust into the bottom and sides of 9-inch springform pan; set aside.

Melt ¼ cup margarine; add apples and lemon juice. Cook, gently stirring, for 3–5 minutes; remove from heat; set aside.

Combine ⅓ cup sugar, 2 tablespoons flour and nutmeg; stir into apple mixture. Spread mixture evenly in crust. Bake at 375 degrees for 35–40 minutes, until crust is brown.

Form reserved crust into a ball; roll ⅛ inch thick. Cut into 10 (1½-inch) star shapes. Sprinkle sugar on stars; bake at 375 degrees for 5–6 minutes or until light brown; cool. Spread melted preserves over top of torte. Top with baked stars. Let stand until preserves are set. Makes 8–10 servings.

Apple Sundae

1 cup brown sugar
1 cup sugar
1 cup cream
4 tablespoons flour
Pinch of salt
¾ teaspoon cinnamon
4 cups apples, sliced

Mix together brown sugar, sugar, cream, flour, salt, cinnamon and apples. Place in a 13 x 9-inch baking dish. Bake at 350 degrees for 30–40 minutes until apples are done. Serve while warm with ice cream.

Orange Cheesecake

2 cups graham cracker crumbs
½ cup butter, melted
⅓ cup sugar
3 (8-ounce) packages cream cheese, softened
¾ cup sugar
2 tablespoons flour
2 tablespoons cornstarch
1 teaspoon vanilla
6 eggs, separated
1 cup orange juice
2 cups sour cream
2 tablespoons grated orange rind
2 tablespoons sugar

Combine graham cracker crumbs, butter and sugar. Press into the bottom of a 13 x 9-inch pan. Beat cream cheese until smooth. Combine sugar, flour and cornstarch. Add to cream cheese with vanilla. Beat until fluffy. Add egg yolks, 1 at a time, beating after each addition; add orange juice.

Beat egg whites until stiff. Gently fold into cream cheese mixture. Pour into pan. Bake at 350 degrees for 45 minutes. Turn off heat; let stand in oven 1 hour. Remove from oven. Combine sour cream, orange rind and sugar; spread over cheesecake. Refrigerate several hours or overnight. Makes 12–15 servings.

Blueberry Cheesecake

2 cups graham cracker crumbs
¼ cup butter, melted
½ cup sugar
2 eggs
1 cup sugar
2 (8-ounce) packages cream cheese
1 teaspoon vanilla
1 can blueberry pie filling

Combine graham cracker crumbs, butter and sugar; pat into 9 x 13-inch pan. Blend eggs and sugar; stir in cream cheese and vanilla; spread over crust. Bake at 375 degrees for 15 minutes. Cool; spread with blueberry pie filling. Refrigerate overnight.

No-Bake Cheesecake

3 tablespoons butter
2 tablespoons sugar
1/4 teaspoon cinnamon
1/4 teaspoon nutmeg
2/3 cup graham cracker crumbs
2 envelopes unflavored gelatin
1 cup sugar, divided
2 eggs, separated
1 cup milk
1 teaspoon grated lemon rind
1 tablespoon lemon juice
1 teaspoon vanilla
3 cups creamed cottage cheese
1 cup heavy cream, whipped

Mix together butter, sugar and spices; blend in graham cracker crumbs; set aside. Combine gelatin and 3/4 cup sugar in saucepan. Beat egg yolks and milk together; stir into gelatin mixture. Cook over low heat stirring constantly until gelatin dissolves and mixture thickens. Remove from heat, stir in lemon rind, juice and vanilla.

Beat cottage cheese on high with an electric mixer until smooth, 3–4 minutes; stir into gelatin mixture. Chill, stirring occasionally, until mixture mounds slightly. Beat egg whites until stiff but not dry; gradually add remaining 1/4 cup sugar and beat until very stiff. Fold into gelatin mixture; fold in whipped cream. Place in 9-inch springform pan; sprinkle with crumbs. Chill 3–4 hours until firm.

Hazelnut Torte

12 medium eggs, separated
2 cups sugar
2 cups ground hazelnuts
12 ladyfingers, grated
   Juice of 1 lemon
   Rind of 1 lemon, grated
   Confectioners' sugar

Beat egg yolks with sugar; add ladyfingers, flavorings and nuts. Beat egg whites; fold into ladyfinger mixture. Bake at 350 degrees in 9 x 13-inch springform pan for 50 minutes. When cooled, sprinkle with confectioners' sugar.

Cocoa Cheesecake

1 1/2 cups graham cracker crumbs
1/3 cup sugar
1/3 cup butter, melted
2 (8-ounce) packages cream cheese, softened
3/4 cup sugar
1/2 cup cocoa
1 teaspoon vanilla
2 eggs
1 cup sour cream
2 tablespoons sugar
1 teaspoon vanilla

Combine crumbs, 1/3 cup sugar and butter. Press mixture onto bottom and halfway up side of 9-inch springform pan. Beat cheese, 3/4 cup sugar, cocoa and vanilla until light and fluffy. Add eggs; blend well. Pour into crust. Bake at 375 degrees for 20 minutes; remove from oven; cool 15 minutes.

Combine sour cream, 2 tablespoons sugar and vanilla; stir until smooth. Spread evenly over baked filling. Bake at 425 degrees for 10 minutes. Cool; chill several hours or overnight. Makes 10–12 servings.

Apple Crumb Pudding

1/2 cup flour
1 teaspoon baking powder
1/2 cup sugar
1 teaspoon cinnamon
1 egg, slightly beaten
1 tablespoon lemon juice
1 teaspoon almond extract
4 cups pared and sliced apples
1/2 cup slivered almonds
1/2 cup raisins
1/2 cup flour
1/4 cup sugar
1/4 cup firmly packed brown sugar
1 teaspoon cinnamon
1/4 teaspoon salt
1 teaspoon grated lemon rind
1/4 cup butter, softened

Sift together 1/2 cup flour, baking powder, 1/2 cup sugar and 1 teaspoon cinnamon; set aside. Combine egg, lemon juice and almond extract; add apples, almonds and raisins. Stir in dry ingredients; mix well. Pour into an 8 x 8 x 2-inch greased pan.

Combine 1/2 cup flour, 1/4 cup sugar, brown sugar, cinnamon, salt and lemon rind; cut in butter until mixture resembles coarse meal. Sprinkle over apples in pan. Bake at 375 degrees for 30–35 minutes.

German Chocolate Cheesecake

1 1/2 cups graham cracker crumbs
2 tablespoons brown sugar
1/4 cup butter, melted
1 cup semisweet chocolate chips, melted
16 ounces cream cheese, softened
2/3 cup packed brown sugar
2 tablespoons cocoa
5 eggs
1 teaspoon vanilla
1 teaspoon almond flavoring

Combine crumbs, sugar and butter. Press into 9-inch springform pan. Chill. Beat cream cheese until fluffy; gradually beat in brown sugar and cocoa. Add eggs, 1 at a time, beating after each addition. Beat in chocolate, vanilla and almond flavoring. Pour into crust and bake at 350 degrees for 45 minutes. Cool; refrigerate overnight. Remove from pan.

Cinnamon-Glazed Baked Apples

1/2 cup sugar
2 tablespoons cinnamon candies
2 large baking apples
1 teaspoon lemon juice
1/2 teaspoon butter

Lightly grease small baking dish. In small saucepan, combine sugar and cinnamon candies with 1/2 cup water; boil, stir until sugar dissolves. Reduce heat; simmer uncovered 2 minutes. Remove from heat. Pare top third of apples . Core apples, leaving bottom intact.

Brush apples with lemon juice; arrange in baking dish. Dot centers with butter; brush generously with sugar and cinnamon glaze. Bake apples at 375 degrees, uncovered, 1 hour, brushing frequently with rest of glaze. Serve warm or cold.

Apple Goodie

½ cup sugar
2 tablespoons flour
¼ teaspoon salt
1 teaspoon cinnamon
1½ quarts apples, sliced
1 cup oatmeal
1 cup brown sugar
1 cup flour
¼ teaspoon baking soda
⅓ teaspoon baking powder
⅔ cup butter

Mix together sugar, flour, salt and cinnamon; add apples and mix well. Place apple mixture on the bottom of a greased pan. Mix the oatmeal, brown sugar, flour, baking soda, baking powder and butter until crumbly. Sprinkle oatmeal mixture on apples and pat firmly. Bake at 350 degrees for 40 minutes or until brown and crust is formed. Serve with milk or cream.

Apple Nut Pudding

2 eggs
1 cup sugar
¾ cup flour
½ teaspoon salt
1 teaspoon baking powder
¼ teaspoon nutmeg
¼ teaspoon cinnamon
1 teaspoon almond extract
¾ cup nuts, chopped
2 cups apples, diced

Beat eggs until light and fluffy. Gradually add sugar, beating thoroughly after each addition. Sift together flour, salt, baking powder, cinnamon and nutmeg. Stir into egg mixture; add almond extract, nuts and apples; mix. Bake in 8 x 8-inch glass dish at 325 degrees for 50 minutes.

Peach Strudel

White bread crumbs
1½ pounds ripe peaches, peeled, diced
½ tablespoon lemon juice
½ cup sugar
¼ teaspoon cinnamon

5 phyllo sheets
6 tablespoons butter
⅓ cup chopped macadamia nuts, toasted

Add lemon juice to peaches. Layer phyllo sheets as described in basic knowledge. Place a 3-inch strip of peach mixture down middle of phyllo sheets. Sprinkle with mixture of cinnamon, sugar and nuts. Fold sides in and roll from the bottom up like jelly roll.

Place seam side down on greased cookie sheet. Score in 6 places diagonally through top few layers of phyllo. Bake at 475 degrees for 10 minutes; reduce heat and bake at 375 degrees an additional 25 minutes. Cool; glaze if desired.

Carrot Pudding

8 carrots, peeled, sliced
2 medium potatoes, peeled and cubed
1 egg
2 tablespoons sour cream
2 tablespoons finely shredded onion
½ teaspoon salt
¼ teaspoon pepper
2 ounces cheddar cheese, cut into small cubes
1 tablespoon butter
Orange slices, halved

Cook carrots in boiling water for 10 minutes. Add potatoes; cook an additional 10–15 minutes; drain; mash. Add egg, sour cream, onion, salt and pepper. Beat until well blended. Stir in cheese. Spoon mixture into a 1½-quart casserole; bake at 350 degrees for 30 minutes. Dot with butter; place under broiler 5 inches from heat, for 3 minutes or until golden brown. Let stand 5 minutes before serving. Makes 6–8 servings.

Ritzy Cherry Dessert

1 white cake mix
Cherry pie filling
Whipped topping

Bake cake according to directions on package. Cool. Layer with cherry pie filling. To serve, add whipped topping.

Piña Colada Cheesecake

Margarine
¼ cup margarine, melted
1 package no-bake cheesecake
3 tablespoons sugar
1 cup cottage cheese, beaten until smooth
1 cup milk
½ teaspoon rum extract
1 (20-ounce) can crushed pineapple, drained
¼ cup flaked coconut
Coconut

Generously coat sides of 8-inch pan with margarine; coat with packaged graham cracker crumbs. Mix ¼ cup margarine with crumbs and sugar. Press into bottom of pan.

Mix together packaged cheesecake filling, cottage cheese, milk and rum extract. Beat on low speed with an electric mixer until blended. Change to medium speed and beat an additional 3 minutes. Mix in pineapple and coconut. Spread in pan. Bake at 350 degrees for 20 minutes. Sprinkle with coconut. Refrigerate.

Apple Kuchen

½ cup butter, softened
1 package yellow cake mix
½ cup flaked coconut
½ (20-ounce) can pie-sliced apples, well drained or 2½ cups sliced, pared baking apples
1 cup sugar
1 teaspoon cinnamon
1 cup dairy sour cream
2 egg yolks or 1 egg

Preheat oven to 350 degrees. Cut butter into dry cake mix until crumbly. Mix in coconut. Pat mixture lightly into ungreased 13 x 9 x 2-inch pan, building up slightly around edges. Bake for 10 minutes.

Arrange apple slices on warm crust. Mix together sugar and cinnamon; sprinkle over apples. Blend sour cream and egg yolks; drizzle over apples. Bake for 25 minutes or until edges are light brown. Do not overbake. Serve warm. Serves 12–15.

Baked Apple Pudding

¼ cup butter, softened

1 cup sugar

1 egg

2 cups apples, pared and thinly sliced

1 teaspoon cinnamon

¼ teaspoon salt

1 teaspoon baking soda

1 cup flour

Vanilla Sauce (recipe follows)

Cream together butter and sugar; add egg; beat well. Stir in apples. Add cinnamon, salt, baking soda and flour to creamed mixture. Bake in greased 8 x 8 x 2-inch pan at 350 degrees for 45 minutes. Serve warm with vanilla sauce.

Vanilla Sauce

½ cup butter

1 cup sugar

½ cup light cream

2 teaspoons vanilla

Heat butter, sugar and cream for 10–15 minutes. Stir until slightly thick. *Do not boil.* Add vanilla.

Almond Delights

2¼ cups flour

½ teaspoon salt

½ cup butter

¼ cup shortening

½ cup sugar

1 egg

1 teaspoon vanilla

1 egg

⅓ cup sugar

¼ teaspoon salt

¾ cup ground blanched almonds

½ teaspoon grated lemon rind

¼ teaspoon almond extract

Sift together flour and salt. Cream butter, shortening and sugar, creaming well. Blend in egg and vanilla. Add sifted dry ingredients; mix well. press dough into bottoms and sides of greased muffin pans, using 1–2 tablespoons for each cup. Leave centers hollow.

Beat egg until light and foamy; add ⅓ cup sugar and ¼ teaspoon salt, beating constantly. Blend in ¾ cup almonds, lemon rind and almond extract. Fill each center with 1 tablespoon almond filling. Bake at 325 degrees 25–30 minutes.

Apple Tapioca

4 cups apples, peeled and sliced

½ cup brown sugar, firmly packed

¾ teaspoon cinnamon

½ teaspoon salt

2 tablespoons minute tapioca

Juice of 1 lemon

1 cup boiling water

Toss apples with sugar, cinnamon, salt and tapioca until the coating is evenly blended. Place apples in 2-quart baking dish. Pour lemon juice over apples; add boiling water. Cover and cook for 1 hour at 300 degrees. Serves 4.

Swedish Kringler

1 cup flour

½ cup margarine

2 tablespoons cold water

1 cup water

½ cup margarine

1 cup flour

3 eggs

1 teaspoon almond extract

Almond Frosting (recipe follows)

Mix together flour, margarine and water; spread dough on ungreased cookie sheet. Pat into a 12 x 6-inch rectangle.

Boil together water and margarine; remove from heat. Over low heat, quickly stir in flour, stirring constantly until mixture forms a ball, about 1 minute. Beat in eggs and extract until smooth and glossy. Spread over crust. Bake at 450 degrees for 5–10 minutes; reduce temperature to 350 degrees and bake 30–35 additional minutes. Cool. Frost with Almond Frosting.

Almond Frosting

1½ cups confectioners' sugar

3 tablespoons margarine

1½ teaspoons almond extract

1–2 tablespoons cream

Blend sugar, margarine and extract; stir in cream until smooth. Frost pastry.

Lemon Torte

2 cups flour

1 cup butter, softened

¼ teaspoon salt

3 tablespoons sugar

8 egg yolks

1 cup sugar

Juice of 2 lemons

Rind of 2 lemons

2 envelopes unflavored gelatin

1 cup cold water

8 egg whites

1 cup sugar

½ pint whipping cream, whipped

Mix together flour, butter, salt and sugar until crumbly. Pat into 9-inch spring-form pan. Bake at 375 degrees for 25 minutes. Cool.

Place egg yolks, 1 cup sugar, lemon juice and lemon rind in double boiler and cook until thickened. Soak gelatin in 1 cup cold water for several minutes; place over boiling water to completely dissolve. Add gelatin to yolk mixture; mix; cool. Beat egg whites until stiff but not dry. Add 1 cup sugar and beat well. Fold into yolk mixture and pour in baked shell. Refrigerate for several hours. Top with whipped cream.

Cranberry Cobbler

2¼ cups flour

2 teaspoons baking powder

½ teaspoon salt

¼ cup sugar

1 cup milk

2 tablespoons butter, melted

¼ cup butter, melted

2 cups hot cranberry sauce

2 tablespoons sugar

¼ teaspoon cinnamon

Sift together flour, baking powder, salt and sugar. Combine milk and 2 tablespoons butter. Pour ¼ cup melted butter into 2-quart casserole; spread in half of dough. Pour cranberry sauce over dough. Drop remaining dough by tablespoonfuls on cranberry sauce. Combine sugar and cinnamon; sprinkle over cobbler. Bake at 350 degrees for 35–40 minutes until brown.

Apple Soufflé

1 tablespoon confectioners' sugar
5 large eggs, separated, room temperature
3 large Granny Smith apples, peeled, cored
2 teaspoons lemon juice
¼ cup butter, divided
½ cup sugar
3 tablespoons flour
¾ cup milk
¼ cup apple brandy
1 teaspoon vanilla extract
½ teaspoon ground nutmeg
⅛ teaspoon salt

Cut half the apples into ¼-inch thick slices. Toss apple slices with 1 teaspoon lemon juice. Melt 1 tablespoon butter on medium heat and sauté apple slices until tender-crisp, about 5 minutes. Sprinkle 1 tablespoon sugar over apples and place in greased soufflé dish dusted with 1 tablespoon confectioners' sugar; set aside.

In same skillet, melt remaining 3 tablespoons butter; stir in flour; cook 1 minute. Beat in milk, stirring constantly until smooth and thickened. Remove from heat and beat in apple brandy, egg yolks, vanilla, nutmeg and salt; set aside.

Beat egg whites until foamy. Gradually beat in remaining 7 tablespoons sugar until stiff peaks form. Fold egg yolk mixture into beaten egg whites. Grate remaining apples into bowl with remaining teaspoon lemon juice. Fold apples into soufflé dish. Bake at 350 degrees for 40–45 minutes until lightly browned on top.

Country Apple Dessert

6 apples, cored and sliced
1½ tablespoons butter or margarine
1 cup sugar
⅓ teaspoon cinnamon
⅓ teaspoon nutmeg
½ cup cream

Arrange apples in shallow baking dish. Dot with butter. Mix together sugar, spices and cream. Pour over apples. Bake at 350 degrees for 30 minutes. Serve warm.

Apple & Brown Rice Pudding

2 cups water
1 cup long-grain brown rice
2 cups milk
1 cup heavy cream
2 large eggs
¼ cup sugar
¼ teaspoon salt
2 large apples, peeled, cored, coarsely chopped
½ cup seedless raisins
½ cup dried quartered apricots
2 tablespoons vanilla

Boil water; stir in rice; cover and cook on low heat for 20 minutes. Add milk to undrained rice; cook, stirring occasionally, about 20 minutes longer or until rice is almost tender.

Beat together cream and eggs; stir in sugar and salt; stir into rice mixture. Add apples, raisins, apricots and vanilla. Cook, stirring constantly, until mixture thickens. Do not boil. Spoon rice mixture into greased 2-quart baking dish and bake at 350 degrees for 30 minutes or until knife comes out clean. Serve warm or cold. Makes 8 servings.

Red Hot Apples

1 cup sugar
1 cup water
2 tablespoons red hots
3 drops red food color
6 medium apples, pared and cored

Mix together sugar, water, red hots and food coloring; place in casserole dish. Cook for 3 minutes in microwave. Combine apples with red syrup. Cook for 7–8 minutes longer, turning dish every 2½ minutes. Cool before serving. Serve with whipped topping.

Easy Apple Dessert

2 medium apples, halved, cored and thinly sliced
½ cup flour
1 teaspoon baking powder
½ teaspoon cinnamon
½ teaspoon nutmeg
¼ teaspoon salt

1 egg
½ cup brown sugar
½ cup honey
1 teaspoon vanilla
½ cup nuts, chopped
½ cup raisins

Soak apple slices in a bowl of cold water; set aside. Combine flour, baking powder, cinnamon, nutmeg and salt; mix well. Beat egg in bowl. Stir in brown sugar, honey and vanilla.

Drain apples. Combine apples with brown sugar mixture; mix in flour mixture. Fold in walnuts and raisins. Spread evenly in a greased 9-inch pie plate. Bake at 350 degrees for 30 minutes. Serve hot and top with French vanilla ice cream.

Cherry Angel Food Torte

2 (1-pound) cans pitted dark sweet cherries, drained (reserve juice)
Water
2 (3-ounce) packages dark cherry gelatin
1 quart vanilla ice cream
1 cup port wine
1 (1½-pound) angel food cake
½ pint whipping cream, whipped

Add water to cherry juice to make 2 cups. Heat liquid to boiling; pour in gelatin and dissolve. Remove from heat. Add ice cream a spoonful at a time and stir until ice cream melts; add wine and cherries. Cut angel food cake in ¾-inch cubes. Fold cake gently into cherry mixture. Place in 9-inch springform pan. Refrigerate; top with whipped cream.

Apple Crisp

½ cup butter, melted
½ cup flour
1 cup oatmeal
¼ cup brown sugar
½ cup water
7–8 apples, sliced

Mix together butter, flour, oatmeal and brown sugar. Put water in bottom of pan. Place apples in water. Sprinkle flour mixture over apples. Bake 45 minutes at 350 degrees.

Cream Puffs

½ cup butter
1 cup boiling water
1 cup flour
¼ teaspoon salt
4 eggs

Combine butter and boiling water in saucepan. Add flour and salt all at once, stirring vigorously. Continue stirring over low heat until mixture forms a ball and leaves sides of pan. Remove from heat; cool slightly; add unbeaten eggs, 1 at a time. Beat well after each addition. Chill thoroughly.

Drop by teaspoonfuls onto lightly greased baking sheet 2 inches apart. Bake at 450 degrees for 15 minutes; reduce heat to 350 degrees and bake an additional 25 minutes. Fill with pudding or ice cream.

Ozark Apple Puddin'

1 egg
¾ cup sugar
2 tablespoons flour
1¼ teaspoons baking powder
⅛ teaspoon salt
1 cup nuts, chopped
½ cup McIntosh apples, chopped
1 teaspoon vanilla

Beat together egg and sugar until smooth. Combine flour, baking powder and salt. Stir into egg mixture. Add nuts, apples and vanilla. Bake in a greased pan at 325 degrees for 30 minutes. Serve with whipped cream.

Sugar-Stuffed Apples

9 apples, cored
½ cup brown sugar, firmly packed
1 teaspoon cinnamon
¼ cup pecans, chopped

Mix sugar, cinnamon and pecans together. Pack sugar mixture into cored apples. Arrange apples in slow cooker. Cover and cook on high for 6–8 hours.

Apple Dessert

6 cups apples, peeled, cored, sliced
1½ cups flour
1 cup brown sugar
1½ teaspoons cinnamon
¼ teaspoon nutmeg
¾ cup margarine
¼ teaspoon ginger

Line bottom of greased slow cooker with apple slices. Mix flour, sugar, cinnamon, nutmeg, ginger and margarine in a bowl. Cover apple slices with mixture. Cover and cook on high setting for 2–3 hours. Serve topped with vanilla ice cream or whipped cream with a cherry on top.

Apple Pudding

2 cups cornflakes
2 cups Winesap apples, thinly sliced
½ cup brown sugar, firmly packed
1 teaspoon cinnamon
2 tablespoons butter

Place a layer of cornflakes in well-buttered baking dish, then a layer of apples. Combine brown sugar and cinnamon; sprinkle this mixture over apples. Dot each layer with butter. Repeat until apples and cornflakes are all used up. Bake at 375 degrees for 30–40 minutes. Serve with cream. Serves 6.

Large Cherry Cheesecake

2 packages graham crackers, finely crushed
4 tablespoons sugar
¾ cup butter
2 (8-ounce) packages cream cheese
2 cups confectioners' sugar
2 envelopes Dream Whip
2 large cans cherry pie filling

Mix together graham crackers, sugar and butter. Press into a 9-inch pie pan. Bake at 350 degrees for 10 minutes. Beat cream cheese until soft; add confectioners' sugar. Whip Dream Whip and add to cream cheese mixture. Place in pie crust. Spoon cherry pie filling on top.

Slow-Cooked Baked Apples

6–8 medium baking apples, cored
Raisins
Pecans, chopped
Brown sugar
1 teaspoon cinnamon
½ teaspoon nutmeg
2 tablespoons butter
½ cup water

Peel top third of apple; place in slow cooker. Fill with raisins, pecans and sugar. Sprinkle with cinnamon and nutmeg. Dot with butter; add water. Cover; cook on low for 8 hours or overnight. Makes 6–8 servings.

Swedish Apple Dessert

1½ cups dry bread crumbs, cubed
½ cup brown sugar
½ teaspoon cinnamon
⅓ cup nuts, chopped
1 teaspoon nutmeg
3 cups applesauce
¼ cup butter

Combine bread crumbs, brown sugar, cinnamon, nutmeg and nuts. In well-greased 8-inch baking pan, alternate with layers of crumbs and applesauce, putting a good layer of crumbs on bottom and top. Dot each layer with butter. Bake at 350 degrees for 25–30 minutes. Serve warm with whipped cream.

Cherries Jubilee

1 (1-pound) can black bing cherries, drained, reserve syrup
½ cup rum
1 teaspoon Leroux Curacao
1 teaspoon cornstarch
Vanilla ice cream

Combine syrup with rum and Leroux Curacao. Marinate cherries in this mixture several hours. Just before serving, make a paste of cornstarch and a little of syrup; add to cherries. Bring cherries to a boil; simmer 1 minute. Lower ladle into hot syrup, fill ladle with rum; set aflame. When flame dies out, serve over vanilla ice cream.

Meat
DISHES

Pork Chops With Apples

6 pork chops, ½-inch thick
Salt and pepper
¼ teaspoon ground mace
2 tablespoons minced orange zest
1 tablespoon butter
4 large tart apples, pared and cut in eighths
⅓ cup dry white wine

Season pork chops with salt and pepper. Rub each side with mace and then with orange zest. Heat butter in skillet. Brown pork on both sides until golden, 2 minutes each side. Spread apples in bottom of buttered 10 x 14-inch baking dish; sprinkle with salt and pepper.

Arrange pork chops on top of apples; pour wine on top and bake until apples are softened and wine has reduced by half—about 30 minutes. Turn chops and bake until tender and thoroughly cooked—another 40 minutes. Serve.

Good Bologna

80 pounds ground hamburger
2 pounds tender quick
3 pounds brown sugar
1 tablespoon garlic salt
1 tablespoon mustard powder
4 tablespoons black pepper

Mix all ingredients together. Let stand overnight. I put into muslin casings and smoke as you do sausage. The casings measure 9 x 24 inches. Sew along sides and one end. Stuff with bologna. Pack in containers or fry in patties. Recipe can be reduced with good results.

Orange-Honey Fish

1 pound fresh or frozen orange roughy, grouper, cod or other fish fillets
2 tablespoons finely chopped green onion
1 teaspoon finely shredded orange peel
2 tablespoons orange juice
2 tablespoons honey
½ teaspoon paprika
¼ teaspoon salt
⅛ teaspoon pepper
Orange slices (optional)

Thaw fish, if frozen. Pat dry. Cut into 4 serving-size portions. Measure thickness of fish.

For glaze, in a small bowl stir together onion, orange peel, orange juice, honey, paprika, salt and pepper.

Place fish on the unheated rack of a broiler pan. Brush some of glaze over fish. Broil 4 inches from heat (allow 4–6 minutes per ½ inch thickness) until fish just flakes with a fork, brushing occasionally with glaze. Garnish with orange slices, if desired. Serves 4. (127 calories per serving)

Summer Sausage

50 pounds ground beef
1 quart salt
2 pounds brown sugar
6 tablespoons black pepper

In very large tub, combine beef, salt, sugar and pepper. Hang up immediately and smoke in smokehouse.

Baked Mushroom Chicken

1 frying chicken, cut up
1 can cream of mushroom soup
1 tablespoon butter
2 tablespoons onion flakes
1 tablespoon paprika
¼ cup chopped parsley

Place chicken pieces with butter in baking dish. Sprinkle with onion, parsley and paprika Pour mushroom soup over tops. Cover and place in 300-degree oven for 2 hours.

Canned Meat

Steak or ham, cubed
1 pint brown sugar
1 cup salt
1 gallon water

Make a brine of brown sugar, salt and water. Heat. Place meat chunks into 14 quarts; fill with hot brine. Process in pressure cooker at 10 pounds pressure for 1½ hours. Cool.

Beer Batter for Fish

¾ cup flour
½ cup Bisquick
Salt and pepper, to taste
1 egg
Beer

Mix flour, Bisquick, salt, pepper and egg. Gradually add beer to make desired thickness for batter.

Fried Hamburger Patties

1 pint canned hamburger
2 eggs
6 little squares crackers, crushed
1/4 cup flour
   Seasoning salt
1/4 cup onions, diced
1/4 cup celery, diced

Mix all ingredients together. Make into patties and fry in little lard.

Curing Hams

   Ham
1 cup salt
1 cup brown sugar
1 teaspoon red pepper
1 teaspoon black pepper, heaping

Clean marrow out of end of ham. Stuff end of bone with salt, brown sugar, red pepper and black pepper mixed together. Rub the mixture over all sides of ham. Wrap in paper and cloth. Hang bone end down so it can drip. Hang meat outside for 30 days.

Canned Hamburger

   Hamburger
1/2 teaspoon salt
1/4 teaspoon pepper

Fill pint jar up to neck with raw hamburger. Add salt and pepper; put on can lid and tighten ring. Cold pack 3 hours or pressure cook at 10 pounds for 1 1/2 hours.

Canned Chunk Beef

   Chunk beef
1/2 teaspoon salt
1/4 teaspoon pepper

Fill pint jar up to neck with raw chunk beef. Add salt and pepper; put on can lid and tighten ring. Cold pack 3 hours or pressure cook at 10 pounds for 1 1/2 hours.

Gravy

1/2 cup bacon drippings
3/4 cup flour
   Salt to taste
1 cup sausage, cooked or canned
1 cup cold water
   Milk

Brown bacon drippings, flour and salt in skillet; remove from stove. Add sausage; return to stove and gently cook meat. Add cold water and stir until real thick. Add milk until desired thickness.

Porcupine Meatballs

1 pound ground beef
1/2 cup cracker crumbs
1/4 cup onions, chopped
2 tablespoons green pepper, chopped
1 (10-ounce) can tomato soup
2 cups boiling water
1 teaspoon salt
1 teaspoon paprika
1/2 cup uncooked rice

Combine meat, crumbs, onions, green pepper, salt and paprika. Mix well; shape into 8 balls. Roll each ball in rice and press the rice into meat so that as it cooks it will cling to the meat. Place meatballs into pan with tomato soup and boiling water. Cover and simmer about 45 minutes. Makes 4–6 servings.

Barbecued Ham

   Ham slices
   Pepper
1/4 teaspoon prepared mustard per ham slice
1/2 teaspoon vinegar per ham slice
1/2 glass wine
1 teaspoon sugar

Lay ham slices flat in frying pan; pepper each, then spread each slice with 1/4 teaspoon mustard. Pour 1/2 teaspoon vinegar on each slice. Fry quickly on both sides. When done, take out and add wine and sugar to gravy. Boil and pour over meat.

Pressed Chicken

3 pounds chicken
1 teaspoon salt
1 tablespoon water
2 tablespoons parsley, minced
3 cups water
1 stalk celery, diced
1 tablespoon plain gelatin per pint of broth

Cook chicken, water, salt and celery in pressure cooker. When done, remove chicken from bones keeping the dark meat separate from the white meat. Strain broth. Dissolve each tablespoon gelatin in 2 tablespoons cold water; add to boiling broth. Stir in parsley.

Alternate layers of white and dark meat in dish or mold. Pour broth over chicken and cover dish. Place in a cool place to set. It helps to cut the chicken up really fine.

Yuminosetti

1 pound noodles
3 pounds hamburger, browned
1 onion, chopped
2 cans mushroom soup
1 can cream of chicken *or* celery soup
1 pint peas, drained
1 cup sour cream

Cook noodles in salted boiling water; drain. In large bowl, add noodles, hamburger, onion, mushroom soup, chicken soup, peas and sour cream. Place in baking dish. Bake at 350 degrees for 1 hour.

Sausage Gravy

4 pounds fresh sausage, fried and chopped
3 cups flour
2 tablespoons salt
1/2 tablespoons pepper
18 cups milk

Add flour to sausage, brown; add salt and pepper. Stir well and add milk. Heat to boiling point and reduce heat and simmer for a few minutes. Makes approximately 5 quarts gravy.

Snappy Pizza

1 pint tomato paste
½ pint water
1 small can mushroom soup
¼ cup sugar
½ teaspoon garlic powder
½ teaspoon oregano
3 pounds ground beef, browned
  Salt to taste
  Cheese

Mix together tomato paste, water, mushroom soup, sugar, garlic powder, salt and oregano; simmer. Add tomato mixture to ground beef. Spread on top of hamburger bun halves. Top with cheese. Bake at 400 degrees until lightly brown, 3–5 minutes.

Summer Sausage

5 pounds hamburger
2½ teaspoons pepper
2½ teaspoons garlic salt
5 teaspoons Morton's Tender quick salt
2½ teaspoons mustard seed
2½ teaspoons liquid smoke

14   AMISH COOKING

Combine hamburger, pepper, garlic salt, quick salt, mustard seed and liquid smoke. Knead 5 minutes every day for 4 days. On the fifth day, put into rolls and bake at 150 degrees for 8 hours. Turn over after 4 hours. Bake on broiler rack. When done, wrap in paper towel to soak up grease. Wrap in plastic. Freezes well. Slice thin and serve.

Mush

16 cups water
4 cups cornmeal
2–3 tablespoons salt
1 cup milk
  Butter
  Maple syrup

Heat water to boiling point. Add cornmeal and salt, stirring constantly. Cook for 20–30 minutes on low heat. Pour into a 9 x 12-inch cake pan to cool. Let set overnight. Slice in pieces and fry in deep fat fryer or in skillet. One cup milk may be added to make golden brown when frying. Serve with butter and maple syrup.

Vegetable Sausage Loaf

1 large carrot
1 egg
4 medium potatoes
½ pound sausage
1 medium onion
¼ cup bread crumbs
4 stalks celery
¼ cup milk
½ teaspoon salt
¼ teaspoon summer savory

Grind vegetables. Beat egg and add with remaining ingredients. Form loaf and bake at 350 degrees for 1 hour. Serves 6.

Meat Loaf

10 pounds hamburger
5 teaspoons salt
1 onion, diced
1 teaspoon pepper
1 quart milk
½ loaf of bread crumbs

Topping

1 cup ketchup
3 tablespoons mustard
6 rounded teaspoons brown sugar

Mix together hamburger, salt, onion, pepper, milk and bread crumbs. Place in loaf pan. Bake at 350 degrees for 90 minutes. Combine ketchup, mustard and brown sugar. Spread on top of meat mixture. Cook an additional 15 minutes.

Baked Chicken

  Chicken
  Salt
  Flour
  Milk

Sprinkle chicken with salt, then roll in flour. Place in baking dish. Pour a little milk over top. Cover and bake at 350 degrees for 1½ hours or until tender. Check once or twice. Add water if liquid is needed.

Paradise Chicken

6 large pieces frying chicken
½ cup chicken broth
¼ cup coffee liqueur
¼ cup red-wine vinegar
2 tablespoons ketchup
1 tablespoon soy sauce
1 tablespoon cornstarch
1 small clove garlic, minced
1 teaspoon grated fresh ginger

Arrange chicken pieces in baking pan. Combine chicken broth, liqueur, vinegar, ketchup, soy sauce, cornstarch, garlic and ginger in saucepan; bring to boil; simmer 2–3 minutes. Spoon half of sauce over chicken. Cover and bake at 375 degrees for 30 minutes. Uncover, spoon on remaining sauce. Bake an additional 15–20 minutes until tender. Makes 4–6 servings.

Roast Beef

5 pounds chuck roast with bone
½ teaspoon salt
¼ teaspoon pepper
1 tablespoon beef base
1 cup tomato juice
  Water

Place roast in 2½-quart baking dish; sprinkle with salt, pepper and beef base. Pour tomato juice over top and add water to barely cover beef. Cover and bake at 350 degrees for 3 hours. Use juice of beef to thicken for gravy.

Chip Chop Ham Sandwiches

2 pounds chipped ham
3 tablespoons brown sugar
1 cup ketchup
¼ cup vinegar
1 cup water
1 tablespoon Worcestershire sauce

Cut meat into bite-size pieces. Fry a little in butter. Sprinkle with a little flour and add brown sugar, ketchup, vinegar, water and Worcestershire sauce. Simmer for 1 hour at 250 degrees. Makes 10–15 sandwiches.

Roast Pork With Apricot & Apple Stuffing

1 (5-pound) pork loin, boned
1 cup dried apricots
2 large apples, peeled, cored, cut into chunks
1 teaspoon salt
1/8 teaspoon white pepper
1 teaspoon powdered ginger
1/4 teaspoon cinnamon
1 1/2 cups water
3 tablespoons flour
Salt and pepper, to taste
1/2 cup sour cream

Cut pocket in side of loin. In a medium-size saucepan, parboil apricots for about 10 minutes to plump. Mix together apricots and apples and stuff them into pocket in loin. Mix together 1 teaspoon of salt, white pepper, ginger and cinnamon; rub on outside of loin. Tie pocket closed by wrapping string around loin several times.

Place loin in roasting pan, fat side up, and roast on bottom shelf of preheated 350-degree oven for 40 minutes per pound. Remove roast from oven; place on platter. Meanwhile, put water in screw-top jar. Spoon flour on top of water, cover and shake to blend. Skim most of fat from roasting pan.

Put pan on burner set on medium heat. Gradually pour in flour-water mixture, stirring constantly with a wooden spoon until thickened. Add more water if necessary to thin gravy. Salt and pepper to taste. Cook at least 5 minutes, stirring occasionally. Remove from heat and stir in sour cream. Slice meat. Serve gravy on roast or serve in gravy bowl.

Glazed Ham

1/2 ham
1 teaspoon dry mustard
3 tablespoons orange marmalade
2 tablespoons rum
Whole cloves

Combine dry mustard, orange marmalade and rum. Moisten ham with rum; spread marmalade paste over fat side of ham. Slash fat in diamonds; stick whole cloves in each diamond. Bake at 325 degrees 60–70 minutes per pound.

Roast Chicken With Sausage-Apple Stuffing

8 ounces bulk sausage
6 tablespoons butter, divided
1/2 cup celery, thinly sliced
1 (8-ounce) package herb-seasoned bread stuffing mix
1 apple, diced
1 cup hot water
1 roasting chicken

In large skillet, brown sausage, breaking up into small pieces; drain fat. Add 2 tablespoons butter; stir in celery, cooking for 5 minutes until celery is tender crisp. In large bowl, combine apples, water and stuffing mix. Stir in celery-sausage mixture. Stuff neck cavity and body cavity. Close with skewers, toothpicks or sew closed. Tie legs close to body.

Place chicken, breast side up, in roasting pan. Brush with remaining melted butter. Roast, uncovered, for 2 hours at 375 degrees. Remove string holding legs together after 1 hour. Cook until done and juices run clear. If chicken browns too quickly, cover with aluminum foil. Remove skewers or toothpicks and string. Cut and serve hot.

Roast Beef With Yorkshire Pudding

4–6 pound boneless beef rib roast
Salt and pepper
Yorkshire Pudding Batter (recipe follows)
Oil

Place rib roast in roasting pan; sprinkle with salt and pepper. Roast uncovered at 325 degrees for 2 1/4 hours. Pour drippings off meat; add enough oil to make 1/4 cup. Place drippings in heated pan; pour in pudding batter. Bake until puffed and golden brown, about 25 minutes. Cut into squares; serve with beef.

Yorkshire Pudding Batter

1 cup flour
1 cup milk
2 eggs
1/2 teaspoon salt

Mix together flour, milk, eggs and salt just until smooth.

Pork With Cranberries & Apple

1 pound boneless pork loin
1/4 teaspoon salt
1/4 teaspoon cracked black peppe
1 large Delicious apple, peeled, cored, sliced
1/4 cup butter, divided
2 tablespoons oil
1/2 cup cranberries
1 cup chicken broth, divided
2 teaspoons sugar
2 tablespoons flour

Cut pork on diagonal into 8 slices. Pound to make 1/4 inch thick. Sprinkle with salt and pepper; set aside. Melt 1 tablespoon butter in large skillet over medium heat; sauté apple wedges until tender-crisp, 5 minutes; remove from heat.

In skillet, heat oil on medium-high; sauté pork until browned on both sides; remove from heat. Reduce heat to medium; add 1 tablespoon butter, cranberries and 2 tablespoons chicken broth; cook until cranberries start to pop. Mix sugar into cranberries; place on platter with apples.

Melt remaining 2 tablespoons butter in skillet. Stir in flour until paste forms; cook 1 minute longer, stirring constantly. Stir in remaining chicken broth and cook until sauce boils and thickens; serve over cutlets.

Creamy White Bass

3–4 pounds white bass
1 (10-ounce) can cream of mushroom soup
1 soup can milk
1 cup diced ham
1 teaspoons lemon juice
1 tablespoon sherry
Biscuits
Paprika

Cover bass with water; simmer 10 minutes. When flaky, remove; break into small pieces; set aside. Drain water. Heat mushroom soup and milk; add fish, ham and lemon juice. Stir in sherry. Serve over biscuits or toast. Sprinkle with paprika.

Holiday Turkey

3 medium onions, finely chopped
3 cups margarine
3 cups croutons, toasted
2 cups chopped walnuts
2 large stalks celery, chopped
2 cups dry white wine
3/4 cup raisins
1/4 cup water
2 1/4 teaspoons salt
1 1/2 teaspoons ground sage
1 12-pound turkey
2 tablespoons margarine, melted
1 teaspoon instant chicken bouillon
1 cup boiling water

Cook onions in margarine until tender; remove from heat; stir in croutons, walnuts, celery, 1 cup of wine, raisins, water, salt and sage. Stuff turkey. Place turkey in roasting pan; brush with margarine. Pour remaining wine on turkey. Dissolve bouillon in boiling water; pour on turkey. Roast uncovered at 325 degrees for 3–5 hours, until done.

Roast Leg of Lamb

5–7 pound leg of lamb
1 clove garlic, cut into slivers
Salt and pepper

Make slits in lamb with tip of knife; insert slivers of garlic into slits. Sprinkle lamb with salt and pepper. Roast at 325 degrees for 2–3 1/2 hours.

Fried Chicken

2 1/2 pound fryer chicken, cut in pieces
1/2 cup flour
1 teaspoon salt
1 teaspoon paprika
1/4 teaspoon pepper
Oil

Mix together flour, salt, paprika and pepper. Coat chicken with flour mixture. Heat oil; cook chicken until brown, 15–20 minutes; reduce heat. Cover and simmer 30–40 minutes, turning once or twice. Remove cover during last 5 minutes of cooking to crisp chicken.

Cornish Game Hens

1/2 cup fresh orange juice
1/4 cup fresh lemon juice
1/2 teaspoon prepared mustard
1/4 teaspoon paprika
3 tablespoons butter
4 Cornish game hens
Salt and pepper
2 thin orange slices, halved
2 thin lemon slices, halved
1 cup seedless grapes

Combine orange juice, lemon juice, mustard and paprika; add butter. Bring to a boil; simmer 1 minute. Remove giblets from hens; rinse in cold water; dry well. Season each cavity with salt and pepper. Add a half slice orange and lemon and 8 grapes to each hen. Truss legs; arrange in shallow pan.

Baste with orange juice mixture and cover loosely with foil. Roast at 375 degrees for 30 minutes, basting occasionally.

To make sauce, remove excess fat from pan; add remaining basting mixture. Bring to boil; simmer until thickened. Spoon over hens. Makes 4 servings.

Duck Oriental

1 (4–5-pound) duckling
1 clove garlic, chopped
Rum
1 orange, pricked all over with fork
1 onion
Butter, melted
1/4 teaspoon ginger
1/2 teaspoon salt
1/4 cup rum
1/2 cup water

Rub duck skin with garlic and sprinkle with rum. In cavity, place orange and onion. Truss up duck. Mix together butter, ginger and salt; brush over duck. Bake at 325 degrees for 2 hours. During last half hour, pour off all fat in pan; baste duck with 1/4 cup rum. Remove duck to platter; skim off excess fat remaining in pan, then add 1/2 cup water to pan essence and boil about 3 minutes. Serve over sliced duck. Makes 4 servings.

Corned Beef & Cabbage

2 pounds corned beef brisket
1 small onion, quartered
1 clove garlic, crushed
1 small head cabbage, cut into 6 wedges

Cover corned beef in 5-quart Dutch oven with water. Add onion and garlic. Heat to boiling; reduce heat. Simmer until beef is tender, about 2 hours. Remove beef to warm platter. Skim fat from broth. Add cabbage; heat to boiling. Reduce heat and simmer 15 minutes.

Oven-Barbecued Chicken

2–3 pound fryer chicken, cut up
3/4 cup chili sauce
2 tablespoons honey
2 tablespoons soy sauce
1 teaspoon dry mustard
1/2 teaspoon prepared horseradish
1/2 teaspoon red pepper sauce

Place chicken in 13 x 9-inch pan. Mix together chili sauce, honey, soy sauce, mustard, horseradish and red pepper sauce; pour over chicken. Bake at 375 degrees for 30 minutes; spoon sauce over chicken; cook, uncovered, until done.

Lemon-Baked Cod

1 pound cod fillets
1/4 cup margarine, melted
2 tablespoons lemon juice
1/4 cup flour
1/2 teaspoon salt
1/8 teaspoon white pepper
Paprika

Combine margarine and lemon juice. Mix flour, salt and white pepper. Dip fish into margarine mixture; coat with flour mixture. Place in ungreased square baking dish; pour margarine over fish; sprinkle with paprika. Bake at 350 degrees for 25–30 minutes, until fish flakes easily with fork.

Swedish Meatballs With Sour Cream Sauce

½ pound ground beef
½ pound ground veal
½ pound ground pork
¼ cup dry bread crumbs
½ cup finely chopped onion
½ cup half-and-half
3 tablespoons snipped parsley
1 teaspoon salt
1 teaspoon Worcestershire sauce
½ teaspoon ground allspice
½ teaspoon grated lemon peel
2 eggs
  Sour Cream Sauce
  (recipe follows)

Combine beef, veal, pork, crumbs, onion, half-and-half, parsley, salt, Worcestershire sauce, allspice, lemon peel and eggs; Shape into 1¼-inch balls. Place in broiler pan. Bake at 375 degrees for 20–25 minutes; pour sauce over meatballs.

Sour Cream Sauce

3 tablespoons margarine
3 tablespoons flour
1½ cups beef broth
1½ teaspoons dried dill weed
¼ teaspoon salt
¼ teaspoon ground nutmeg
½ cup sour cream

Melt margarine over low heat. Stir in flour; cook, stirring constantly, until smooth and bubbly; remove from heat. Stir in broth, dill weed, salt and nutmeg. Heat to boiling, stirring constantly. Boil, stirring constantly, 1 minute; remove from heat. Mix in sour cream.

Chicken or Ribs

½ cup chili sauce
1 cup pineapple juice
2 tablespoons cornstarch
3 pounds chicken, cut up *or* spare *or* beef ribs

Combine chili sauce and pineapple juice; slowly stir in cornstarch. Heat until thoroughly mixed. Baste chicken with sauce. Barbecue over low-medium coals, turning and basting every 8 minutes for 30–40 minutes. Makes 4–6 servings.

Rock Cornish Hens With Cumberland Sauce

4 (1-pound) Rock Cornish hens
2 cups seasoned bread crumbs
½ cup wheat germ
½ cup celery and leaves, finely cut
½ cup chicken broth
⅓ cup butter, melted
1 teaspoon sugar
1 teaspoon salt
1 (10-ounce) jar red currant jelly
½ cup golden raisins
¼ cup butter
2 teaspoons lemon juice
¼ teaspoon allspice
1 (16-ounce) jar spiced crabapples, drained for garnish

Preheat oven to 375 degrees. From each hen remove giblets and necks. Rinse and drain hens. Tuck neck skin under wings to secure it. In large bowl, combine bread crumbs, wheat germ, celery, chicken broth, 2 tablespoons butter, sugar and salt.

Spoon mixture into cavity of hens. With string, tie legs and tail of each hen together. Brush hens generously with butter. Place hens breast-side up on rack in roasting pan. Bake 1–1½ hours, or until leg can be moved up and down easily. Baste with remaining melted butter.

Make Cumberland sauce by combining jelly, raisins, ¼ cup butter, lemon juice and allspice in saucepan. Stir until mixture is well-blended. During last half hour of baking, brush hens with sauce. Serve hens garnished with crabapples, and pass the sauce.

Basted Apple Juice Ham

3 tablespoons brown sugar
1 tablespoon dry mustard
1 (5-pound) canned *or* smoked ham
  Whole cloves
1 pint apple juice

Mix brown sugar and mustard together. Rub into ham. Score ham; insert whole cloves around edge. Pour apple juice over ham. Baste frequently while baking. Bake at 350 degrees for 2 hours or until ham is done.

Applesauce Chili

1 pound ground beef
1 teaspoon salt
1 large onion, chopped
1 clove garlic, minced
1 tablespoon chili powder
1 teaspoon oregano
1 (1-pound) can stewed tomatoes
1¾ cups applesauce
1 (1-pound) can red kidney beans, drained

Brown beef in large skillet. Add salt, onion, garlic, chili powder, oregano, tomatoes and applesauce. Bring to a boil. Cover and let simmer for 1 hour. Add beans and simmer, uncovered, for 10 minutes more. Serves 6.

Turkey With Rum-Sausage Stuffing

1 (10–12 pound) turkey
  Rum
  Butter, melted
2 (8-ounce) packages herb-seasoned bread stuffing
1 pound sausage meat, crumbled
¼ cup light cream
¼ cup rum

Sprinkle rum inside and outside of turkey. Combine stuffing, sausage meat, cream and rum; stuff turkey; truss and sew. Sprinkle with more rum; brush with melted butter. Place turkey in roasting pan and loosely cover; roast at 325 degrees for 4–4½ hours.

Smothered Fish

3 pounds fish
  Salt and pepper
⅓ cup dry sherry
½ pound sliced fresh mushrooms
6 tablespoons butter, divided
½ cup grated Parmesan cheese
1 cup sour cream
  Paprika

Season fish with salt and pepper; sprinkle with sherry. Sauté mushrooms in 2 tablespoons butter; spread over fish. Combine 4 tablespoons melted butter, Parmesan cheese and sour cream. Spoon sour cream mixture on top of fish; sprinkle with paprika. Bake in shallow baking dish at 350 degrees for 30–40 minutes or until fish flakes easily.

Chicken & Gravy

2–3 pounds chicken
1 tablespoon margarine, softened
½ teaspoon salt
¼ teaspoon allspice
1 tablespoon margarine
¼ cup water
Gravy (recipe follows)

Mix together margarine, salt and allspice; brush over chicken. Heat 1 tablespoon margarine in 4-quart Dutch oven over medium heat; cook chicken until brown on all sides; add water. Cook, covered, over medium heat until chicken is done, 30–40 minutes. Remove chicken; reserve drippings.

Gravy

Milk
½ cup milk
¼ cup flour
½ teaspoon salt
⅛ teaspoon allspice
1 (4-ounce) can mushroom stems and pieces, drained
1 teaspoon currant jelly

Add enough milk to chicken drippings to make 1½ cups; place in Dutch oven. Combine ½ cup milk, flour, salt and allspice in jar; shake; gradually add to drippings until mixed. Stir in mushrooms and jelly. Heat to boiling, stirring constantly. Boil 1 minute, stirring constantly.

Savory Roast Beef

¼ cup chopped onion
2 tablespoons butter
1 (16-ounce) can tomatoes, cut up
1 (10-ounce) can tomato soup
1 (4-ounce) can sliced mushrooms
½ teaspoon salt
½ teaspoon dried crushed basil
½ teaspoon dried crushed oregano
¼ teaspoon pepper
2 cups cooked beef, thinly sliced into bite-size strips
Hot cooked rice

Cook onion in butter until tender. Add undrained tomatoes, tomato soup, undrained mushrooms, salt, basil, oregano and pepper. Bring to boil; reduce heat; simmer, uncovered, 20 minutes. Add meat; continue cooking until just heated through. Serve over rice. Makes 4–6 servings.

Beef With Rum Sauce

2 pounds boneless chuck, cut in chunks
4 tablespoons rum, divided
2 tablespoons butter
2 tablespoons flour
1½ teaspoons salt
1 (6-ounce) can mushrooms with liquid
1 tablespoon tomato ketchup
1 bay leaf
1 tablespoon currant jelly
1 tablespoon wine vinegar
2 cups water

Sprinkle meat with 2 tablespoons rum; let stand 1 hour; brown meat in butter. Sprinkle with remaining 2 tablespoons rum; cook an additional minute. Place meat in Dutch oven. Add flour to butter in skillet, blending well. Add salt and remaining ingredients. Pour sauce over meat; cover tightly. Bring sauce to boil; simmer gently for 30 minutes or until meat is very tender. Makes 4–6 servings.

Buffet Ham

4–5 pound boneless smoked ham, cooked, cut into ¼-inch slices, tied
3 tablespoons corn syrup
2 tablespoons brown sugar
1 teaspoon prepared mustard
Mustard Sauce (recipe follows)

Bake ham at 325 degrees for 1–1¼ hours. Mix together corn syrup, brown sugar and mustard. Brush mixture on ham during last 15 minutes of baking.

Mustard Sauce

1 tablespoon margarine, melted
1 tablespoon flour
½ teaspoon salt
¼ teaspoon pepper
1 cup milk
3 tablespoons prepared mustard
1 tablespoon prepared horseradish

Blend flour, salt and pepper with margarine. Cook over low heat, stirring constantly, until smooth and bubbly. Stir in milk, boil 1 minute, stirring constantly. Stir in mustard and horseradish; heat until hot.

Chicken & Biscuits

1 (10-ounce) package frozen green peas
2 cups cooked, cut-up chicken or turkey
1 (10-ounce) can cream of chicken soup
½ cup sour cream
½ cup milk
½ teaspoon salt
⅛ teaspoon pepper
2 cups buttermilk baking mix
½ cup cold water
1¼ cups shredded cheddar cheese

Rinse peas under cold water until separated; drain. Heat peas, chicken or turkey, soup, sour cream, milk, salt and pepper, stirring frequently; keep warm.

Combine baking mix and water; beat 20 strokes. Knead 5 times; roll ½ inch thick. Cut with 2-inch cutter. Place mixture into 2-quart baking dish. Sprinkle with cheese. Place biscuits on cheese. Bake at 425 degrees for 20 minutes.

Pork Chops With Apples

½ teaspoon garlic powder
1½ teaspoons caraway seeds
¼ teaspoon salt
¼ teaspoon thyme
¼ teaspoon pepper
1 medium onion, sliced, separated into rings
3 cups sauerkraut, drained
4 pork chops, cut ½-inch thick, trimmed, browned
¾ cup apple juice
1 cup apple slices, unpeeled and cored

Stir together garlic powder, caraway seeds, salt, thyme and pepper. Place half of onion rings and sauerkraut in bottom of slow cooker; sprinkle with half of the spice mixture. Place pork chops on top of onion rings. Lay rest of onion rings and sauerkraut on top of pork chops; sprinkle with remaining spice mixture. Pour apple juice over all. Top with apple slices. Bake on high 6–8 hours or 10–12 hours on low. Makes 4 servings.

Bake
A PIE

Cheesy Beef Pie

- 1 pound ground beef
- ½ cup chopped onions
- 2 teaspoons cornstarch
- 10 ounces mild taco sauce
- ¼ cup parsley
- 1 (3-ounce) can mushrooms, chopped
- 3 eggs, separated
- 1½ cups grated cheese
- 2 (9-inch) pie crusts

Brown beef and onion together; drain. Sprinkle meat with cornstarch; blend. Add taco sauce, parsley and mushrooms. Spread ½ beaten egg whites over bottom crust.

Spoon meat into pie shell; sprinkle top with cheese. Pour remaining egg whites over cheese. Add top crust and brush with slightly beaten egg yolks. Bake at 350 degrees for 50–55 minutes. Let stand 10 minutes before serving.

Old-Fashioned Cream Pie

- 1 (9-inch) unbaked pie crust
- 3 heaping tablespoons flour
- ½ cup brown sugar
- 1 cup white sugar
- 1 egg
- 1½ cups milk
- Lump of butter
- ½ teaspoon nutmeg

Mix together white sugar and flour. Add brown sugar, egg and milk; stir in nutmeg. Pour into pie crust and dot with butter. Bake at 325 degrees until light brown and smells done.

Chocolate Pie Crust

- 1½ cups flour
- 3 tablespoons sugar
- 3 tablespoons unsweetened cocoa
- ½ cup butter
- 2 tablespoons shortening
- 3–4 tablespoons cold water

Combine flour, sugar and cocoa. Cut in butter and shortening until mixture resembles coarse crumbs. Sprinkle water over mixture, 1 tablespoon at a time, tossing until moistened. Form into a ball and roll out crusts. Bake at 400 degrees for 10–12 minutes. Makes 2 crusts.

Graham Cracker Crust

- 10 graham crackers, crushed
- 4 tablespoons sugar
- 4 tablespoons butter, melted

Mix together crackers, sugar and butter. Press into 9-inch pie pan. Refrigerate 15 minutes.

Cookie Crust

- ¾ cup flour
- ⅓ cup margarine, softened
- 3 tablespoons confectioners' sugar
- ¼ teaspoon vanilla

Mix together flour, margarine, sugar and vanilla. Press in bottom of ungreased pan. Bake at 350 degrees for 10–13 minutes; cool.

Oreo Cookie Pie

- 1 large package Oreo cookies, crushed
- 1 stick margarine, melted
- 1 (8-ounce) package cream cheese
- 2 large cartons non-dairy whipped topping
- ½ cup sugar
- 1 large package chocolate instant pudding mix
- 3 cups milk

Mix together cookie crumbs and margarine; spread half of mixture into a 9 x 10-inch cake pan. Mix cream cheese, whipped topping and sugar; spread on top of cookie crumb mixture. Mix chocolate pudding and milk; spread on top of cream cheese mixture. Sprinkle remaining cookie crumbs on top; refrigerate.

Never-Fail Pastry

- 1 cup flour
- ¼ teaspoon baking powder
- ¼ teaspoon salt
- 4 tablespoons ice water
- 3 tablespoons shortening

Mix together flour, baking powder and salt. Cut in shortening; add enough water to make a stiff dough. Roll out onto floured surface; place in pie pan. Makes 1 crust.

Hazelnut Chocolate Mousse

½ cup finely chopped hazelnuts
½ cup flour
1 tablespoon firmly packed brown sugar
6 tablespoons cold unsalted butter
1–2 teaspoons ice water
1 pound semisweet chocolate, melted
2 large eggs, room temperature
4 egg yolks, room temperature
3 ounces hazelnut liqueur
6 egg whites, room temperature
Dash cream of tartar
Dash salt
¼ cup confectioners' sugar
1 pint whipping cream

In food processor, combine nuts, flour and brown sugar until blended. Cut butter in 6 pieces and process into mixture until crumbly. Add 1–2 teaspoons ice water and mix just until mixture begins to hold together. Press into the bottom of an ungreased 9 x 13-inch springform pan. Bake at 400 degrees for 12–15 minutes or until lightly browned. Cool completely before filling.

Cool chocolate; mix in whole eggs 1 at a time. The mixture will be thick and stiff. Mix in egg yolks and liqueur; set aside. Beat egg whites until frothy. Add salt and cream of tartar; continue beating until soft peaks form. Beat in confectioners' sugar, a tablespoon at a time until stiff.

In a separate bowl, whip cream until soft peaks form; do not overbeat. Fold chocolate and cream into whites. Pour into cooled crust. Refrigerate at least 4 hours. (Pie may be refrigerated 2 days or frozen and thawed in refrigerator overnight before serving.)

Nancy's Pie Crust

2 cups sifted flour
1 teaspoon salt
2/3 cup shortening
5–7 tablespoons cold water

Combine flour and salt; cut in shortening until crumbly. Add water 1 tablespoon at a time until flour forms a ball. Roll out on floured board. Makes 2 pie crusts.

Peach Cream Pie

1 unbaked pie crust
1 quart canned peaches, drained, sliced
1 cup sugar
2 tablespoons flour
1 cup cream
1 teaspoon vanilla

Place peach slices in pie crust. Stir together sugar and flour; mix in cream and vanilla. Mix well. Pour over peaches in crust. Bake at 350 degrees for 40 minutes or until cream thickens and is delicate brown.

Lime Pie

1 (9-inch) baked graham cracker crust
2 (12-ounce) containers whipped topping
1 (14-ounce) can sweetened condensed milk
1 (6-ounce) can limeade
4 drops green food coloring

Mix together whipped topping, sweetened condensed milk, limeade and food coloring. Pour into graham cracker crust and cool until firm and set.

Cantaloupe Pie

1 large cantaloupe
1 cup sugar
2 tablespoons cornstarch
2 eggs, separated
¼ teaspoon salt
¼ cup cold water
4 tablespoons sugar
1 (9-inch) baked pie shell
4 tablespoons sugar

Cut cantaloupe in half; remove seeds. Scoop out pulp and place in top of double boiler; add sugar. Mix cornstarch with cold water; add to cantaloupe. Cook over medium heat until thickened; add beaten egg yolks and salt; cook 1 minute more. Remove from heat; cool 10 minutes; pour into baked pie shell.

Beat egg whites with 4 tablespoons sugar until stiff; spread on pie. Bake at 350 degrees for 15 minutes. Cool before serving.

Chocolate Pie

1 (4½-ounce) package instant chocolate pudding
1 envelope Dream Whip
1¾ cups milk
½ small package cream cheese
1 graham cracker crust
Whipped topping

Mix together pudding, Dream Whip and milk. Melt cream cheese in bowl and add to pudding mixture. Put in graham cracker crust; place in refrigerator to set. Serve with whipped topping.

Oatmeal Pie

3 eggs
¼ cup butter
½ cup sugar
½ cup corn syrup
1 cup rolled oats
1½ teaspoons vanilla
1 (9-inch) unbaked pie crust

Beat together eggs, butter, sugar, corn syrup and vanilla. Stir in rolled oats. Pour into prepared pie crust. Bake at 350 degrees for 30–40 minutes or until done.

Ice Cream Pie

1 chocolate cookie pie crust
1 gallon praline and cream ice cream
1 jar hot fudge

Let ice cream set at room temperature for 5–10 minutes to soften. Spoon ice cream into crust until half full. Spread about half of hot fudge over ice cream. Add another layer of ice cream. Cover and freeze for at least 2 hours. Just before serving spread remaining hot fudge on top.

Oil Pie Crust

2 tablespoons sugar
1½ cups flour
½ cup oil
½ teaspoon salt
2 tablespoons cold milk

Combine sugar, flour, oil, salt and milk in pie pan; mix with fork. Press into pan with fingers to cover bottom and sides of pie pan. For a crumbly crust, press lightly with a fork.

Dutch Apple Pie

1 graham cracker crust
1 large egg yolk, slightly beaten
5½ cups peeled and sliced cooking apples
1 tablespoon lemon juice
½ cup sugar
¼ cup firmly packed light brown sugar,
3 tablespoons flour
¼ teaspoon salt
½ teaspoon cinnamon
¼ teaspoon nutmeg
¾ cup flour
¼ cup sugar
¼ cup firmly packed brown sugar
⅓ cup butter, softened

Brush graham cracker crust with egg yolk. Place on baking sheet and bake at 375 degrees until lightly brown; remove from oven. Combine apples, lemon juice, ½ cup sugar, ¼ cup brown sugar, 3 tablespoons flour, salt, cinnamon and nutmeg.

Mix well; spoon into crust. Mix together remaining flour, sugars and butter with fork until crumbly. Sprinkle mixture evenly over apples. Place pie on baking sheet and bake an additional 50 minutes. Cool. Serve at room temperature.

Harvest Moon Fruit Pie

2 (9-inch) unbaked pie crusts
4 cups pared and thinly sliced apples
1 cup ground fresh cranberries
1 cup ground dried apricots
½ teaspoon grated orange rind
1¼ cups sugar
2 tablespoons flour
¼ teaspoon salt
½ teaspoon cinnamon
¼ teaspoon nutmeg
1 tablespoon butter

Place 1 pie crust in 9-inch pie pan. Combine apples, cranberries, apricots and orange rind. Blend together sugar, flour, salt, cinnamon and nutmeg; add to fruit mixture. Pour into pastry shell. Dot with butter. Place remaining crust on top of pie; cut slits for steam to escape; seal. Bake at 375 degrees for 40–50 minutes.

Crisscross Apple Pie

2 cups flour
1 teaspoon salt
⅔ cup shortening
2 egg yolks, slightly beaten
3 tablespoons cold water
1 tablespoon lemon juice
4 cups pared and sliced apples
¾ cup sugar
2 tablespoons flour
¼ teaspoon salt
½ teaspoon cinnamon
½ teaspoon nutmeg
Confectioners' Sugar Icing (recipe follows)

Sift together flour and salt; cut in shortening until mixture resembles coarse crumbs. Blend together egg yolks, water and lemon juice; sprinkle over flour mixture, tossing until dough is moist enough to hold together.

Roll out ⅔ of dough to a 14 x 10-inch rectangle. Place into bottom of a 10 x 6-inch pan. Roll remaining dough to a 11 x 7-inch rectangle. Cut X-shaped slits to allow steam to escape; set aside.

Combine apples, sugar, 2 tablespoons-flour, salt cinnamon and nutmeg; turn into pastry-lined pan. Place crust over filling; seal. Bake at 450 degrees for 10 minutes; lower temperature to 375 degrees and bake for 25–30 minutes. Cool slightly before icing.

Confectioners' Sugar Icing

½ cup confectioners' sugar, sifted
1 tablespoon milk
¼ teaspoon vanilla

Mix together sugar and milk; blend in vanilla; beat until smooth.

Spiced Pie Crust

1 cup flour
½ teaspoon salt
1 teaspoon allspice
⅓ cup shortening
2–3 tablespoons cold water

Mix together flour, salt and allspice. Cut in shortening. Sprinkle with water, stirring to mix with fork. Roll out on floured surface. Place in pie pan.

Date Macaroon Pie

3 egg whites
1 cup sugar
½ teaspoon baking powder
1 teaspoon vanilla
1 teaspoon water
½ cup finely chopped dates
12 saltines, finely crushed
Whipped cream
Maraschino cherries

Beat together egg whites until stiff peaks are formed. Add sugar, baking powder, vanilla and water to egg white mixture; fold in dates and saltines. Pour into 9-inch buttered pie plate. Bake at 325 degrees for 30 minutes. Serve topped with whipped cream and cherry.

Blackberry Pie

3¼ cups blackberries
1¼ cups sugar
3 tablespoons flour
2 (9-inch) unbaked pie crusts
Margarine
Sugar

Sprinkle 1 tablespoon flour over crust bottom. Mix together 2 tablespoons flour with sugar. Place blackberries in crust; sprinkle with flour/sugar mixture. Shake berries to let mixture work down. Dot with pieces of margarine. Add top crust, cut slits for steam and seal edge; sprinkle sugar over crust before baking. Bake at 350 degrees for 60 minutes or until nicely browned.

Apple Crumb Pie

⅔ cup sugar
2 tablespoons flour
¾ teaspoon cinnamon
1 (9-inch) unbaked pastry shell
6–8 apples, peeled and sliced
½ cup flour
¼ cup sugar
½ cup butter

Combine sugar, flour and cinnamon; stir in apples. Place in pastry shell. Combine remaining ½ cup flour and ¼ sugar; cut in butter until crumbly. Sprinkle over apples. Bake at 400 degrees for 45–50 minutes.

Golden Peach Pie

1 cup flour
½ teaspoon salt
¼ teaspoon nutmeg
⅓ cup shortening
2–3 tablespoons cold water
12 fresh or canned peach halves, well drained
1 cup firmly packed brown sugar
⅓ cup flour
3 tablespoons butter
1 cup whipping cream
½ teaspoon vanilla
1 tablespoon caramelized syrup from pie
   Nutmeg

Sift together flour, salt and nutmeg. Cut in shortening until mixture is crumbly. Sprinkle with water and toss until dough is moist. Form into a ball. Roll into circle. Place in 9-inch pie pan. Fold edge to form standing rim.

Arrange peach halves in pie shell cut side up. Combine brown sugar with ⅓ cup flour; cut in butter. Sprinkle evenly over peaches. Bake at 425 degrees for 10 minutes. Cover pie; bake at 375 degrees for 35–40 minutes. Cool thoroughly.

Beat whipping cream. Add vanilla and caramelized syrup from pie. Place whipped cream around edge of pie; sprinkle with nutmeg.

French Pear Pie

1 (9-inch) unbaked pie shell
1 (1-pound, 13-ounce) can pear halves, drained
3 tablespoons flour
½ cup sugar
¼ teaspoon ginger
1½ cups sour cream
½ cup flour
¼ cup firmly packed brown sugar
½ teaspoon nutmeg
¼ cup butter

Arrange pears, cut side up, in pastry shell. Combine 3 tablespoons flour, sugar, ginger and sour cream, mixing well; pour over pears. Mix together ½ cup flour, brown sugar and nutmeg; cut in butter; sprinkle over filling. Bake at 400 degrees for 25–30 minutes until golden brown.

Cranberry-Apple Pie

2 (9-inch) unbaked pie crusts
1¾ cups sugar
¼ cup flour
3 cups pared and sliced tart apples
2 cups fresh cranberries
2 tablespoons margarine

Mix together sugar and flour; gently mix with apples and cranberries. Place in pie shell; dot with margarine. Cover with top crust; cut slits for steam. Seal edge and cover with aluminum foil. Bake at 425 degrees for 40–50 minutes, removing foil during last 15 minutes.

Icebox Cherry Pie

1 can sweetened condensed milk
   Juice of 2 lemons
¼ cup sugar
1 can sour pitted red pie cherries, drained
1 cup nuts
1 cup whipped cream
1 graham cracker pie crust
   Whipped topping

Mix together milk, lemon juice and sugar. Add cherries and nuts. Fold in whipped cream. Pour into pie crust. Top with whipped topping.

Apple Crumb Pie

1 cup sugar
1 teaspoon cinnamon
6 tart apples, pared, cut in eighths
¾ cup flour
⅓ cup butter
1 (9-inch) unbaked pastry shell

Mix together ½ cup sugar and cinnamon; sprinkle over apples. Place apple mixture into unbaked pastry shell. Combine remaining sugar and flour; cut in butter until mixture resembles coarse crumbs. Sprinkle crumbs over apples. Bake at 425 degrees for 10 minutes; reduce temperature to 350 degrees and bake for an additional 35 minutes.

Lemon Cake Pie

1 (9-inch) unbaked pie crust
3 eggs, separated
2 tablespoons grated lemon peel
⅔ cup lemon juice
1 cup milk
1¼ cups sugar
⅓ cup flour
¼ teaspoon salt

Beat egg whites until stiff peaks form; set aside. Beat egg yolks; add lemon peel, lemon juice and milk. Stir in sugar, flour and salt; beat until smooth. Blend lemon mixture into egg whites with an electric mixer on low for 1 minute. Pour into pie crust. Bake at 350 degrees for 45–50 minutes.

Lattice-Topped Raspberry Pie

2 (9-inch) unbaked pie crusts
1 cup sugar
⅓ cup flour
4 cups fresh raspberries
2 tablespoons margarine *or* butter
   Milk
   Sugar

Mix together sugar and flour; gently stir in raspberries; pour into 1 pie crust; dot with margarine. Cut strips using remaining crust and place on filling; seal crust. Brush pastry with milk; sprinkle with sugar. Cover pastry edges with foil. Bake at 425 degrees for 35–45 minutes, removing foil during last 15 minutes.

Lemon Pie

2 cups water
1 cup sugar
5–6 tablespoons powdered fruit pectin
3 egg yolks
¼ cup lemon juice
   Pinch of salt
1 teaspoon butter

Bring water, sugar and pectin to boil. Stir with wire whisk; add egg yolks, lemon juice, salt and butter, blending until smooth. Pour into unbaked pie shell. Bake at 350 degrees for 30–40 minutes until crust is golden brown.

Apple a la Cream Pie

1 9-inch unbaked pie crust
1 tablespoon finely chopped almonds
4 cups pared and sliced apples
1/3 cup sugar
2 tablespoons flour
2 eggs, slightly beaten
1 cup cream
1/2 teaspoon cinnamon
1/4 teaspoon nutmeg
1/4 cup sugar
3 tablespoons sugar
2 tablespoons finely chopped almonds
2 tablespoons butter

Sprinkle 1 tablespoon almonds over bottom of pastry-lined pan; combine apples, 1/3 cup sugar and flour and arrange on crust. Press a circle of foil firmly over filling only. Bake at 400 degrees for 25–30 minutes. Remove foil.

Combine eggs, cream, cinnamon, nutmeg and 1/4 cup sugar. Pour over apples. Combine 3 tablespoons sugar, 2 tablespoons almonds and 2 tablespoons butter; make crumb mixture. Sprinkle over pie. Bake at 400 degrees for 15–20 minutes until knife comes out clean.

Cashew Pie

1 cup flour
1/2 teaspoon salt
1/3 cup shortening
2–3 tablespoons cold milk
1 cup firmly packed brown sugar
3 tablespoons butter, softened
3/4 cup light corn syrup
1 teaspoon vanilla
3 eggs, well beaten
1 cup crushed salted cashew nuts

Sift together flour and salt; cut in shortening until mixture is crumbly. Sprinkle with milk until dough is moist. Form into ball and roll out. Fill a 9-inch pie pan.

Cream sugar with butter; stir in corn syrup and vanilla; mix well. Blend in eggs; add nuts. Pour into pie shell. Bake at 350 degrees for 50–55 minutes.

Applescotch Cheese Pie

1 1/2 cups flour
1/2 teaspoon salt
2/3 cup shortening
4–5 tablespoons cold water
1/4 cup butter
1 cup sugar
3 eggs
1 cup apple butter
1/4 cup flour
1/4 teaspoon salt
3/4 cup grated American cheese

Sift together flour and salt; cut in shortening until it resembles coarse crumbs.

Sprinkle with cold water and toss with fork until dough is moist. Form into a ball. Roll out dough and place in a 9-inch pie pan. Prick crust with fork. Cut remaining pastry into fancy shapes with cookie cutter. Place on ungreased baking sheet. Bake pie shell and cutouts at 400 degrees for 10 minutes. Cool.

Cream together butter and sugar; blend in eggs, apple butter, flour, salt and cheese. Fill pastry shell. Bake at 350 degrees for 45–50 minutes. Arrange baked pastry cutouts over filling.

Rhubarb Orange Custard Pie

1 (9-inch) unbaked pie crust
2 cups cut up rhubarb
1/2 cup water
1 cup sugar
2 tablespoons cornstarch
3 eggs, separated
Juice of 1 large orange
1 teaspoon grated orange peel
Pinch salt
6 tablespoons sugar
1/8 teaspoon cream of tartar
1/2 teaspoon vanilla

Cook rhubarb with water until tender. Mix together sugar, cornstarch, egg yolks, orange juice, orange peel and salt. Pour this mixture into hot rhubarb. Cook until thickened. Pour into pie crust. Beat egg whites until frothy; add cream of tartar and vanilla. Continue beating until stiff; slowly beat in sugar until dissolved. Bake at 350 degrees for 40–50 minutes until lightly browned.

Apple Cheese Pie in Coconut Crust

1 cup shredded coconut
1/2 cup wheat germ
2 tablespoons butter, melted
4 cups thinly sliced apples
1/2 teaspoon cinnamon
2 tablespoons butter, softened
3 eggs
1/4 cup honey
4 ounces cream cheese
1 teaspoon vanilla
2/3 cup whole-wheat flour
1/4 teaspoon cinnamon
1 tablespoon butter
1 tablespoon oil
2 teaspoons honey
1 tablespoon finely chopped walnuts

Combine coconut and wheat germ with butter; toss with 2 forks until coconut is thoroughly coated. Press mixture firmly into a 9-inch pie plate. Refrigerate until firm.

Toss apples with cinnamon; arrange on bottom of crust. Cream butter, eggs and honey together. Add cream cheese and vanilla; blend just until smooth. Pour over apples.

Combine flour, cinnamon, butter, oil, honey and walnuts. Sprinkle on apple filling. Bake at 350 degrees for 45 minutes or until apples are tender. Cool; refrigerate.

Raisin Pie

2 (9-inch) unbaked pie crusts
3 cups raisins
6 cups water
3/4 cup sugar
2 tablespoons cornstarch
Pinch salt
1 egg

Cook raisins with 6 cups water until softened; cool. Mix together sugar, cornstarch and salt; add to raisin mixture. Add egg; beat well. Bring mixture to a boil; pour into crust. Clut remaining pie crust into strips and use to form lattice over top of raisin mixture. Bake at 350 degrees for 1 hour.

Pineapple Upside-Down Pie

2 (9-inch) unbaked pie crusts
1 (1 pound 4½-ounce) can pineapple tidbits, drained, reserve juice
   Water
3 tablespoons cornstarch
¾ cup brown sugar, divided
2 tablespoons lemon juice
6 tablespoons butter
½ cup pecan halves

Add water to pineapple juice to make 1½ cups; set aside. Combine cornstarch and ¼ cup brown sugar in saucepan; add lemon juice and pineapple mixture. Cook, stirring constantly, until mixture is thick and clear. Remove from heat and add 2 tablespoons butter, stirring until melted.

Place remaining 4 tablespoons butter in bottom of 9-inch pie pan; place in 425-degree oven until butter is melted. Sprinkle with remaining ½ cup brown sugar and 1 tablespoon water. Arrange pecan halves, rounded side down, on bottom and sides of pie pan. Carefully line pan with pastry. Spoon in pineapple mixture; cover with top crust; cut vent for steam and seal edges.

Bake at 425 degrees for 25 minutes. Turn pie upside down immediately. Cool before cutting.

Chocolate Chip Walnut Pie

2 eggs
½ cup flour
½ cup sugar
½ cup firmly packed brown sugar
1 cup butter, melted, cooled to room temperature
1 (6-ounce) package chocolate chips
1 cup chopped walnuts
1 (9-inch) unbaked pie crust

Beat eggs until foamy; beat in flour and sugars until well blended. Stir in butter; fold in chocolate chips and walnuts.

Spoon into unbaked pie crust. Bake at 325 degrees for 1 hour or until knife comes out clean. Do not overbake. Serve warm.

Limelight Pie

¾ cup flour
¼ teaspoon salt
2 tablespoons sugar
¼ cup shortening
½ ounce chocolate, melted
1–2 tablespoons cold water
1 (15-ounce) can sweetened condensed milk
¼ cup lime juice
¼ teaspoon salt
1 (9-ounce) can crushed pineapple, drained
4 drops green food coloring
¾ cup heavy cream
1 tablespoons confectioners' sugar
½ teaspoon vanilla
1 tablespoon grated chocolate

Sift together flour, salt and sugar; cut in shortening until it resembles coarse crumbs. Drip melted chocolate over mixture; mix lightly. Add enough cold water to make dough moist. Form into a ball and roll out to fit an 8-inch pie pan. Prick crust with fork. Bake at 400 degrees for 10–12 minutes. Cool.

Mix together milk, lime juice and salt. Stir in pineapple and food coloring, mixing well. Pour into pie shell. Chill 2–3 hours. Whip cream until stiff; fold in sugar and vanilla. Spread on chilled pie. Sprinkle with chocolate.

Peach-Praline Pie

1 (9-inch) unbaked pie crust
4 cups sliced peaches
½ cup sugar
2 tablespoons tapioca
½ cup chopped pecans
1 teaspoon lemon juice
¼ cup firmly packed brown sugar
½ cup sifted flour
¼ cup margarine

Combine peaches, sugar, tapioca and lemon juice; let stand 15 minutes. Mix together flour, brown sugar and pecans; cut in butter with fork until crumbly. Sprinkle ⅓ of pecan mixture over bottom of pie crust; cover with peach mixture; sprinkle remaining pecan mixture over peaches.

Bake at 425 degrees for 10 minutes. Reduce heat to 350 degrees and bake an additional 20 minutes.

Pineapple Cheese Pie

1 (9-inch) unbaked pie crust
⅓ cup sugar
1 tablespoon cornstarch
1 (8¼-ounce) can crushed pineapple, undrained
1 (8-ounce) package cream cheese, softened
½ cup sugar
½ teaspoon salt
½ cup milk
2 eggs
½ teaspoon vanilla
¼ cup chopped pecans
   Pineapple slices
   Maraschino cherries

Combine sugar and cornstarch in saucepan; gradually add pineapple. Cook, stirring constantly, until clear and thickened. Cool; spread onto pie crust. Combine cream cheese, sugar and salt; mix until well-blended. Blend in milk, eggs and vanilla. Pour over pineapple mixture; sprinkle with nuts. Bake at 400 degrees for 15 minutes. May garnish with pineapple slices and maraschino cherry halves.

Pecan Praline Pie

⅓ cup butter
⅓ cup brown sugar
½ cup chopped pecans
1 (9-inch) baked pie crust
1 (5-ounce) package vanilla pie filling (not instant)
3 cups milk
1 envelope whipped topping

Heat butter, sugar and nuts in pan until melted; spread on bottom of pie crust. Bake at 450 degrees for 5 minutes. Cool. Prepare pie filling with milk; cool 5 minutes, stirring occasionally. Measure 1 cup of pudding; cover with waxed paper and chill.

Pour remainder of filling into pie crust and chill. Prepare whipped topping as package directs. Fold 1⅓ cups topping into reserved, chilled pudding and spread over filling in pie; chill. Garnish with remaining whipped topping and pecans.

Pineapple Coconut Pie

1 (9-inch) unbaked pie crust
1 (8¾-ounce) can crushed pineapple, reserve juice
3 eggs, slightly beaten
½ cup sugar
1 teaspoon vanilla
¼ teaspoon salt
¼ teaspoon nutmeg
2 cups light cream, hot
Coconut Topping (recipe follows)

Combine eggs, sugar, vanilla, salt, nutmeg and ⅓ cup reserved juice. Gradually add cream, mixing well. Pour into pie crust and bake at 400 degrees for 25–30 minutes or until knife inserted in center comes out clean. Top with pineapple and Coconut Topping. Cover crust edges with foil and broil for 1–2 minutes, until mixture bubbles and begins to brown. Cool.

Coconut Topping

½ cup flaked coconut
¼ cup firmly packed brown sugar
3 tablespoons cream
2 tablespoons butter, melted

Combine coconut, sugar, cream and butter. Sprinkle on pie.

Mystery Pecan Pie

1 (9-inch) unbaked pie crust
1 (8-ounce) package cream cheese
⅓ cup sugar
¼ cup sugar
4 eggs, divided
2 teaspoons vanilla, divided
¼ teaspoon salt
1¼ cups pecan halves
1 cup corn syrup

Beat together cream cheese, ⅓ cup sugar, 1 egg, 1 teaspoon vanilla and salt; set aside. Beat remaining 3 eggs well; add ¼ cup sugar, corn syrup and 1 teaspoon vanilla; blend well. Spread cream cheese mixture in pie crust. Sprinkle pecans over cheese layer. Pour corn syrup mixture gently over top of pecans. Bake at 375 degrees for 40 minutes or until center is firm to touch.

Maple Walnut Pie

1 cup maple syrup
4 eggs, beaten
½ cup sugar
⅓ cup margarine, melted
Dash salt
1⅓ cups broken walnuts
1 (9-inch) unbaked pie crust

Beat together syrup, eggs, sugar, margarine and salt. Mix until smooth. Add walnuts; pour into pie crust. Cover crust edges with foil. Bake at 350 degrees for 15 minutes; remove foil; bake an additional 25 minutes until filling is set. Cool.

Nutty Chocolate Pie

3 eggs
1 cup light corn syrup
1 cup coarsely chopped walnuts
1 cup semisweet chocolate chips
½ cup sugar
2 tablespoons butter, melted
1 teaspoon vanilla
1 (9-inch) unbaked pie crust

Beat eggs; add corn syrup, walnuts, chocolate chips, sugar, butter and vanilla. Mix until well blended. Pour into pie crust. Bake at 350 degrees for 50–60 minutes. Cool.

Mini Pecan Pies

½ cup margarine
1 (3-ounce) package cream cheese, softened
1 cup flour
¾ cup firmly packed brown sugar
1 egg
1 teaspoon vanilla
¾ cup chopped pecans

Combine margarine and cream cheese; mix until well blended. Add flour; mix well. Chill. Combine brown sugar, egg and vanilla; mix well. Stir in nuts.

Divide dough into 24 balls. Press into miniature muffin pans. Fill each cup ¾ full of brown sugar mixture. Bake at 325 degrees for 25–30 minutes or until lightly browned. Cool for 5 minutes; remove from pan.

Pie Dough

5½ cups flour
2 cups shortening
1 teaspoon salt
1 teaspoon sugar
1 egg, slightly beaten
Water

Blend together flour, shortening, sugar and salt with pastry blender. Place egg in cup and fill with water to make 1 cup. Pour over flour mixture; mix to make dough. Roll out on floured surface and place in pie pans. Makes 3 double crusts. May be kept in refrigerator for 2 weeks.

Macadamia Coconut Pie

1 (9-inch) unbaked pie crust
¼ pound butter
¾ cup sugar
3 eggs
¾ cup dark corn syrup
½ cup coconut
¼ teaspoon salt
1 teaspoon vanilla
1 cup chopped unsalted macadamia nuts

Cream together butter and sugar; add eggs. Blend in corn syrup. Add coconut, salt, vanilla and nuts. Mix well; pour into pie crust. Bake at 350 degrees for 35–40 minutes.

Cranberry Walnut Pie

3 eggs, slightly beaten
1 cup light corn syrup
⅔ cup sugar
2 tablespoons margarine, melted
⅛ teaspoon salt
1 cup chopped cranberries
¾ cup coarsely chopped walnuts
1 tablespoon grated orange rind
1 (9-inch) unbaked pie crust

Stir together eggs, corn syrup, sugar, margarine and salt. Gently stir in cranberries, nuts and rind. Pour into pastry shell. Bake at 350 degrees for 1 hour or until knife comes out clean.

Peach-Raspberry Streusel Pie

1 (9-inch) unbaked pie crust
1 (10-ounce) package frozen sliced peaches, thawed
1 (10-ounce) package frozen raspberries, thawed
1/4 cup sugar
3 tablespoons cornstarch
1/4 teaspoon cinnamon
1 tablespoon lemon juice
Streusel Topping
(recipe follows)

Mix together peaches and raspberries; combine sugar, cornstarch and cinnamon; add to fruit. Sprinkle with lemon juice; mix well. Pour into pie crust. Bake at 375 degrees for 30–35 minutes or until filling is partially set in center. Sprinkle with Streusel Topping. Bake an additional 10–15 minutes until golden brown.

Streusel Topping

1/4 cup butter
3/4 cup flour
1/2 cup firmly packed brown sugar

Mix together butter, flour and brown sugar. Sprinkle on pie.

Spectacular Pecan Pie

1 (9-inch) pie crust
1/4 cup butter
3/4 cup sugar
1 teaspoon vanilla
2 tablespoons flour
3 eggs
1/2 cup coffee liqueur
1/2 cup dark corn syrup
3/4 cup evaporated milk
1 cup pecans

Cream together butter, sugar and vanilla; add flour; mix well. Beat in eggs, 1 at a time. Blend in coffee liqueur, corn syrup, milk and pecans. Mix well; pour into pie crust. Bake at 400 degrees for 10 minutes; reduce heat to 325 degrees and bake an additional 40 minutes, until firm. Chill.

Date Walnut Pie

1 (9-inch) unbaked pie crust
3 egg yolks
2/3 cup sugar
1 tablespoon flour
1/2 teaspoon salt
1 1/3 cups whipping cream
1 cup cut up dates
1 cup chopped walnuts
1 teaspoon vanilla

Beat together egg yolks, sugar, flour and salt until light and fluffy. Stir in whipping cream, dates, walnuts and vanilla. Pour into pie crust. Bake at 350 degrees for 50–60 minutes. Cool slightly.

Chocolate Pecan Pie

1 (9-inch) unbaked pie crust
1/3 cup margarine
2 (1-ounce) squares unsweetened chocolate
3 eggs
2/3 cup sugar
1/2 teaspoon salt
1 cup corn syrup
1 cup pecan halves

Melt margarine and chocolate over low heat. Beat together eggs, sugar, salt and syrup; stir in chocolate mixture and pecans. Pour into pie crust. Bake at 375 degrees for 40–50 minutes. Cool slightly. Keep refrigerated.

Brownie Fudge Nut Pie

1 3/4 cups coarsely chopped pecan halves
1 (14-ounce) can sweetened condensed milk
1/4 cup margarine
3 eggs, beaten
1 teaspoon vanilla extract
1/2 cup unsweetened cocoa
3 tablespoons flour
1 (9-inch) unbaked pastry shell

Combine milk, margarine and cocoa over low heat until margarine melts and mixture is warm; remove from heat. Stir in eggs, flour, vanilla and nuts; pour into crust. Bake at 350 degrees for 50 minutes or until center is firm.

Dixie Pecan Pie

1/3 cup shortening
1/2 cup brown sugar
1 cup pecans
1 cup corn syrup
3 eggs
1/4 teaspoon salt
1/2 cup milk
1/2 teaspoon vanilla

Blend together shortening and sugar; stir in pecans; set aside. Mix together corn syrup, eggs, salt, milk and vanilla; pour over shortening mixture; mix well. Pour into pie crust. Bake at 425 degrees for 10 minutes, then at 350 degrees for 30 minutes.

Ice Cream Pie With Fruit Sauce

3/4 cup vanilla wafer crumbs
1/2 cup wheat germ
2 tablespoons sugar
1/2 teaspoon nutmeg
1/4 cup butter, melted
1/2 cup diced mixed candied fruit
2 tablespoons rum
1 quart vanilla ice cream, softened
Fruit Sauce (recipe follows)

Combine crumbs, wheat germ, sugar, nutmeg and butter. Press in bottom of buttered 9-inch pie pan. Bake at 350 degrees for 5 minutes; cool completely.

Mix together fruit and rum; fold into ice cream; spread over crust. Freeze until ice cream is firm. Serve with Fruit Sauce.

Fruit Sauce

1/2 cup apricot preserves
1/2 cup diced mixed candied fruit
1/4 cup light corn syrup
1/4 cup rum, divided

Mix together apricot preserves, candied fruit, corn syrup and all but 2 tablespoons rum; heat over low heat until hot. Heat remaining 2 tablespoons rum in a small saucepan to produce fumes (do not boil). Ignite; pour over rum-fruit mixture, stirring until flames die down. Serve immediately. Makes 1 cup.

Lemon Coconut Meringue Pie

1 (9-inch) baked pie crust
4 eggs, separated
2/3 cup sugar
1/4 cup lemon juice
2 teaspoons grated lemon rind
1/4 teaspoon nutmeg
2/3 cup sugar
1/2 cup coconut
Nutmeg

Beat egg yolks in top of double boiler until thick and lemon colored. Gradually beat in 2/3 cup sugar; cook until mixture begins to thicken around sides of pans, about 5–7 minutes. Blend in lemon juice, lemon rind and nutmeg. Cook another 10 minutes until thick, stirring constantly.

Beat egg whites until foamy; gradually beat in 2/3 cup sugar. Continue beating until meringue stands in peaks. Blend 1/3 of meringue into lemon mixture; cool. Place in cooled pie shell. Fold coconut into remaining meringue. Spread on top of filling. Sprinkle with nutmeg. Brown at 350 degrees for 12–15 minutes.

Fruit Ice Cream Pie

Crust
1/3 cup unsalted butter
2 cups crushed vanilla wafers
4 cups butter brickle ice cream, slightly softened

Topping
1 pint fresh strawberries, hulled, sliced in half
1 pint fresh blueberries
2 tablespoons apple jelly, melted

Heat oven to 375 degrees. In 2-quart saucepan melt butter; stir in crushed wafers. Press mixture firmly against bottom and sides of 9-inch pie pan. Bake for 8 minutes; cool completely. Spread ice cream over cooled pie crust. Cover; freeze until firm (6–8 hours, or overnight).

Arrange fruit on top of ice cream. Place strawberries around outer edge. Place double ring of blueberries inside strawberry circle. Brush fruit with jelly to glaze, being careful not to get glaze on ice cream. Serves 8.

Chilled Lemon Pie

1 (9-inch) graham cracker crust, baked
1 envelope unflavored gelatin
1/2 cup cold water
2 (8-ounce) containers lemon flavored yogurt
1 cup salad dressing
1 cup whipped topping

Stir gelatin and water over low heat until dissolved; set aside. Beat yogurt and salad dressing at medium speed with electric mixer until well blended. Gradually add gelatin, mixing until blended. Fold in whipped topping. Pour into crust; chill until firm.

Banana Cream Pie

10 graham crackers, crushed
4 tablespoons sugar
4 tablespoons butter, melted
1 cup cream, whipped
1 tablespoon confectioners' sugar
1/2 teaspoon vanilla
2 bananas, thinly sliced
Grated coconut

Mix together graham crackers, sugar and butter; pack firmly into 9-inch pie pan. Refrigerate 15 minutes. Beat cream until thickenend; slowly add confectioners' sugar and vanilla; fold in bananas. Just before serving, spoon into pie shell; sprinkle with coconut.

Banana Cream Cheese Pie

1 baked pie shell
3 medium bananas
1 (8-ounce) package cream cheese, room temperature
1 can sweetened condensed milk
1/2 cup lemon juice
1 tablespoon vanilla

Slice 2 bananas; place in pie shell. Beat cream cheese until light and fluffy. Add milk gradually and continue beating until mixture is smooth. Stir in lemon juice and vanilla. Pour in pie shell; chill until filling is firm. Just before serving, slice remaining banana; arrange slices on top of pie filling.

Apple Galette

1 1/2 cups flour
6 tablespoons cold water
1 stick butter, softened
1/4 teaspoon salt
4 large Golden Delicious apples, peeled, cored
1/3 cup confectioners' sugar
2 tablespoons butter
Glacé (recipe follows)

Break butter into flour with fingers, until butter is small marble size. Add water and mix with a spoon. Put on a lightly floured board. Work with hands until the pastry holds together. Wrap in waxed paper. Chill for several hours. Roll out until very thin.

Place on cookie sheet; chill again. Cut apples in half and slice, not too thin. Using ends and broken pieces, chop and place in center of pastry. This will make a little mound.

Arrange remaining apple slices in circles to the center. Fold sides of pastry up around the outside of apples. Pastry will look flowerlike. Sprinkle with sugar. Dot with butter. Bake at 400 degrees for 1 hour.

Glacé
4 tablespoons apricot preserves
1 tablespoon brandy

Mix together preserves and brandy; spread on Galette while warm.

Pecan Pumpkin Pie

3 eggs
1 cup pumpkin
1/3 cup sugar
1 teaspoon pumpkin pie spice
2/3 cup corn syrup
1/2 cup sugar
3 tablespoons butter, melted
1/2 teaspoon vanilla
1 cup pecan halves
1 (9-inch) unbaked pie crust

Stir together 1 slightly beaten egg, pumpkin, 1/3 cup sugar and pie spice. Spread over pie crust. Combine 2 beaten eggs, corn syrup, 1/2 cup sugar, butter and vanilla. Stir in nuts. Spoon over pumpkin mixture. Bake at 350 degrees for 50 minutes or until filling is set.

Golden Apricot Creme Pie

1 (8-ounce) package cream cheese
1/4 cup sugar
1 cup heavy cream
1 teaspoon vanilla extract
1/8 teaspoon almond extract
1 (10 1/2-ounce) can apricot halves, drained, reserve juice
1 envelope unflavored gelatin
1 graham cracker crust
1/2 cup currant jelly, melted

Beat cream cheese with sugar until light and fluffy. Slowly add cream; stir in vanilla and almond extracts. Soften gelatin in 1/2 cup reserved apricot syrup and heat to dissolve gelatin; stir into cream cheese mixture. Pour into pie shell; chill until set. Arrange apricot halves on top of pie; Spoon melted jelly over apricots before serving. Chill.

Raisin Nut Pie

3 eggs, slightly beaten
3/4 cup light corn syrup
1/2 cup firmly packed brown sugar
1/4 cup margarine, melted
1 teaspoon vanilla
1/4 teaspoon salt
1 cup raisins
1/2 cup chopped pecans
1 (9-inch) unbaked pie crust

Beat together eggs, corn syrup, brown sugar, margarine, vanilla and salt. Stir in raisins and nuts. Pour into pastry shell. Bake at 350 degrees for 45–55 minutes or until knife comes out clean. Cool.

Ice Cream Pie

2 cups crispy rice cereal
1 cup coconut
3/4 cup chopped walnuts
1 stick butter, melted
1 pint vanilla ice cream, softened
Chocolate sauce

Combine cereal, coconut, walnuts and butter. Press into an 8-inch pie pan, saving a bit to use as topping; fill with ice cream. Freeze for 2–3 hours. Sprinkle with reserved crust and drizzle with chocolate sauce.

Chocolate Mousse Pie

1 (8-ounce) chocolate bar, finely chopped
1/3 cup milk
2 tablespoons sugar
3 ounces cream cheese, softened
3 1/2 cups whipped topping
1 chocolate pie crust, baked

Heat 5 ounces of chocolate and milk over low heat; stir until melted. Beat sugar into cream cheese; add melted chocolate mixture and beat until smooth. Fold in whipped topping; blend until smooth. Stir in chopped chocolate. Spoon into pie crust. Freeze for 4 hours until firm. Let stand 1 hour before serving. Store in freezer.

Cherry Cheese Pie

1 (9-inch) graham cracker crumb crust
1 (8-ounce) package cream cheese, softened
1 (14-ounce) can sweetened condensed milk
1/3 cup lemon juice
1 teaspoon vanilla extract
1 (21-ounce) can cherry pie filling chilled

Beat cream cheese until fluffy. Gradually beat in milk until smooth. Sti in lemon juice and vanilla. Pour into pie crust. Chill for at least 3 hours or until set. Top with cherry pie filling before serving. Keep refrigerated.

Rich Pecan Pie

1 1/2 cups maple syrup
1/4 cup margarine
1/4 cup sugar
1 1/2 cups pecan halves
1 (9-inch) unbaked pie crust
3 eggs, slightly beaten
1 teaspoon vanilla
Dash salt

Combine syrup, margarine and sugar in saucepan; bring to boil; boil gently 5 minutes, stirring occasionally. Cool slightly. Place pecans in pie shell. Mix eggs, vanilla and salt; gradually stir into cooled syrup mixture. Pour over pecans in pie crust. Bake at 375 degrees for 35–40 minutes or until knife comes out clean.

Creamy Coconut Pie

1 (3-ounce) package cream cheese, softened
2 tablespoons sugar
1/2 cup milk
1 1/3 cups flaked coconut
1 (8-ounce) container whipped topping
1/2 teaspoon almond extract
1 (8-inch) graham cracker crust

Blend cream cheese, sugar, milk and coconut in an electric blender for 30 seconds. Fold into topping and add extract. Spoon into crust. Freeze 4 hours, until firm. Sprinkle with additional coconut. Let stand at room temperature 5 minutes before cutting. Store in freezer.

Cranberry Cream Cheese Pie

1 (3-ounce) package raspberry gelatin
1 cup boiling water
1/2 cup cold water
1 (3-ounce) package cream cheese
2 tablespoons milk
1 (16-ounce) can whole cranberry sauce, broken into pieces
1 (9-inch) baked pie shell
Whipped cream

Dissolve gelatin in 1 cup boiling water, stirring until dissolved. Add 1/2 cup cold water. Refrigerate 1–2 hours to thicken. Soften cream cheese with milk and spread into baked pie shell. Whip refrigerated gelatin until fluffy; fold in cranberry sauce. Pour into cream cheese-lined pie shell; refrigerate until set. Serve with whipped cream.

Lemon Cream Pie

1 (9-inch) graham cracker pie crust
1 (8-inch) carton whipped topping
1 (6-ounce) can frozen lemonade
1 (14-ounce) can sweetened condensed milk

Beat whipped topping, lemonade and condensed milk together thoroughly. Pour into pie crust. Refrigerate 1 hour before serving.

Apple & Cheese Tarts

- 2 cups flour
- 2 cups shredded cheddar cheese
- ½ teaspoon salt
- ½ cup butter
- ⅓ cup milk
- 1 cup canned apple pie filling
- ¼ cup raisins

Combine flour, cheese and salt; cut in butter until crumbly. Sprinkle with milk to make dough. Form into ball; wrap in waxed paper. Chill ½ hour. Roll out to ⅛-inch thickness. Cut with 3-inch cookie cutter. Place half of rounds on ungreased cookie sheets.

Mix together apple pie filling and raisins; place a rounded teaspoonful of apple filling in center of each pastry round. Cut a cross in remaining rounds; place over filling. Seal. Bake at 400 degrees for 12–15 minutes until light golden brown. Makes 2 dozen tarts.

Brickle Bits Pie

- 1 (3-ounce) package cream cheese
- 2 tablespoons sugar
- ½ cup milk
- 1 (6-ounce) package brickle bits
- 1 (8-ounce) container whipped topping
- 1 (9-inch) graham cracker crust

Blend cream cheese, sugar and milk; add brickle bits; fold in whipped topping. Place in crust. Refrigerate several hours before serving.

Mint Chocolate Pie

- 1 (9-inch) chocolate crumb crust
- 1 quart mint chocolate chip ice cream, softened
- 1 jar hot fudge topping
- 1 (4-ounce) container whipped topping

Fill crumb crust with 2 cups ice cream. Freeze until hardened. Spread ¾ cup hot fudge topping on hardened ice cream. Freeze. Repeat with second layer using remaining 2 cups ice cream. Spread with whipped topping and serve frozen. May garnish with chocolate curls.

Pecan Tassies

- 1 (8-ounce) package cream cheese, softened
- 1 cup butter
- 2 cups flour
- 2 eggs, beaten
- 1½ cups firmly packed brown sugar
- 2 teaspoons vanilla
- 1½ cups chopped pecans

Combine cream cheese and butter, mixing until well blended. Add flour and mix well. Chill. Divide dough into quarters. Divide each quarter into 12 balls. Press each ball into the bottom and sides of miniature muffin pans.

Combine eggs, brown sugar and vanilla and mix well. Stir in pecans. Spoon into pastry shells, filling each cup. Bake at 325 degrees for 30 minutes until pastry is golden brown.

Strawberry Pie

- ½ cup boiling water
- 1 envelope unflavored gelatin
- ½ cup sugar
- 1 (10-ounce) package frozen strawberries, partially thawed
- Juice of ½ lemon
- 1 cup heavy cream, whipped
- 1 baked pie crust

Dissolve gelatin in boiling water. Add lemon juice, sugar and strawberries. Stir with fork; fold in whipped cream. Pour filling into pie crust; refrigerate 2–3 hours before serving.

Blueberry Cheesecake Pie

- 8 ounces sour cream
- 8 ounces cream cheese
- ⅓ cup sugar
- 2 large eggs
- ¼ cup milk
- 1 teaspoon vanilla
- 1 (9-inch) baked pie crust
- 1 (21-ounce) can blueberry pie filling, chilled

Beat together sour cream, cream cheese, sugar, eggs, milk and vanilla. Pour into crust. Bake at 375 degrees for 30 minutes. Top with blueberry pie filling. Keep refrigerated.

Chess Pie

- 1 (9-inch) unbaked pie crust
- 3 egg yolks
- ⅔ cup sugar
- 1 tablespoon flour
- ½ teaspoon salt
- 1⅓ cups whipping cream
- 1 cup cut up dates
- 1 cup chopped walnuts
- 1 teaspoon vanilla

Beat together eggs, sugar, flour and salt; stir in whipping cream, dates, nuts and vanilla. Pour into pie crust. Bake at 350 degrees for 50–60 minutes, until crust is golden brown.

Chocolate Cheese Pie

- 1–1½ cups graham cracker crumbs
- ¼ cup packed light brown sugar
- ⅛ teaspoon nutmeg
- ⅓ cup butter, melted
- 1 (1-ounce) square unsweetened chocolate, melted
- 1 (6-ounce) package semisweet chocolate chips
- 1 (8-ounce) package cream cheese, softened
- ¾ cup firmly packed light brown sugar, divided
- ⅛ teaspoon salt
- 1 teaspoon vanilla
- 2 eggs, separated
- 1 cup heavy cream, whipped

Combine graham cracker crumbs with brown sugar, nutmeg, butter and melted chocolate. Press into a 9-inch pie pan. Chill until firm.

Melt semisweet chocolate chips over hot water; cool 10 minutes. Blend together cream cheese, ½ cup brown sugar, salt and vanilla; beat at high speed using an electric mixer. Beat in egg yolks, 1 at a time, mixing well after each addition; beat in cooled chocolate. In another bowl, beat egg whites until stiff peaks form. Gradually mix in remaining brown sugar; beat until stiff, glossy peaks form.

Fold chocolate mixture into egg whites; then fold in whipped cream. Reserve ¼ of mixture and pour the rest into crust. Chill until filling sets slightly. With tapered spoon, drop reserved mixture in mounds over top of pie. Chill overnight.

Brazil Nut Mocha Pie

1 cup flour
1/4 teaspoon salt
1/3 cup shortening
1/3 cup chopped Brazil nuts
3 tablespoons cold water
1/4 teaspoon almond extract
1 envelope unflavored gelatin
1/4 cup milk
3 eggs, separated
3/4 cup milk
1/3 cup cold coffee
1/2 cup sugar
1/4 teaspoon salt
1/2 teaspoon vanilla
1/4 cup sugar
1 cup whipped cream
1/2 cup shaved Brazil nuts

Sift together flour and salt; cut in shortening until mixture is crumbly. Add chopped Brazil nuts. Combine water and almond extract; make into dough. Roll out and place in a 9-inch pie pan. Prick crust. Bake at 425 degrees for 12–15 minutes. Cool.

Soften gelatin in 1/4 milk; set aside. In double boiler, combine slightly beaten egg yolks, 3/4 cup milk, coffee, sugar and salt; cook over boiling water until mixture thickens, stirring constantly.

Remove from heat. Add vanilla and gelatin; beat well. Chill until mixture begins to thicken.

Beat egg whites until stiff; gradually add 1/4 cup sugar and beat until dissolved. Fold cream, shaved Brazil nuts and egg whites into gelatin mixture. Pour into cooled pie crust. Chill 3–5 hours before serving.

Lemon Tartlets

24 baked tart shells
1/3 cup butter
1/3 cup sugar
1 teaspoon grated lemon rind
1/3 cup lemon juice
1/4 teaspoon salt
4 egg yolks, slightly beaten

Melt butter; add sugar, lemon rind, lemon juice, salt and egg yolks; cook 10 minutes, stirring constantly. Cool until thickened. Pour into cooled tart shells.

Swiss Butterhorns

2 cups flour
1/4 teaspoon salt
1/3 cup butter
1/3 cup margarine
1 egg yolk
3/4 cup sour cream
1/2 cup finely chopped nuts
3/4 teaspoon cinnamon
1/2 cup sugar
Frosting (recipe follows)

Combine flour and salt; cut in butter and margarine. Stir in egg yolk and sour cream; mix well. Shape dough into ball and wrap in waxed paper. Chill 1 hour or overnight.

Divide dough into 3 parts. On lightly floured board roll each in 12-inch circles; cut in 12 pie-shaped wedges. Blend sugar, nuts and cinnamon. Sprinkle each wedge with sugar mixture.

Starting at wide edge, roll up. Place on greased baking sheet with point tucked underneath. Bake at 375 degrees for 20–25 minutes. Remove from oven. Frost.

Frosting

1 cup confectioners' sugar
2 tablespoons hot water
1/4 teaspoon vanilla

Blend together sugar, water and vanilla. Drizzle on pastry.

Rhubarb Custard Pie

2 (9-inch) unbaked pie crusts
3 eggs, slightly beaten
3 tablespoons milk
1 3/4 cups sugar
1/4 cup flour
1/2 teaspoon nutmeg
4 cups fresh rhubarb, cut in 1/2-inch pieces
1 tablespoon butter

Place bottom crust in pie pan. Mix together eggs, milk, sugar, flour, nutmeg and rhubarb. Pour into pie pan and dot with butter. Cut strips with remaining dough. Make lattice top on pie; seal ends. Bake at 400 degrees for 50–60 minutes on bottom rack of oven, until crust is golden brown.

Mocha Sundae Pie

1 1/4 cups crushed chocolate wafers
1 tablespoon sugar
1/4 cup butter, melted
1 cup evaporated milk
1 cup miniature marshmallows
1 cup semisweet chocolate chips
Dash salt
1 quart coffee ice cream, softened and divided

Combine wafers, sugar and butter. Press firmly into a 9-inch pie plate. Bake at 300 degrees for 12–15 minutes. Cool, then chill. Over low heat, stir evaporated milk, marshmallows, chocolate chips and salt until melted and thick. Cool. Spoon half the ice cream into crust; drizzle with half the filling; spoon on remaining ice cream; drizzle with remaining filling. Freeze 4 hours.

Peanut Butter Pie

1 cup chunky peanut butter
1 (8-ounce) package cream cheese, softened
3/4 cup sugar
2 tablespoons butter, melted
1 tablespoon vanilla
1 cup whipped cream
1 graham cracker crust
1/3 cup hot fudge topping, melted

Cream together peanut butter, cream cheese and sugar. Add butter and vanilla; blend well. Fold in whipped cream; stir well. Pour into a graham cracker crust. Chill 4–5 hours until set. Drizzle top with hot fudge topping. Chill at least 30 minutes.

Nut Basket Tarts

18 baked tart shells
3 eggs
1 1/4 cups firmly packed brown sugar
1 cup chopped walnuts
1/2 cup shredded coconut
2 tablespoons flour
1/2 teaspoon baking powder
1 teaspoon salt

Combine eggs, brown sugar, walnuts, coconut, flour, baking powder and salt; mix well. Spoon into tart shells. Bake at 325 degrees for 20–25 minutes.

Little Surprise Pies

18 unbaked tart shells
¾ cup firmly packed brown sugar
1 egg, slightly beaten
1 teaspoon rum flavoring
6 semisweet chocolate chips per tart
1⅓ cups grated coconut
½ cup sweetened condensed milk

Combine brown sugar, egg and rum; blend well. Spoon 2 teaspoonfuls into each tart. Top with 6 chocolate chips. Combine coconut and milk. Spoon over chocolate chips. Bake at 350 degrees for 20–25 minutes until lightly browned.

Maple Syrup Tarts

1 cup maple syrup
6 tablespoons flour
½ cup water
2 egg yolks, beaten
1 tablespoon butter
¼ cup chopped walnuts
12 tart shells
Whipped cream
Walnut halves

Heat maple syrup. Mix flour and water until smooth; gradually stir into heated syrup and cook 10 minutes until thickened, stirring constantly. Mix a little of hot mixture with egg yolks; stir into syrup mixture and continue cooking 3–4 minutes. Remove from heat; stir in butter and walnuts; cool slightly. Pour into tart shells. Top with whipped cream and walnut halves.

Key Lime Pie

1 (8-inch) graham cracker crust
3 egg yolks
1 (14-ounce) can sweetened condensed milk
½ cup lime juice
Green food coloring, optional
Whipped topping

Beat together egg yolks, milk, lime juice and food coloring. Pour into prepared pie crust. Bake at 325 degrees for 30 minutes; cool. Refrigerate; top with whipped topping. Keep refrigerated.

Carrot Pie

1 (9-inch) unbaked pie crust
2 cups cooked and mashed carrots
1 cup honey
¾ cup evaporated milk
½ teaspoon salt
1 teaspoon cinnamon
½ teaspoon nutmeg
½ teaspoon ginger
Dash cloves
3 eggs, slightly beaten

Combine carrots, honey, evaporated milk, salt, cinnamon, nutmeg, ginger and cloves; mix well. Fold in eggs. Pour into pie crust. Bake at 400 degrees for 40–45 minutes until knife comes out clean. Cool 30 minutes, then refrigerate.

Mini Pecan Dreams

1 (3-ounce) package cream cheese
1 stick margarine
1 cup flour
1 egg, beaten
¾ cup packed brown sugar
1 teaspoon vanilla
1 tablespoon butter, melted
Pecans, chopped

Mix together cream cheese, margarine and flour; chill 2 hours. Press into muffin tins. Beat egg, brown sugar, vanilla and butter until foamy. Fill shells ⅔ full. Sprinkle tops with pecans. Bake at 350 degrees for 15 minutes; reduce temperature to 250 degrees for 10 minutes. Let stand a few minutes before removing.

Peanut Butter Ice Cream Pie

1 quart vanilla ice cream, slightly softened
½ cup chunky peanut butter
½ cup crushed unsalted peanuts, divided
1½ tablespoons vanilla
1 (10-inch) graham cracker crust
Whipped cream
Maraschino cherries

Combine ice cream, peanut butter, ¼ cup peanuts and vanilla; mix well. Turn into crust; sprinkle with remaining peanuts. Freeze. Garnish with whipped cream and cherries.

Pineapple Tarts

½ cup butter
2 tablespoons sugar
1 (3-ounce) package cream cheese
1½ cups flour
½ cup chopped pecans
2 eggs, slightly beaten
1 cup firmly packed brown sugar
⅔ cup crushed pineapple
2 tablespoons butter, melted
¼ cup chopped pecans

Cream butter, sugar and cream cheese; gradually stir in flour, mixing thoroughly. Form into ball; chill 30 minutes. Press in 12 muffin cups. Sprinkle muffin cups with pecans.

Combine eggs, brown sugar, pineapple and butter; spoon into muffin cups, filling ¾ full. Sprinkle with ¼ cup pecans. Bake at 350 degrees for 30–35 minutes until golden brown. Cool 15 minutes before removing from pan.

Strawberry Daiquiri Pie

1 (9-inch) baked graham cracker crust
1 pint strawberries, hulled
¾ cup sugar
1 envelope unflavored gelatin
⅓ cup lime juice
⅓ cup light rum
½ pint whipping cream, whipped
Whole strawberries

In blender, combine 1 pint strawberries and sugar; process until berries are puréed; set aside for 15 minutes. Stir gelatin into lime juice in saucepan; let stand 5 minutes to soften. Stir over medium heat until gelatin is dissolved. With blender running at medium speed, add gelatin mixture to pureed mixture; process until blended.

Strain through fine sieve into bowl. Stir rum into mixture. Refrigerate, stirring often, until mixture begins to mound when spooned on top of itself. Fold in whipped cream. Spoon into crust. Freeze 4 hours. Garnish with whole berries.

Tropical Pie

2 cups graham cracker crumbs
1 stick butter, melted
1 (12-ounce) container whipped topping
2 cans sweetened condensed milk
½ cup lemon juice
1 (20-ounce) can crushed pineapple, drained
2 (3-ounce) cans mandarin oranges, drained
½ cup pecans, chopped
Toasted coconut

Mix together graham cracker crumbs and butter. Press into a 9 x 13-inch baking pan. Bake at 350 degrees for 10 minutes. Cool.

Mix together whipped topping, milk, lemon juice, pineapple, oranges and pecans. Pour into crust. Top with toasted coconut. Refrigerate overnight.

Fabulous Pumpkin Pie

1 (9-inch) unbaked pie crust
1 cup evaporated milk
½ cup light brown sugar, firmly packed
¼ cup coffee liqueur
¼ cup light corn syrup
1½ teaspoons pumpkin pie spice
½ teaspoon salt
1½ cups pumpkin
2 large eggs, beaten
Coffee Liqueur Cream Topping (recipe follows)

Combine milk, sugar, coffee liqueur, corn syrup, spice and salt. Add pumpkin and eggs; blend well; set aside. Bake pie crust at 450 degrees for 7–8 minutes. Pour pumpkin mixture slowly into crust. Reduce oven heat to 325 degrees; bake an additional 40 minutes. Serve with Coffee Liqueur Cream Topping.

Coffee Liqueur Cream Topping

1 cup whipping cream
2 tablespoons coffee liqueur
Coffee liqueur

Beat whipping cream and liqueur until stiff peaks form. Drizzle with coffee liqueur.

Grasshopper Tarts

1 (12-ounce) package semisweet chocolate chips
2 tablespoons shortening
32 large marshmallows
½ cup milk
¼ cup créme de menthe
3 tablespoons white créme de cacao
1½ cups whipping cream
Few drops green food coloring

Melt chocolate chips and shortening. Coat bottom of 12 paper-lined muffin cups with chocolate mixture. Refrigerate until firm. Fill in with remaining chocolate. Refrigerate until firm. Gently remove paper cups from chocolate shells, returning shells to muffin cups.

Melt marshmallows and milk over medium heat; refrigerate until mixture mounds slightly; stir in liqueurs. Beat whipping cream until stiff; fold in marshmallow mixture; stir in food coloring. Pour mixture into chocolate shells. Refrigerate until set, 2–3 hours.

Praline Pumpkin Custard Pie

1 (9-inch) unbaked pie crust, pricked with fork
⅓ cup finely ground, firmly packed pecans
⅓ cup firmly packed brown sugar
2 tablespoons butter, softened
2 eggs, well beaten
1 cup cooked pumpkin
⅔ cup firmly packed brown sugar
1 tablespoon flour
¼ teaspoon cloves
⅛ teaspoon mace
½ teaspoon salt
½ teaspoon cinnamon
½ teaspoon ginger
1 cup coffee cream

Combine pecans, ⅓ cup brown sugar and butter; press firmly into pie crust. Bake at 450 degrees for 10 minutes. Combine eggs, pumpkin, brown sugar, flour, cloves, mace, salt, cinnamon and ginger. Blend in coffee cream; beat until mixture is smooth and creamy. Pour into partially baked pie crust. Bake at 325 degrees for 40–45 minutes.

Cranberry-Nut Tart

1 cup plus 2 tablespoons finely chopped walnuts
¼ cup sugar
1½ cups flour
½ cup butter
1 egg, slightly beaten
1 teaspoon vanilla extract
1 envelope unflavored gelatin
¼ cup cold water
3 cups fresh cranberries
1 cup sugar
¼ cup red currant jelly
¼ cup whipping cream, whipped

Combine walnuts, sugar and flour; cut in butter until crumbly. Add egg and vanilla; stir with a fork until dry ingredients are moistened. Press mixture in lightly greased 9-inch springform pan; chill 30 minutes. Bake at 350 degrees for 15–20 minutes or until golden brown. Cool completely.

Sprinkle gelatin over water; set aside. Combine cranberries, 1 cup sugar and jelly in saucepan; cook 10 minutes over low heat or until cranberry skins pop. Remove cranberry mixture from heat and let cool 5 minutes; add softened gelatin and stir until dissolved. Cool completely.

Pour cranberry mixture into tart shell. Chill several hours. Place tart on a seving platter, and remove from springform pan. Garnish with whipped cream.

Easy Pecan Tarts

2 eggs
1 cup firmly packed light brown sugar
2 tablespoons butter, melted
1 tablespoon water
1 teaspoon vanilla extract
Pinch of salt
1 cup chopped pecans
8 (2-inch) unbaked tart shells
Whipped cream
Pecan halves

Combine eggs, brown sugar, butter, water, vanilla and salt; beat well. Stir in pecans. Spoon pecan mixture into tart shells. Bake at 425 degrees for 15–17 minutes. Garnish with whipped cream and pecan halves if desired.

Green Tomato Pie

    4 cups thinly sliced green
      tomatoes
    2 tablespoons white vinegar
    ¼ cup honey
    1 cup sugar
    ¼ teaspoon salt
    ¼ teaspoon cinnamon
    ½ teaspoon nutmeg
    ¼ cup flour
    2 unbaked pie crusts

Mix together green tomatoes, vinegar and honey. Cook over low heat until tomatoes are soft; cool until just warm. Mix together sugar, salt, cinnamon, nutmeg and flour; pour into pastry-lined pan. Cover with top crust; slit for steam to escape. Sprinkle lightly with sugar. Bake at 350 degrees for 45–50 minutes until crust is golden.

Strawberry Cream Cheese Pie

    1 (10-ounce) package strawberry
      halves in syrup, thawed,
      drained, reserve liquid
    2 (8-ounce) packages cream
      cheese
    ¼ cup sugar
    1 teaspoon vanilla
    2 cups whipped topping
    1 chocolate crumb crust

Beat together cream cheese, ¼ cup strawberry liquid, strawberries, sugar and vanilla until smooth. Fold in whipped topping. Spoon into crust. Refrigerate several hours.

Custard Pie

    1 (9-inch) unbaked pie crust
    4 eggs, slightly beaten
    ⅔ cup sugar
    ½ teaspoon salt
    ¼ teaspoon nutmeg
    2⅔ cups milk
    1 teaspoon vanilla

Beat together eggs, sugar, salt, nutmeg, milk and vanilla. Pour into pie crust. Bake at 450 degrees for 20 minutes. Reduce temperature to 350 degrees and bake an additional 15–20 minutes, until knife comes out clean. Cool. Keep refrigerated.

Apple Butter Pumpkin Pie

    1 cup cooked and mashed
      pumpkin
    1 cup apple butter
    ⅓ cup firmly packed brown sugar
    ½ teaspoon cinnamon
    ¼ teaspoon salt
    ¼ teaspoon ginger
    ¼ teaspoon nutmeg
    3 eggs
    1 (5-ounce) can evaporated milk
    ⅓ cup milk
    1 (9-inch) unbaked pie shell
      Whipped cream

Combine pumpkin, apple butter, brown sugar, cinnamon, salt, ginger and nutmeg. Add eggs. With fork, lightly beat eggs into pumpkin mixture. Stir in evaporated milk and milk. Pour into pie crust. Cover edges of crust with foil. Bake at 375 degrees for 50 minutes, removing foil during last 25 minutes. Cool.

Coconut Custard Pie

    1 (9-inch) baked pie crust
    ¼ cup flour
    ½ teaspoon salt
    1 cup sugar
    3 eggs, separated
    1 egg, slightly beaten
    ½ cup cold milk
    1 cup milk, scalded
    1 teaspoon vanilla
    1 cup moist shredded coconut
    6 tablespoons sugar

Sift together flour, salt and sugar. Beat egg yolks; add 1 egg and cold milk; blend into dry ingredients. Add scalded milk. Cook over boiling water until thick, stirring constantly. Remove from heat. Add vanilla. Cool. Sprinkle coconut in bottom of pie crust; pour cooled custard over coconut; set aside.

Beat 3 egg whites until frothy; gradually add sugar; beat until it stands in shiny heavy points. Spread on pie; bake at 350 degrees for 15 minutes until browned. Cool.

Chocolate Meringue Pie

    4 tablespoons cocoa
    1¼ cups sugar
    6 tablespoons flour
    ½ teaspoon salt
    2½ cups milk
    3 eggs, separated
    2 tablespoons butter
    1 teaspoon vanilla
    1 (9-inch) baked pie crust
    ½ teaspoon cream of tartar
    1 tablespoon water
    6 tablespoons sugar

Combine cocoa, sugar, flour, salt and milk in double boiler; cook until thickened, stirring often. Stir in small amount of cocoa mixture into egg yolks; pour all of this into rest of cocoa mixture. Cook 2 minutes; add butter and vanilla; cool. Pour in pie crust.

Beat egg whites until frothy. Add cream of tartar and water; beat until whites are stiff. Gradually add sugar, beating well after each addition. Pile meringue onto pie, spreading to edge of crust. Bake at 325 degrees for 20 minutes or until brown.

Chocolate Pie

    1 (9-inch) baked pie crust
    1 envelope unflavored gelatin
    ¼ cup milk
    4 eggs, separated
    1¼ cups milk
    ⅓ cup sugar
    ½ teaspoon salt
    1 teaspoon vanilla
    ¼ cup sugar
      Whipped cream

Soften gelatin in milk. Combine egg yolks, 1¼ cups milk, sugar and salt. Cook over boiling water until mixture thickens, stirring constantly. Remove from heat. Add vanilla with gelatin and beat well. Chill until mixture begins to thicken.

Beat egg whites until stiff; gradually beat in ¼ cup sugar. Carefully fold egg whites into gelatin mixture. Pour into cooled pie crust. Chill 3–5 hours. Serve with whipped cream.

Pumpkin Cheese Pie

1 (8-ounce) package cream cheese
3/4 cup brown sugar
1 teaspoon cinnamon
1 teaspoon nutmeg
1/2 teaspoon ginger
1/2 teaspoon cloves
1/2 teaspoon salt
1/4 cup flour
3 eggs, beaten
1 can pumpkin
1 cup evaporated milk
1 teaspoon vanilla
1 (9-inch) unbaked pie crust

Beat cream cheese, sugar, cinnamon, nutmeg, ginger, cloves, salt and flour; add eggs. Stir in pumpkin, milk and vanilla. Pour into pie crust. Bake at 375 degrees for 45 minutes.

French Silk Chocolate Pie

1 (8-inch) baked pie crust
1/2 cup butter
3/4 cup sugar
1 (1-ounce) square chocolate, melted, cooled
1 teaspoon vanilla
2 eggs

Cream butter and sugar; blend in chocolate and vanilla. Add eggs, 1 at a time, beating 5 minutes after each addition with an electric mixer on medium speed. Pour into pie crust. Chill 1–2 hours.

Chocolate Chip Pie

1 cup sugar
1/2 cup flour
2 eggs, well beaten
1 stick margarine, melted
1 teaspoon vanilla
1 cup semisweet chocolate chips
3/4 cup pecans
1/2 cup coconut
1 unbaked deep dish pie crust

Blend together flour, sugar, eggs, margarine and vanilla. Stir in chocolate chips, pecans and coconut. Pour into pie crust. Bake at 350 degrees for 30–35 minutes, until firm.

Chocolate Brownie Pie

1 (9-inch) baked pie crust
2 (2-ounce) squares chocolate
1/2 cup butter
3/4 cup sugar
1/4 teaspoon salt
2 eggs
1 teaspoon vanilla
1/2 cup flour
1/2 cup chopped pecans
   Whipped cream, sweetened
   Chocolate, grated
   Pecan halves

Melt chocolate squares, butter, sugar and salt in top of double boiler until well blended. Cool 5 minutes. Add eggs, stirring until smooth. Blend in vanilla. Combine flour and pecans; add to chocolate mixture, blending well. Pour into pie crust. Bake at 325 degrees for 25–35 minutes. Chill thoroughly. Top with whipped cream, grated chocolate and pecan halves before serving.

Maple Almond Pie

1 (10-inch) unbaked pie crust
2 tablespoons butter, melted
3/4 cup light brown sugar
3/4 cup maple syrup
1/4 teaspoon salt
4 large eggs
1/2 cup canned milk
1/2 teaspoon maple extract
1/2 teaspoon lemon extract
3/4 cup quick rolled oats
1/2 cup slivered almonds
   Whipped topping
   Maraschino cherries

Melt butter, brown sugar and maple syrup together over low heat; stir until sugar is dissolved. Add extracts and salt; set aside to cool. Beat eggs and milk together; add to sugar mixture. Blend well. Stir in oats and nuts; pour into pie crust.

Bake at 400 degrees for 20 minutes; reduce heat to 350 degrees and bake an additional 20–25 minutes until middle is firm. Serve with whipped cream and maraschino cherries.

Strawberry Glaze Pie

6 cups strawberries
1 cup sugar
3 tablespoons cornstarch
1/2 cup water
1 (3-ounce) package cream cheese, softened
1 (9-inch) baked pie shell

Mash enough strawberries to measure 1 cup. Over medium heat, stir and heat sugar, cornstarch, water and mashed strawberries until mixture thickens and boils. Noil 1 minute,, stirring constantly; cool.

Beat cream cheese until smooth; spread on bottom of pie shell. Place remaining whole strawberries in bottom of pie crust; pour cooked strawberry mixture over top. Refrigerate at least 3 hours, or until set.

Chocolate Creme Mint Pie

1 (8-inch) baked pie crust
3/4 cup butter, softened
1 cup sugar
3 eggs, well beaten
3 (3-ounce) squares chocolate, melted, cooled
1/2 teaspoon peppermint extract
   Whipped cream

Cream butter and sugar; blend in eggs. Fold in chocolate; beat until smooth. Add peppermint extract. Pour into cooled pie crust. Chill several hours. Top with whipped cream.

Peanut Butter Pie

1 (9-inch) unbaked pie crust
2/3 cup sugar
1/2 teaspoon salt
1 cup dark corn syrup
1/3 cup creamy peanut butter
3 eggs
1 cup salted peanuts

Beat sugar, salt, corn syrup, peanut butter and eggs; stir in peanuts. Pour into pie crust. Bake at 375 degrees for 40–50 minutes until golden brown; cool slightly; refrigerate.

Macaroon Pie

3 egg whites
½ teaspoon baking powder
1 cup sugar
1 teaspoon vanilla extract
1 dozen graham crackers, finely crushed
½ cup finely chopped dates
1 cup chopped pecans
   Whipped cream

Beat egg whites until frothy; sprinkle baking powder over whites and continue beating until stiff. Gradually beat in sugar; add vanilla. Mix together graham cracker crumbs, dates and pecans; fold into egg white mixture. Spread in 9-inch pie pan. Bake at 300 degrees for 30 minutes or until set and very lightly browned. Cool; spread with whipped cream.

Fudge Brownie Pie

2 eggs
1 cup sugar
½ cup butter, melted
½ cup flour
⅓ cup cocoa
¼ teaspoon salt
1 teaspoon vanilla
½ cup chopped nuts
   Ice cream
   Hot Fudge Sauce (recipe follows)

Beat eggs; blend in sugar and margarine. Combine flour, cocoa and salt; add to butter mixture. Stir in vanilla and nuts. Bake in lightly greased 8-inch pie pan at 350 degrees for 25–30 minutes or until almost set. Cool. Serve topped with ice cream and Hot Fudge Sauce.

Hot Fudge Sauce

¾ cup sugar
½ cup cocoa
1 (5-ounce) can evaporated milk
⅓ cup light corn syrup
⅓ cup butter
1 teaspoon vanilla

Combine sugar and cocoa in saucepan; blend in evaporated milk and corn syrup. Cook over medium heat, stirring constantly until mixture boils; boil, stirring constantly, 1 minute. Remove from heat; stir in butter and vanilla. Serve warm.

Mocha Pie

1 cup flour
2 tablespoons sugar
½ teaspoon salt
⅓ cup shortening
1 egg yolk
   Water
40 marshmallows
¼ cup sugar
2 teaspoons instant coffee
¼ cup evaporated milk
2 cup semisweet chocolate chips
1 cup whipping cream

Sift together flour, sugar and salt; cut in shortening until crumbly. Combine egg yolk and enough water to make ¼ cup; sprinkle over flour mixture, making dough. Roll into crust; place in 9-inch pie pan. Prick crust and bake at 375 degrees for 12–15 minutes until golden brown. Cool.

Combine marshmallows, sugar, coffee and milk in top of double boiler; cook until marshmallows are melted. Stir in chocolate chips; cool slightly. Spread ¾ of mixture in bottom of baked crust. Fold cream into remaining chocolate mixture. Spoon over pie. Chill at least 2 hours before serving.

Four-Cheese Pie

½ cup shredded Swiss cheese
½ cup shredded cheddar cheese
1 cup shredded mozzarella cheese
1 cup shredded Monterey Jack cheese
1 medium onion, chopped
2 tablespoons flour
1 (10-inch) unbaked pie crust
4 eggs, slightly beaten
1 cup milk
½ teaspoon salt
½ teaspoon dry mustard
½ teaspoon Worcestershire sauce
2 medium tomatoes, sliced

Mix together cheeses, onion and flour. Spread in 10-inch pie crust. Beat together eggs, milk, salt, mustard and Worcestershire sauce. Pour over cheese mixture. Bake uncovered at 350 degrees for 35–40 minutes. Let stand 10 minutes; garnish with tomato slices.

Broccoli-Cheese Pie

1 egg, separated
3 ounces macaroni rings, cooked
1 tablespoon snipped chives
1 cup shredded Cheddar cheese
1 (10-ounce) package frozen chopped broccoli, cooked
4 eggs
1 cup creamed cottage cheese
1 tablespoon snipped chives
1 teaspoon salt
   Paprika

Combine 1 egg yolk, macaroni and chives. Press against bottom of greased pie pan. Bake at 375 degrees for 10 minutes; cool 10 minutes. Sprinkle cheese over crust. Arrange broccoli on cheese. Beat 4 eggs, 1 egg white, cottage cheese, 1 tablespoon chives and 1 teaspoon salt; pour over broccoli. Sprinkle with paprika.

Bake uncovered at 425 degrees for 15 minutes; reduce temperature to 300 degrees and bake 30 additional minutes or until knife comes out clean. Cool 10 minutes before serving.

Molasses Crumb Pie

½ cup molasses
1 egg yolk
½ teaspoon baking soda
¾ cup boiling water
¾ cup flour
2 tablespoons shortening
½ teaspoon cinnamon
⅛ teaspoon nutmeg
⅛ teaspoon ginger
⅛ teaspoon cloves
½ cup firmly packed brown sugar
¼ teaspoon salt
1 (9-inch) unbaked pie crust

Combine molasses and egg yolk; dissolve baking soda in water; add to molasses mixture; set aside.

Mix together flour, sugar, spices and salt; cut in shortening until crumbly. Put alternate layers of crumbs and filling into an unbaked pie shell. Top with crumbs. Bake at 450 degrees until edges of crust begin to brown. Reduce heat to 375 degrees and bake 20 minutes until firm.

Pumpkin Chiffon Pie

1 envelope unflavored gelatin
¼ cup bourbon
3 eggs, separated
1 (16-ounce) can pumpkin
¾ cup firmly packed brown sugar
½ teaspoon salt
2 teaspoons pumpkin pie spice
½ cup milk
¼ teaspoon cream of tartar
¼ cup plus 2 tablespoons sugar
1 (9-inch) baked pie crust
  Ginger Cream Topping
  (recipe follows)

Combine gelatin and bourbon; let soften 5 minutes. Combine gelatin mixture, beaten egg yolks, pumpkin, brown sugar, salt, pumpkin pie spice and milk in top of a double boiler; cook over boiling water, stirring occasionally, for 10 minutes or until mixture is thoroughly heated. Chill until thickened.

Beat egg whites (at room temperature) with cream of tartar until foamy. Gradually add sugar, beating until stiff peaks form. Fold into pumpkin mixture; spoon into pastry shell. Chill several hours until firm. To serve, top with Ginger Cream Topping.

Ginger Cream Topping

½ teaspoon ginger
1 tablespoon sugar
1 cup whipping cream

Beat together ginger, sugar and cream until stiff peaks form. Makes 2 cups.

Pumpkin Cream Pie

1¾ cups cold milk
1 cup pumpkin
2 tablespoons sugar
½ teaspoon cinnamon
¼ teaspoon cloves
⅛ teaspoon nutmeg
1 (6-ounce) package vanilla instant pudding mix
1 (9-inch) baked pie crust

Beat together milk, pumpkin, sugar, cinnamon, cloves, nutmeg and pudding for 30 seconds or until smooth. Pour into baked pastry crust and refrigerate until thoroughly chilled.

Buttermilk Pie

1 stick butter
2 cups sugar
5 eggs
2 tablespoons flour
  Juice of 1 lemon
1 teaspoon vanilla extract
1 cup buttermilk
1 (10-inch) pie crust

Cream together butter and sugar. Add eggs, 1 at a time. Stir in flour, lemon juice, vanilla and buttermilk, mixing thoroughly. Place in pie crust. Bake at 400 degrees for 10 minutes; lower temperature to 325 degrees and bake an additional 45–50 minutes until set.

Beef Mushroom Pie

1 (9-inch) baked pie crust
1 can mushroom soup
2 eggs, lightly beaten
½ cup milk
2 tablespoons onion *or* chives
¼ teaspoon salt
  Dash pepper
½ pound ground beef, browned, drained
¾ cup shredded Swiss cheese

Mix together soup, eggs, milk and spices; add beef and cheese. Pour into pie crust. Cover edge of pie shell with foil. Bake at 350 degrees for 60 minutes until knife comes out clean.

Dried Apple Pie

1½ cups boiling water
1½ cups dried apples
½ cup sugar
½ teaspoon cinnamon
½ teaspoon nutmeg
2 tablespoons butter
1 double crust for pie

Pour boiling water over dried apples; let set a half day. Add sugar, either brown or white, spices and stir well. Line pie pan with bottom crust then pour apple-spice mixture into this. Dot well with butter and put on top crust. Bake in fairly hot oven for 45–60 minutes, or until golden brown.

Deluxe Pecan Pie

3 eggs
1 cup sugar
¼ teaspoon salt
2 tablespoons butter, melted
½ cup dark corn syrup
½ cup heavy cream
1 teaspoon vanilla extract
¼ cup bourbon or brandy
2 tablespoons chopped pecans
1 cup pecan halves
1 (9-inch) unbaked pie shell

Beat eggs, sugar, salt, butter, corn syrup and heavy cream. Stir in vanilla, bourbon, pecans and pecan halves. Pour mixture into pie crust. Bake at 375 degrees for 40–50 minutes, until set in middle.

Apple Betty Pie

1 stick butter *or* margarine
4 cups apples, cored and sliced
¼ cup orange juice
1 cup sugar
¾ cup flour
½ teaspoon cinnamon
¼ teaspoon nutmeg
  Dash salt

Melt butter in long cake pan. Mix apples with orange juice, sugar, flour, cinnamon, nutmeg and salt; place in pan. Bake at 375 degrees for 25–35 minutes.

Pumpkin Ice Cream Pie

1 pint vanilla ice cream, softened
1 (9-inch) baked graham cracker crust
1 cup pumpkin
¾ cup sugar
½ teaspoon ginger
½ teaspoon cinnamon
½ teaspoon salt
¼ teaspoon nutmeg
1 cup whipping cream

Spoon ice cream into crust; freeze. Combine pumpkin, sugar, ginger, cinnamon, salt and nutmeg. Whip cream to stiff peaks. Fold into pumpkin mixture. Spread evenly over ice cream. Freeze for 2 days. Serve frozen.

Lemon Buttermilk Pie

¼ cup butter
1 cup sugar
1 tablespoon flour
1 tablespoon cornmeal
4 eggs
⅓ cup lemon juice
1 tablespoon grated lemon peel
½ cup buttermilk
1 (8-inch) unbaked pie crust

Melt butter; add sugar, flour and cornmeal. Add eggs, 1 at a time, beating well after each addition. Add lemon juice, lemon peel and buttermilk. Pour into unbaked 8-inch pie shell. Bake for 45 minutes at 350 degrees or until knife comes out clean.

Apple Crunch Pie

8–9 tart apples, sliced
½ cup sugar
2 tablespoons flour
Dash salt
¾ teaspoon cinnamon
¾ cup flour
⅓ cup butter
½ cup sugar

Mix together apples, sugar, flour, salt and cinnamon. Place in 9 x 9-inch pan. Mix flour, butter and sugar together until crumbly and spread over apples. Bake at 400 degrees for 20 minutes; lower temperature to 350 degrees and bake for 30–40 additional minutes.

Apple Juice Concentrate Pie

6 apples, sliced
1 (6-ounce) can frozen apple juice concentrate
2 tablespoons cornstarch
2 teaspoons cinnamon
2 (9-inch) unbaked pie crusts

Combine concentrate with cornstarch and cinnamon; add sliced apples. Mix thoroughly. Place in pie shell and cover with crust. Bake at 350 degrees for 1 hour.

Holiday Rum Pie

1 (8-inch) graham cracker crust
4 (3-ounce) packages cream cheese, softened
½ cup sugar
2 large eggs
1 tablespoon rum
1 cup sour cream
3 tablespoons sugar
1 tablespoon rum

Beat eggs; add sugar. Mix together cream cheese and rum; add to egg mixture; beat until creamy. Pour into crust and bake at 350 degrees for 25 minutes. Mix together sour cream, 3 tablespoons sugar and 1 tablespoon rum; mix well and spread on top of pie. Return pie to oven and bake an additional 5 minutes to heat cream.

Dutch Apple Pie

3 cups tart apples, sliced
1 cup sugar
1 teaspoon cinnamon
¾ cup flour
⅓ cup butter
1 (9-inch) unbaked pie shell

Sprinkle apples with mixture of ½ cup sugar and cinnamon. Sift ½ cup sugar with flour and cut in butter until crumbly. Put crumbs on top of pie and bake 10 minutes at 450 degrees, then 30 minutes at 350 degrees.

Traditional Pumpkin Pie

3 eggs, beaten
½ teaspoon salt
⅔ cup brown sugar
⅓ cup sugar
1½ cups milk
1½ cups cooked pumpkin
2 teaspoons cinnamon
1 teaspoon ginger
½ teaspoon nutmeg
⅛ teaspoon allspice
1 (9-inch) unbaked pie crust

Mix together eggs, salt, sugars and milk. Add pumpkin and spices. Mix well; pour into pie crust. Bake at 425 degrees for 35–45 minutes until center firms up.

Boston Cream Pie

1½ cups flour
1 cup sugar
1½ teaspoons baking powder
½ teaspoon salt
¾ cup milk
⅓ cup shortening
1 egg
1 teaspoon vanilla
Cream Filling (recipe follows)
Chocolate Glaze (recipe follows)

With an electric mixer, beat flour, sugar, baking powder, salt, milk, shortening, egg and vanilla on low speed for 30 seconds. Turn to high speed and beat 3 minutes. Pour into greased and floured 9-inch round pan.

Bake at 350 degrees for 35 minutes; cool for 10 minutes before removing from pan. Cool completely. Split cake in half horizontally. Fill layers with Cream Filling. Spread top of cake with Chocolate Glaze; refrigerate.

Cream Filling

⅓ cup sugar
2 tablespoons cornstarch
⅛ teaspoon salt
1½ cups milk
2 egg yolks, slightly beaten
2 teaspoons vanilla

Mix together sugar, cornstarch and salt in saucepan. Combine milk and egg yolks; gradually stir into sugar mixture. Cook over medium heat, stirring constantly, until mixture thickens and boils. Boil 1 minute, stirring constantly. Remove from heat. Blend in vanilla. Cool.

Chocolate Glaze

3 tablespoons margarine
2 (1-ounce) squares unsweetened chocolate
1 cup confectioners' sugar
¾ teaspoon vanilla
1–2 tablespoons hot water

Heat together margarine and chocolate in saucepan over low heat until chocolate is melted; stir constantly. Remove from heat; blend in confectioners' sugar and vanilla. Add water, 1 teaspoon at a time, until smooth.

Apple Pie

2 cups flour
1 teaspoon salt
2/3 cup lard
1/4 cup water
Pie Filling (recipe follows)

Combine flour and salt; cut in lard. Stir water in with fork to make dough. Divide in half and roll out to make two 9-inch crusts.

Pie Filling

1 cup sugar
1 teaspoon cinnamon
6–8 apples, sliced
1 1/2 tablespoons butter

Preheat oven to 425 degrees. Mix together sugar and cinnamon; toss with apples. Place apples in pie shell; dot with butter; sprinkle with cinnamon. Cover with top crust and cut slits to allow steam to escape. Bake for 15 minutes at 425 degrees; lower temperature to 350 degrees and cook an additional hour.

Christmas Apple Pastry

2 cups flour
1/2 cup sugar
1/2 teaspoon baking powder
1/2 teaspoon salt
1 cup butter
2 eggs, separated
4 cups apples, pared, sliced 1/8-inch thick
1/2 cup sugar
1/4 cup flour
1 teaspoon cinnamon
1/4 teaspoon nutmeg

Combine flour, sugar, baking powder and salt; cut in butter until crumbly. Mix in slightly beaten egg yolks. Press half of the mixture in 15 x 10-inch jelly roll pan. Set aside remaining half of mixture.

Combine apples, sugar, flour, cinnamon and nutmeg; arrange over bottom crust. Sprinkle remaining crust mixture over filling. Brush beaten egg whites over all. Bake at 350 degrees for 30–40 minutes. May drizzle with confectioners' sugar glaze.

Aunt Amy's Favorite Pie

1 (9-inch) unbaked pie crust
4 eggs, separated
1 1/4 cups milk
1 1/3 cups sugar
3 tablespoons butter, melted
3 tablespoons flour
1/2 teaspoon cinnamon
1/4 teaspoon nutmeg
1/4 teaspoon cloves
1/2 teaspoon salt

Prick bottom of pie crust. Bake at 450 degrees for 10–12 minutes. Combine beaten egg yolks, milk, sugar, butter, flour, cinnamon, nutmeg and cloves; mix well. Beat egg whites; add salt and beat until stiff but not dry. Gently fold into egg yolk mixture. Pour into warm pie crust. Bake at 350 degrees for 40–50 minutes.

Little Jack Horner Plum Pudding Pie

1 (9-inch) unbaked pie shell
1 cup unsifted flour
1 teaspoon ground cinnamon
1/4 teaspoon salt
1/4 teaspoon ground cloves
1/3 cup butter *or* margarine
1/3 cup dark corn syrup
1/4 cup chopped candied fruit
1 1/2 cups prepared mincemeat
1/2 cup chopped walnuts
3 eggs, separated

In large bowl, mix together flour, cinnamon, salt and cloves. Cut in butter with pastry blender or 2 knives until coarse crumbs form. Mix corn syrup and candied fruit. Stir fruit mixture, mincemeat and walnuts into flour mixture. Beat egg whites until soft peaks form when beater is raised.

Beat egg yolks until thick and lemon-colored; stir into flour mixture. Fold in egg whites. Pour into pastry shell. Bake in a 350-degree oven for about 1 hour, or until cake tester inserted in center comes out clean. Serve warm. Decorate with whipped cream or whipped topping and candied cherries or bits of candied fruit.

Kart-Wheels

1 1/2 cups flour
1/2 cup margarine, softened
1/4 cup confectioners' sugar
1/2 teaspoon baking powder
2 tablespoons milk
1 can apple pie filling

Combine flour, margarine, confectioners' sugar, baking powder and milk. Knead this like dough until well mixed. Make into 6 balls. Make into tart shells, with the sides at least 1/2-inch high. Fill with pie filling. Bake at 375 degrees for 20 minutes or until lightly browned.

Rum Pumpkin Pie

1 (9-inch) pie crust
2 eggs, slightly beaten
1 cup brown sugar
1/2 teaspoon ginger
1/2 teaspoon cinnamon
1/4 teaspoon nutmeg
1/4 teaspoon mace
1 3/4 cups pumpkin
1/2 cup milk
1/2 cup cream
4 tablespoons rum

Bake pie crust at 400 degrees for 5 minutes. Combine eggs, brown sugar, spices, pumpkin, milk, cream and rum. Pour into partially baked crust. Bake at 350 degrees for 1 hour or until knife comes out clean.

Apple Crumb Pie

2/3 cup sugar
2 tablespoons flour
3/4 teaspoon cinnamon
6–8 tart apples, peeled and sliced (6 cups)
1 (9-inch) unbaked pie shell
1/2 cup flour
1/4 cup sugar
1/4 cup butter

Combine sugar, flour and cinnamon; stir in apples and place in pie shell. Combine flour and sugar; cut in butter until crumbly. Sprinkle over apples. Bake at 400 degrees for 45–50 minutes or until done.

Caramel Apple Pie

1 (21-ounce) can apple pie filling
1 (9-inch) pie crust
12 caramel candies
¼ cup butter
1 tablespoon lemon juice
2 tablespoons milk

Pour apple pie filling into prepared 9-inch pie shell. Combine caramels, butter, lemon juice and milk in saucepan; head over low heat stirring constantly until smooth and caramels are melted. Pour over apples. Bake at 400 degrees until brown, 25–30 minutes.

Caramel Apple Streusel

20 vanilla caramels
3 tablespoons milk
2¼ cups flour
1 cup butter, softened
1 cup sugar
1 cup pecans, chopped
1 egg
3 cups apples, peeled and sliced
¼ cup flour
¾ cup sugar
1 cup water
1 teaspoon cinnamon

In top part of double boiler, place caramels and milk; heat until melted, stirring constantly; set aside. In saucepan, place apples and 1 cup water. Cook until apples are cooked through but not mushy. Stir together ¾ cup sugar, ¼ cup flour and cinnamon.

Remove apples with slotted spoon, leaving only the juice in the pan. Over medium heat, stir in the flour mixture, stirring constantly, until thickened. Fold in apples. Cool. In large bowl, combine 2¼ cups flour, butter, 1 cup sugar, pecans and egg.

Beat on low speed with mixer, scraping bowl often, until mixture is crumbly. Set aside 1½ cups crumbly mixture. With the remaining crumbs, press on bottom and sides of 9-inch springform pan. Spoon pie filling mixture onto crust. Drizzle caramel sauce over pie filling. Sprinkle with reserved crumbs. Bake at 350 degrees for 45–50 minutes. Cool. Remove form and serve.

Dutch Apple Crisp Pie

5 large tart cooking apples, pared, cored and sliced
1 cup sugar
½ cup plus 2 tablespoons flour
½ teaspoon nutmeg
¼ teaspoon cinnamon
1 (9-inch) unbaked pastry shell
¼ teaspoon lemon juice
½ stick butter *or* margarine
½ cup nuts, chopped

Combine apples with mixture of ½ cup sugar, 2 teaspoons flour, nutmeg and cinnamon. Spoon into pastry shell; sprinkle with lemon juice. Combine remaining sugar and flour; cut in butter until crumbly. Add nuts; sprinkle over apples. Bake at 400 degrees for 45–55 minutes or until apples are tender. Cool.

Apple Pastry

1 batch pie dough, enough for 2 pies
3–4 medium, tart, apples, pared and cored
⅔ cup sugar
1½ cups water
1 tablespoon butter
¼ teaspoon cinnamon
1 cup sugar
2 teaspoons cinnamon
2 teaspoons butter

Preheat oven to 425 degrees. Combine ⅔ cup sugar, water, 1 tablespoon butter and ¼ teaspoon cinnamon in saucepan; bring to a boil and set aside. Roll out pastry to a little less than ⅛-inch thick; cut into 7-inch squares. Stir together 1 cup sugar and 2 teaspoons cinnamon. Fill apple cavities evenly. Dot each with butter. Bring opposite points of pastry up over the apple. Overlap edges, moisten and seal.

Place in baking dish. Pour hot syrup around dumplings. Bake immediately 40–45 minutes or until crust is nicely browned and apples are cooked through (test with fork). Serve warm with syrup and with cream or whipped cream.

French Apple Pie

½ cup sugar
3 teaspoons flour
¼ teaspoon ground nutmeg
¼ teaspoon ground cinnamon
Dash of salt
5 cups apples, thinly sliced
1 cup flour
½ cup firm butter
½ cup brown sugar

Mix together sugar, flour, nutmeg, cinnamon and salt. Stir in apples. Turn into 8-inch pie plate. Mix together 1 cup flour, butter and brown sugar until crumbly. Sprinkle over apples. Bake for 50 minutes at 375–400 degrees until done.

Norwegian Pie

¾ cup sugar
½ cup flour
1 teaspoon baking powder
¼ teaspoon salt
1 egg
¼ teaspoon vanilla
¼ teaspoon cinnamon
1 cup Winesap apples, diced
½ cup black walnuts, chopped
1 (9-inch) pie shell

Mix together sugar, flour, baking powder and salt. Add 1 unbeaten egg and stir well. Add vanilla, cinnamon, apples and walnuts. Place in 9-inch pie pan. Bake at 350 degrees for 30–35 minutes.

September Apple Pie

2 (9-inch) pie crusts
¾ cup sugar
2 tablespoons flour
½ teaspoon cinnamon
½ teaspoon nutmeg
Dash of salt
4 cups apples, thinly sliced
2 tablespoons butter

Stir together sugar, flour, cinnamon, nutmeg and salt; mix with apples. Place on pie crust; dot with butter. Cover with remaining crust. Bake at 400 degrees for 50 minutes or until done.

Unique Dutch Apple Pie

- 1 (9-inch) unbaked pie crust
- 3 cups apples, sliced
- 1 cup sugar
- 3 tablespoons flour
- ½ teaspoon cinnamon
- ½ cup sugar
- ½ cup flour
- ¼ cup Parmesan cheese
- 3 tablespoons margarine

Mix together sugar, flour and cinnamon; sprinkle over apples placed in unbaked pie shell. Bake at 350 degrees for 1 hour. Combine and mix together ½ cup sugar, ½ cup flour, Parmesan cheese and margarine until crumbly. Sprinkle over baked apple pie; return to oven; bake until golden brown.

Apple Fritters

- 2 egg yolks
- ⅔ cup milk
- 1 tablespoon butter, melted
- 1 cup flour
- 1 tablespoon sugar
- ¼ teaspoon salt
- 2 egg whites
  Apple slices, ½-inch thick
  Confectioners' sugar

Beat together egg yolks, milk and butter. Sift in flour, sugar and salt; mix. Cover batter and refrigerate at least 2 hours. Beat egg whites until stiff and fold into batter. Dip apple slices in confectioners' sugar, then in batter. Deep-fry at 375 degrees, flipping slices over when golden brown. Drain on paper toweling. Dust with confectioners' sugar. Makes 8–10 servings.

Crazy Crust Apple Pie

- 1 cup flour
- 2 tablespoons sugar
- 1 teaspoon baking powder
- ½ teaspoon salt
- ¾ cup water
- ⅔ cup shortening
- 1 egg

Preheat oven to 425 degrees. Combine flour, sugar, baking powder, salt, water, shortening and egg; blend at lowest speed and beat for 2 minutes at medium speed. Spread batter in 9 or 10-inch pie pan.

Pie Filling

- 1 can apple pie filling
- 1 tablespoon lemon juice
- ½ teaspoon cinnamon

Mix together pie filling, lemon juice and cinnamon. Carefully spoon filling in center of batter. Do not stir. Bake until crust is golden brown, 40–45 minutes.

Sweet Potato Pie

- 1 (9-inch) unbaked pie crust
- 2 eggs, slightly beaten
- 2 cups cooked and mashed sweet potatoes
- ¾ cup sugar
- ½ teaspoon salt
- 1 teaspoon cinnamon
- ⅓ teaspoon ginger
- ¼ teaspoon cloves
- 1⅔ cups evaporated milk

Beat together eggs, sweet potatoes, sugar, salt, cinnamon, ginger, cloves and milk. Pour into pie crust. Bake at 425 for 15 minutes. Lower temperature to 350 degrees and bake an additional 45 minutes or until knife comes out clean. Cool. Keep refrigerated.

Candy-Cane Pie

- 1 envelope unflavored gelatin
- ¼ cup cold water
- ¾ cup milk, scalded
- ½ cup sugar
- ¼ teaspoon salt
- 1 cup crushed candy canes
- 4 egg yolks, slightly beaten
- 4 egg whites
- 1 (9-inch) cookie crumb crust
  Whipped cream

Soak gelatin in cold water. Stir together milk, sugar, salt and peppermint candy. Add egg yolks to mixture; cook over boiling water until mixture coats spoon. Stir in gelatin. Chill until thick and syrupy. Beat egg whites until stiff; fold into custard. Pour into crumb crust. Chill until firm, about 3 hours. Serve with whipped cream.

Cream Cheese Pumpkin Pie With Pecan Crust

- ¾ cup flour
- 6 tablespoons firmly packed brown sugar
- ¼ teaspoon salt
- 6 tablespoons butter, chilled, cut into pieces
- 1 tablespoon cold water
- ½ cup finely chopped pecans
- 1 (8-ounce) package cream cheese, [1] room temperature
- 6 tablespoons sour cream
- ½ cup sugar
- 2 large eggs
- 1 cup pumpkin
- ¾ teaspoon cinnamon
- ¼ teaspoon ginger
- ⅛ teaspoon cloves

Blend flour, sugar and salt in processor using on/off turns. Add butter until mixture resembles coarse cornmeal. Add water until moist clumps form. In large bowl combine flour mixture and pecans. Knead until pecans are incorporated and dough comes together. Press dough on bottom and sides of buttered 9-inch tart pan with removable bottom. Refrigerate until firm, about 30 minutes.

Place rack in center of oven. Line crust with foil and weigh down with beans or pie weights. Bake at 375 degrees for 10 minutes, until sides are firm. Remove weights and bake an additional 10 minutes until crust begins to brown.

Beat cream cheese and sour cream until smooth. Gradually add sugar; beat until blended. Add eggs, 1 at a time, beating just to blend after each addition. Set aside ⅓ cup cheese mixture. Add pumpkin, cinnamon, ginger and cloves to cream cheese mixture. Beat until well blended. Spread in crust.

Drop reserved ⅓ cup cream cheese mixture by teaspoonfuls over pumpkin filling. Using tip of knife, gently swirl cheese mixture into pumpkin in a decorative pattern. Bake at 350 degrees for 30 minutes or until firm in center.

Colonial Innkeeper's Pie

1 cup flour
½ teaspoon salt
⅓ cup shortening
2–4 tablespoons cold water
1½ (1-ounce) squares
    unsweetened chocolate
½ cup water
⅔ cup sugar
¼ cup butter
1½ teaspoons vanilla
1 cup flour
¾ cup sugar
1 teaspoon baking powder
½ teaspoon salt
¼ cup shortening
½ cup milk
½ teaspoon vanilla
1 egg
½ cup finely chopped nuts

Mix together 1 cup flour and ½ teaspoon salt; cut in ⅓ cup shortening. Add water 1 tablespoon at a time, mixing with fork to form ball. Roll out pastry and place in a 9-inch pie pan; cover while preparing pie.

Melt chocolate with water; add ⅔ cup sugar and bring to a boil, stirring constantly. Remove from heat; stir in butter and 1½ teaspoons vanilla; set aside to cool.

Sift together 1 cup flour, ¾ cup sugar, baking powder and ½ teaspoon salt. Add ¼ cup shortening, milk and ½ teaspoon vanilla. Beat 2 minutes, at medium speed, with an electric mixer. Add egg and beat 2 more minutes. Pour into pie crust. Stir chocolate mixture and carefully pour over pie. Sprinkle with nuts. Bake at 350 degrees for 55–60 minutes, until knife comes out clean.

Apple Pie in Cheddar Cheese Crust

2 cups flour
1 cup cheddar cheese, shredded
½ teaspoon salt
⅔ cup shortening
6 tablespoons cold water
1 egg yolk, beaten
1 tablespoon water
    Pie Filling (recipe follows)

Combine flour, cheese and salt in large bowl. Cut in shortening with pastry blender until mixture is course crumbs. Add cold water 1 tablespoon at a time until dry ingredients are moistened. Divide dough in half. Roll out on floured surface. Place in pie plate.

Pie Filling

9 cups tart apples, sliced
⅓ cup brown sugar, packed
⅓ cup sugar
2 tablespoons flour
1 teaspoon cinnamon
¼ teaspoon nutmeg
¼ teaspoon salt
2 tablespoons butter
1 egg yolk
1 tablespoon water

Combine apples, with brown sugar, sugar, flour, cinnamon, nutmeg and salt; place in pie shell. Dot with butter. Place top crust over apples. Mix together egg yolk and water; brush crust with this mixture. Cut slits in top crust before baking to allow steam to escape. Bake at 400 degrees for 40 minutes. Makes 1 9-inch pie.

Christmas Lime Parfait Pie

1 (6-ounce) package lime gelatin
2 cups boiling water
1 teaspoon grated lime peel
⅓ cup fresh lime juice
1 quart vanilla ice cream
1 (10-inch) baked pie crust
    Whipped cream
    Cherries

Dissolve gelatin in boiling water; stir in peel and juice. Add ice cream by spoonfuls, stirring until melted. Chill until slightly thickened and mixture mounds slightly when dropped from a spoon. Pour into pie crust. Chill until firm. Garnish with whipped cream and cherries.

Canned Apple Pie Filling

9 cups water
5 cups sugar
1 cup cornstarch
3 teaspoons cinnamon
2 teaspoons nutmeg
    Cloves (optional)
    Ginger (optional)
7 quarts apples, peeled and sliced

Heat water, sugar, cornstarch, cinnamon, nutmeg, cloves and ginger until sugar is dissolved; pour over apples. Process until cooker reaches 10 pounds pressure. Remove from heat.

Peanut Crust Pie

1 cup flour
½ teaspoon baking powder
½ teaspoon salt
⅓ cup shortening
⅓ cup crushed salted peanuts
3–4 tablespoons cold water
1 envelope unflavored gelatin
¼ cup milk
2 (1-ounce) squares chocolate
¾ cup sugar
2 eggs, separated
¼ teaspoon cinnamon
¼ teaspoon salt
¾ cup milk
½ teaspoon vanilla
2 tablespoons sugar
¾ cup heavy cream
    Whipped cream
    Peanuts, crushed

Sift together flour, baking powder and ½ teaspoon salt. Cut in shortening until crumbling; add peanuts. Sprinkle with water, making dough. Form into ball. Roll into crust for 9-inch pie pan. Prick crust and bake at 425 degrees for 12–15 minutes.

Soften gelatin in cold milk. Melt chocolate in double boiler; add ¾ cup sugar, egg yolks, cinnamon and ¼ teaspoon salt. Gradually blend in ¾ cup milk. Cook over boiling water until mixture thickens, stirring constantly. Remove from heat; add vanilla and gelatin mixture; stir until dissolved. Chill until mixture begins to thicken. Mix well.

Beat egg whites until stiff; add 2 tablespoons sugar and beat until dissolved. Whip cream until stiff; fold into beaten egg whites. Fold into chocolate mixture. Pour into pie crust. Chill 2–3 hours. Top with whipped cream and crushed peanuts.

Salad
BOWL

Salad Bowl Sandwich

1 (7-ounce) can tuna, drained and flaked
1 cup cherry tomatoes, halved
1 medium-size green pepper, halved, seeded and diced
1/4 cup diced red onion
1/4 cup sliced pitted black olives
1 (8-ounce) package mozzarella cheese, diced
1/2 cup bottled oil-and-vinegar dressing
2 teaspoons dried basil, crumbled
6 white pita bread, (whole-wheat, if preferred)

Combine tuna, cherry tomatoes, green pepper, red onion, olives, mozzarella cheese, oil-and-vinegar dressing and basil in a large bowl; toss to mix. To serve, open pocket of each pita bread with a small knife and tuck tuna filling into pockets. Serves 6.

Applesauce Fruit Salad

1 envelope plain gelatin
1/2 cup applesauce
1 (3-ounce) box apricot gelatin
1 cup boiling water
1 (15–20-ounce) can fruit cocktail, drained
1 cup whipped topping, prepared
1 cup miniature marshmallows
1 fresh red apple

Lightly oil large salad mold. In bowl, dissolve plain gelatin in applesauce. Beat well. In separate large bowl, dissolve apricot gelatin in boiling water.

Stir together fruit cocktail and applesauce mixture. Chill until slightly thickened. Fold in whipped cream and marshmallows. Pour half of mixture into salad mold. Slice apple and place in attractive pattern. Pour rest of mixture over top of apples; chill until firm. Unmold and serve.

Frozen Daiquiri Salad

1/2 cup mayonnaise
1/2 cup liquid daiquiri mix
1 (4 1/2-ounce) package no-bake custard mix
8 ounces cream cheese, softened
Few drops green food coloring
1 (20-ounce) can crushed pineapple, drained
1 (4-ounce) jar maraschino cherries, drained and chopped

Blend together mayonnaise, daiquiri mix, custard mix and cream cheese until smooth. Add green food coloring; fold in pineapple and cherries. Pour into oiled 5-cup mold. Freeze.

Pistachio Fruit Salad

1 (12-ounce) container non-dairy whipped topping
2 packages pistachio pudding mix
1 (13-ounce) can crushed pineapple
1 can fruit cocktail
1 can mandarin orange segments
1 small bottle maraschino cherries
Iceberg lettuce leaves
Few mandarin orange segments

Mix together pineapple with pudding and pineapple juice. Drain orange segments and fruit cocktail. Blend remaining ingredients, except cherries and lettuce, with whipped topping. Chill in refrigerator overnight and serve on Iceberg lettuce leaves, with orange and cherry garnish.

Cranberry Gelatin Mold

1 (3-ounce) box cherry gelatin
1 (No. 2) can crushed pineapple, reserve juice
1 can whole jellied cranberries
1 tablespoon vinegar
1 (11-ounce) can mandarin oranges
Pecans

Melt gelatin in pineapple juice over low heat; remove from heat. Add cranberries and vinegar; stir. Mix in pineapple and drained orange sections and nuts. Pour into mold and refrigerate.

Cottage Cheese Apple Salad

4 apples
1/2 cup golden raisins
1/2 cup walnuts
1 tablespoon sugar
1 tablespoon lemon juice
1 cup cottage cheese
1/2 cup sour cream

In large bowl, combine apples, raisins and walnuts. In separate bowl, stir together sugar, lemon juice, cottage cheese and sour cream; fold into apple mixture. Chill and serve.

Oriental Seafood Salad

1 pound fresh *or* frozen seafood (use a combination of fish and shrimp, scallops or lobster)
2 tablespoons oil, divided
2 green onions, chopped
1/4 teaspoon ground ginger
3/4 cup chicken broth
1/4 cup ketchup
2 tablespoons cider vinegar
2 tablespoons dry sherry
1 teaspoon sugar
  Dash pepper
  Dash hot pepper sauce (Tabasco)
2 teaspoons cornstarch
1 tablespoon water
  Lettuce leaves

If frozen, thaw seafood. Cut into 1-inch pieces.

Heat 1 tablespoon of the oil in a large frying pan or wok. Add seafood and stir-fry gently until cooked through. Remove to a large bowl and set aside. Into same pot or wok, add remaining 1 tablespoon oil; sauté onion and ginger for 1 minute. Stir in next 7 ingredients; heat to boiling.

Combine cornstarch and water; pour into broth mixture and cook 1 minute, or until slightly thickened. Pour sauce over seafood. Cover and refrigerate at least 4 hours or overnight.

To serve, arrange lettuce leaves on serving plate. Place seafood mixture in a mound on lettuce. Serves 4.

Gelatin Tapioca

2 quarts water
1 cup tapioca
  Sprinkle salt
1/2 cup sugar
1 (3-ounce) package gelatin
1 can Rich's Topping *or* 2 large whipped topping

Bring water to boil and add tapioca and salt. Cook for 20 minutes uncovered. Remove from heat and add sugar and gelatin. Stir until dissolved. Let set. When cold, stir in topping. Can add strawberries and bananas with strawberry gelatin and pineapples with orange gelatin.

Raspberry Pineapple Salad

2 cups boiling water
2 (3-ounce) packages raspberry-flavored gelatin
1 (16-ounce) package frozen raspberries, partially thawed
1 (8 1/4-ounce) can crushed pineapple, drained

Add boiling water to gelatin and stir until dissolved. Add raspberries immediately; separate berries with a fork and mix gently. Add pineapple and mix; pour into lightly oiled 6 1/2-cup ring mold and chill. Unmold and garnish with greens and fruit. Serves 8.

Winter White Gelatin

1 (8-ounce) package cream cheese, softened
1/2 cup granulated sugar
1/2 teaspoon vanilla *or* almond extract
1/2 cup milk
1 envelope unflavored gelatin
1/4 cup cold water
  Boiling water
1 cup whipped topping
  Fruit *or* berries for decoration (strawberries are great)

Blend cream cheese, sugar and vanilla or almond extract. Gradually add milk. Set aside. Dissolve gelatin in cold water. Add boiling water to make 1 cup. After slightly cooled, stir into cream cheese mixture. Chill until slightly thickened and fold in whipped topping. Chill in 1 1/2-quart mold. Unmold and garnish before serving.

Orange Toss

2 (11-ounce) cans mandarin orange segments, drained
1/2 small head iceberg lettuce, coarsely shredded
2 green onions, thinly sliced
  Fresh salad dressing

Mix together all but 4 orange segments and lettuce. Divide lettuce mixture among 4 bowls; sprinkle with sliced onions. Garnish each salad with reserved orange segment; drizzle with dressing.

Holiday Cranberry Mousse

1 (20-ounce) can crushed pineapple, drained, reserve juice
1 (6-ounce) package strawberry gelatin
1 cup water
1 (1-pound) can whole-berry cranberry sauce
3 tablespoons fresh lemon juice
1 teaspoon fresh grated lemon peel
1/4 teaspoon ground nutmeg
2 cups sour cream
1/2 cup chopped pecans

Add pineapple juice to gelatin in saucepan. Stir in water. Heat to boiling, stirring to dissolve gelatin. Remove from heat. Blend in cranberry sauce. Add lemon juice, lemon peel and nutmeg. Chill until mixture thickens slightly. Blend sour cream into gelatin mixture. Fold in pineapple and pecans; pour into 2-quart mold. Chill until firm. Unmold onto serving plate.

Christmas Cherry Freeze

2 cups whipping cream, whipped
1 can sweetened condensed milk
1 (21-ounce) can cherry pie filling
1 (1-pound, 4-ounce) can crushed pineapple, drained
1/4 cup lemon juice
1/4 teaspoon almond extract

Whip cream. Combine remaining ingredients and fold in whipped cream. Freeze. Serves 8.

Sauerkraut Salad

1/4 cup water
1 cup sugar
3-4 cups sauerkraut, drained
1 onion, chopped
1 cup celery, chopped
1 green pepper, chopped

Bring water and sugar to a boil. Cool. In bowl, combine sauerkraut, onion, celery and green pepper. Pour sugar mixture over vegetables; stir well. Chill 12 hours before serving.

Frozen Cranberry Salad

1 pound cranberries, ground
1 cup marshmallows, cut up
2 cups crushed pineapple, drained
½ cup chopped nuts
2 cups sugar
1 carton whipped topping

Mix together cranberries, marshmallows, pineapple, nuts and sugar until sugar is dissolved. Fold in whipped topping. Freeze.

Crystal Salad

1 package lemon gelatin
1¼ cups boiling water
½ cup pineapple juice
½ cup whipping cream
½ cup salad dressing
½ cup apples, diced
½ cup crushed pineapple, drain and reserve juice
½ cup celery, diced
2 cups miniature marshmallows

Dissolve gelatin in boiling water. Add pineapple juice. Whip cream. Add whipped cream to congealed gelatin. Stir together salad dressing, apples, pineapple, celery and marshmallows. Fold into gelatin. Chill until firm.

Confetti Waldorf Salad

2 carrots, grated
2 apples, diced
¾ cup celery, thinly sliced
½ cup raisins
½ cup pecans, chopped
½ cup coconut, shredded
3 tablespoons mayonnaise
2 teaspoons sugar
¼ teaspoon salt
1½ teaspoons cream
1 teaspoon lemon juice

In large bowl, combine carrots, apples, celery, raisins, coconut and pecans. In small bowl, combine mayonnaise, sugar, salt, cream and lemon juice. Pour over apple mixture. Chill and serve.

Flo's Broccoli Cabbage Salad

2 cups shredded cabbage
1 head fresh broccoli, cut into florets
1 small onion, diced
1 cup diced celery
¼ teaspoon salt
¼ teaspoon Mrs. Dash (herbs and spices)
1 tablespoon vinegar
Mayonnaise (enough to moisten salad)
½ pound bacon, fried, drained and crumbled

Combine cabbage, broccoli, onion and celery. Sprinkle salt and Mrs. Dash on mixture and mix well. Add vinegar and mix well. Add mayonnaise. Place in a serving dish; refrigerate until ready to serve. Add crumbled bacon to top of salad. Serves 4.

Cottage Cheese Salad

2 (3-ounces) boxes lime gelatin
2 cups hot water
1 (8-ounce) package cream cheese
2 cups cold water
1 (24-ounce) carton cottage cheese
1 (15-ounce) can crushed pineapple, drained

In a bowl, place lime gelatin and hot water; stir to dissolve. Beat in cream cheese; add 2 cups cold water. Stir in cottage cheese and pineapple. Chill until firm.

Watergate Salad

1 (9-ounce) box of whipped topping
1 box of pistachio pudding
1 (20-ounce) can of crushed pineapple
1 cup small marshmallows
½ cup nuts, chopped
Few drops green food coloring, optional

Combine whipped topping, pudding, pineapple, marshmallows, nuts and food coloring. Blend together and chill.

Holiday Lime Salad

1 large box lime gelatin
1 cup hot water
2 cups miniature marshmallows
⅔ cup mayonnaise
½ cup cold water
3 stalks celery, diced
1 cup chopped maraschino cherries
1 cup chopped nuts
1 apple, diced
1 small can crushed pineapple
2 bananas, thinly sliced

Dissolve gelatin in hot water, then add marshmallows; stir to melt marshmallows. Add cold water, and when cooled, add cherries, mayonnaise, celery, apple, pineapple, nuts and bananas. Mix in a 13 x 9 x 2-inch glass dish. Place in refrigerator until set.

Pea Salad

1 head lettuce, shredded
2 pounds bacon, crisply fried
4 cups canned peas
12 eggs, hard-boiled and chopped
1 medium onion, chopped
1 quart salad dressing
2 cups Swiss cheese, grated

Mix peas, bacon, eggs, onion and salad dressing together well. Spread on top of lettuce and sprinkle with Swiss cheese. Chill.

Sunflower Seed & Raisin Apple Salad

2 stalks celery, thinly sliced
4 apples, cored and diced
¼ cup sunflower seeds
⅓ cup seedless raisins
½ cup mayonnaise
Lettuce for garnish

In large bowl, combine celery, apples, sunflower seeds, raisins and mayonnaise. Add a little more mayonnaise if needed. Serve on bed of lettuce.

Glistening Garden Salad

1 (3-ounce) package lemon gelatin
1 (3-ounce) package lime gelatin
2 cups boiling water
1½ cups cold water
3 tablespoons lemon juice
1 cup shredded carrots
1 cup finely chopped, unpeeled cucumber
¼ cup sliced celery
1½ teaspoons prepared horseradish
   Lettuce leaves (optional)
   Mayonnaise (optional)

Dissolve gelatin in boiling water; add cold water, lemon juice and horseradish. Chill until partially set. Fold in vegetables. Pour into 5½-cup mold or in dish equivalent to mold size. Chill until set.

Unmold onto lettuce leaves or cut in squares. Serve with mayonnaise, if desired. Serves 8.

Pickled Mushrooms

3 pounds small, fresh button mushrooms
   Water
3 tablespoons salt
2 large cloves garlic, chopped
2 onions, finely chopped
25 crushed peppercorns
2 teaspoons dried thyme
3 lemons, juice and rind
6 cups white wine
2 cups cider vinegar
4 bay leaves
2 tablespoons salt
½ cup snipped parsley
1 cup olive oil

Cover mushrooms with water containing 3 tablespoons salt. Soak for 10 minutes; drain; add to the marinade (containing all remaining ingredients). Heat. When mixture boils, turn down heat to simmer for 10 minutes, or until mushrooms are tender. Discard lemon rinds and chill.

These may be put into jars for preserving if they are ladled into sterilized jars while boiling hot and sealed with rubber rings.

Sweet Potato Salad

1 pound sweet potatoes *or* yams
   Water to cover potatoes
2 green onions, sliced
½ cup mayonnaise
¼ cup chopped, toasted pecans
1 stalk celery, diced
1 tablespoon lemon juice
   Parsley for garnish (optional)

Prepare potatoes and cube them. Place in pot of water to cover. Simmer until tender, about 30 minutes. Drain well and cool. In small bowl combine potatoes with onions and celery. Mix mayonnaise and lemon juice. Blend into potato mixture. Sprinkle with pecans.

Serve immediately or cover and refrigerate 1 hour. Sprinkle with parsley, if desired.

Christmas Eve Salad

1 (8¼-ounce) can sliced beets
1 (8-ounce) can chunk pineapple, packed in juice
1 medium orange, pared and sectioned
1 pink grapefruit, pared and sectioned
2 bananas, sliced
1 (8-ounce) can water chestnuts, drained and sliced
2 tablespoons lemon juice
1 teaspoon sugar substitute, divided
3 cups shredded lettuce
1 lime, cut into wedges
¼ cup blanched almond slivers
1 tablespoon anise seed

Drain beets and pineapple, reserving liquid. In large bowl, combine beets, pineapple, orange, grapefruit, bananas and water chestnuts. In small bowl, combine reserved beet and pineapple liquids, lemon juice and ½ teaspoon sugar substitute. Pour over fruit.

Let stand 10 minutes; drain. In serving bowl, arrange fruit on shredded lettuce. Garnish with lime wedges and almonds. In cup, combine anise seed and remaining ½ teaspoon sugar substitute; sprinkle over salad. Serves 8. (115 calories per serving)

Spinach Apple Toss

½ cup salad oil
¼ cup lemon juice
1 tablespoons green onion, sliced
1 teaspoon sugar
½ teaspoon salt
½ teaspoon dried mint
   Dash pepper
10 ounces fresh spinach
2 medium apples, sliced
1 small cucumber, sliced
⅓ cup radishes, sliced
2 tablespoons sunflower seeds, shelled

In screw-top jar, combine oil, lemon juice, green onion, sugar, salt, mint and pepper. Cover; shake well and chill. In large salad bowl, combine spinach, apples, cucumber, radishes and sunflower seeds. Shake dressing and pour over salad. Toss to coat.

Salad Dressing

⅓ cup cornstarch
1¾ cup water
⅓ cup vinegar
¾ cup vegetable oil
1 small egg yolk plus enough water to make ¼ cup
½ teaspoon dry ground mustard
2 teaspoons salt
3 tablespoons sugar
   Red pepper (optional)

In saucepan, combine cornstarch, water and vinegar; bring to boil. Let cool to lukewarm. In another bowl, mix oil, egg yolk plus water, mustard, salt, sugar and red pepper. Beat until creamy and add to cornstarch mixture while still warm, not hot. Beat well. Makes 1 quart.

Apple Salad

Apples, cubed
Marshmallows
Nuts
Grapes
Salad dressing

Mix together apples, marshmallows, nuts, grapes and salad dressing. Serve.

Soups & STEWS

Zesty Pumpkin Soup

¼ cup butter
1 cup chopped onion
1 garlic clove, crushed
1 teaspoon curry powder
½ teaspoon salt
¼ teaspoon ground coriander
⅛ teaspoon crushed red pepper
3 cups chicken broth
1¾ cups pumpkin
1 cup half-and-half
    Sour cream
    Chives

Sauté onion and garlic in butter until soft; add curry powder, salt, coriander and red pepper; cook 1 minute. Add broth; boil gently, uncovered, for 15–20 minutes. Stir in pumpkin and half-and-half; cook an additional 5 minutes. Blend in blender until creamy. Garnish with sour cream and chives.

Amish Pea Soup

1 cup split green peas
2½ pints water
1 cup ham, diced
1 onion, diced
    Bay leaf
1 tablespoon chopped parsley
    Salt and pepper
    Butter

Soak peas in enough water to cover; let stand overnight. Drain. Cover with water again and add ham, onion, bay leaf, parsley, salt, pepper and butter. Cook over low heat for 2–3 hours.

Vichyssoise

1 medium onion, sliced
2 teaspoons margarine
2 medium potatoes, thinly sliced
1 small stalk celery, chopped
¼ teaspoon salt
1 (10-ounce) can condensed chicken broth
1 cup half-and-half
¼ teaspoon salt
⅛ teaspoon pepper
½ cup half-and-half
    Snipped chives

Sauté onion in margarine until tender; reduce heat. Stir in potatoes, celery, ¼ teaspoon salt and broth. Cover; simmer 15–20 minutes until potatoes are tender.

Blend potato mixture in blender on medium speed until smooth, about 45 seconds; return to saucepan. Stir in 1 cup half-and-half, ¼ teaspoon salt and pepper. Heat over medium heat, stirring constantly, until hot and bubbly. Refrigerate at least 4 hours. To serve, stir ½ cup half-and-half into soup. Garnish with snipped chives.

Corn Chowder

    Bacon bits
    Yellow canned corn
    Potatoes, cubed
    Onions, diced
    Salt
    Pepper
    Milk

Combine bacon bits, corn, potatoes, onions and milk in saucepan. Simmer until potatoes are done. Salt and pepper to taste.

Homemade Noodles

5 cups flour
5 eggs
¼ cup water
2 teaspoons salt

In large bowl, combine 2 cups flour, eggs, water and salt. Mix well. Add the rest of the flour 1 cup at a time. Use more if needed. The dough should be stiff. Cover bowl and let rest for 30 minutes. On floured surface, roll dough thin. Cut into thin strips. Let noodles dry for a few hours. Duck eggs make wonderful noodles, if you can get them.

Broccoli Soup

1 small head of broccoli, finely diced
2 onions, diced
1 teaspoon celery flakes
    Salt and pepper
2 teaspoons chicken soup base
3 tablespoons flour
2 quarts milk
    Cheese, cubed
    Crackers

Place broccoli, onions, celery flakes, salt, pepper and chicken soup base in saucepan. Cover with water and let cook 5–10 minutes. Make a thickening with flour and part of milk. Add to vegetables and let cook a little. Add rest of milk and cheese to your desire. Serve over crackers. For a thicker soup use more flour.

112

Squash Soup With Chives

½ cup unsalted butter

3 pounds yellow crookneck squash, sliced

3 large onions, sliced

1 tablespoon crumbled, dried thyme

6 (14½-ounce) cans chicken broth

Sour cream

Minced fresh chives

Melt butter in heavy large pot over medium-low heat. Add squash, onion and thyme. Cover and cook until vegetables are tender, stirring occasionally, about 30 minutes. Add broth and simmer, uncovered, 30 minutes. Purée soup in batches in blender. (May be prepared 1 day ahead. Cover and refrigerate.) Return soup to pot and bring to simmer. Ladle into bowls. Top with dollop of sour cream. Sprinkle with chives. Makes 12 servings.

Nautical Chowder

½ cup chopped onion

½ cup sliced celery

¼ cup butter

3 cups diced, peeled raw potatoes

2 cups water

2 tablespoons flour

2 cups milk

2 teaspoons salt

½ teaspoon fine herb blend

⅛ teaspoon pepper

1 (1-pound) can pink salmon *or*

2 (7-ounce) cans tuna, drained and flaked

Chopped parsley

Lemon juice

Sauté onion and celery in butter until tender and lightly browned. Add potatoes and water. Simmer until potatoes are just tender, about 15 minutes. Blend flour into ½ cup milk. Add to remaining milk and stir into potato mixture. Add salt, herbs and pepper.

Cook until soup is smooth and slightly thickened. Add fish and allow to heat. Garnish with chopped parsley and serve with a few drops lemon juice for each serving. Serves 6–8.

Sausage Cheddar Chowder

3 cups water

2 chicken bouillon cubes

1 (12-ounce) package smoked sausage, thinly sliced

2 cups thinly sliced carrots

2 cups thinly sliced celery

1 teaspoon onion salt

½ cup ground oat flour*

2 cups milk

1½ cups (6 ounces) shredded cheddar cheese

Combine water and bouillon cubes in a 4-quart kettle. Bring to a boil over medium heat, stirring occasionally until bouillon cubes are dissolved; reduce heat. Stir in meat, celery, carrots and onion salt. Cover; simmer 10 minutes.

Bring to a boil; gradually add milk and oat flour, stirring constantly. Reduce heat and simmer 10 minutes, stirring occasionally. Remove from heat. Add cheese; mix until cheese is melted. Makes 8 (1 cup) servings.

*Oat flour; Place 1¼ cups quick or old-fashioned oats, uncooked, in blender or food processor. Cover; blend 60 seconds. Store in a tightly covered container in a cool dry place up to 6 months. May also be used for breading, thickening or gravies, dredging or browning.

Sausage Chowder

2½ cups diced potatoes

½ cup chopped celery

1 medium onion, chopped

½ pound sausage meat *or* links

2½ tablespoons flour

3½ cups milk

Salt and pepper to taste

Cook potatoes, celery and onion in a small quantity of boiling salted water until tender; do not drain. Cut sausage in small pieces and fry slowly; pour off most of the fat, leaving 2–3 tablespoons. Add flour to sausage and mix well. Add milk all at once and cook, stirring constantly, until thickened. Add potatoes. Season with salt and pepper. Reheat slowly. If held for a period of time, keep hot in a double boiler. Serves 6.

Mexican Potato Soup

4 cups chopped, peeled potatoes

½ cup chopped onion

2 tablespoons margarine

2 tomatoes, seeded and chopped

2 tablespoons margarine

4 cups hot water

6 chicken bouillon cubes

1 pound chopped ham

1½ cups sour cream

Cook potatoes in water to cover in saucepan for 12–15 minutes; drain. Sauté chopped onion in 2 tablespoons margarine in skillet. Remove onion with slotted spoon. Sauté tomatoes in 2 tablespoons margarine in skillet. Add onion, tomatoes, hot water, bouillon, ham and sour cream to potatoes. Simmer for 15 minutes; do not boil. Serves 6.

Country-Minestrone Soup

Combine in 3-quart glass casserole

5 cups water

1 (10½-ounce) can condensed beef bouillon

5 teaspoons instant bouillon granules

1 clove garlic, finely chopped

1 small onion, chopped

1 (16-ounce) can tomatoes, undrained

1 cup broken, uncooked spaghetti pieces

1 teaspoon salt

⅛ teaspoon pepper

¼ teaspoon oregano

¼ teaspoon basil

Cover with casserole lid. Microwave on high for 22–25 minutes, or until spaghetti is tender.

Add:

1 cup frozen peas

Cover; microwave on high for 5–6 minutes, or heated through. If desired, sprinkle individual servings with shredded mozzarella cheese just before serving.

Chili Chicken

1 large finely chopped onion
1 cup finely chopped green pepper
1 clove crushed garlic
1 tablespoon chili powder
¼ teaspoon dried oregano
1 teaspoon cumin powder
2 tablespoons oil
½ cup tomato purée (not paste)
½ ounce unsweetened chocolate, grated
1 cup chicken broth
⅓ cup slivered, blanched almonds
Salt and pepper to taste
4 cups coarsely chopped, cooked and boned chicken

In a saucepan over moderate heat, sauté onion, pepper, garlic, chili powder, oregano and cumin in hot oil until vegetables are tender. Add tomato purée and chocolate; cook over low heat, stirring constantly, until chocolate melts. Add chicken broth; cook 5 minutes. Pulverize almonds and stir in slowly. Season. Add chicken; simmer for 10 minutes. Serve over steamed rice. Serves 6–8.

Wild Rice Soup

1 cup uncooked wild rice
3 cups boiling water
2 strips smoked bacon
¼ cup chopped onion
¾ cup sliced celery
½ cup sliced carrots
1 (14½-ounce) can chicken broth
2 (10¾-ounce) cans cream of mushroom soup
2 soup cans milk
1 (4-ounce) can mushrooms, *plus* liquid
1 teaspoon seasoned salt
Pepper to taste

Combine rice and boiling water in large saucepan; simmer, covered, 50–60 minutes. Drain off excess liquid; set rice aside. Fry bacon until crisp; remove bacon and sauté onion, celery and carrots in small amount of bacon fat. Combine broth, soup, milk, mushrooms, salt and pepper, reserved crumbled bacon, sautéed vegetables and wild rice. Simmer, covered, 1 hour. Serves 8.

Cream of Broccoli Soup

3½ cups milk
1 (10-ounce) package frozen broccoli, partially thawed
1 envelope chicken noodle soup mix with diced white chicken meat
1 tablespoon flour

In medium saucepan, bring 3 cups milk and broccoli to the boiling point; then simmer, stirring occasionally, for 5 minutes. Stir in chicken noodle soup mix and flour blended with remaining milk. Bring to boiling point; then simmer, stirring occasionally, for 10 minutes, or until soup is slightly thickened and broccoli is tender. Serves 4.

Chicken Deluxe Soup

2 quarts potatoes, diced
3–4 large carrots, diced
1 small onion, diced
1 teaspoon celery flakes
1 quart chicken meat with broth
¾ pound noodles
Salt and pepper to taste
Chicken soup base

Place potatoes, carrots, onions and celery flakes in 6 quart saucepan. Add chicken and broth and fill about ¾ full of water. Bring to boil. After about 5 minutes add noodles and cook until noodles and potatoes are soft. Season with salt and chicken soup base.

Winter Bean Soup

2 cups mixed dried beans
2 tablespoons salt
1 quart water
2 cups ham, diced
1 large onion, chopped
1 clove garlic, minced
1 teaspoon chili powder
1 (28-ounce) can tomatoes, chopped
1–2 tablespoons lemon juice
Salt and pepper

Rinse beans. Cover with water; add salt and soak overnight. Drain; place beans in slow cooker. Add 1 quart water and ham. Cook on high for 4–6 hours. Add onion, garlic, chili powder, tomatoes and lemon juice. Cook an additional 1½ hours on high. Salt and pepper to taste.

Autumn Corn & Pumpkin Chowder

½ cup butter *or* margarine
2 onions, chopped
½ cup all-purpose flour
7 ears corn, kernels cut off
1½ cups cooked pumpkin
2 cups chicken broth
¼ teaspoon salt
1 cup cubed cooked ham
¼ teaspoon allspice
2 cups light cream

In a deep pot melt butter; cook onions. Add next 5 ingredients; simmer 10 minutes; add ham. Pour half the chowder into food processor or blender; mix until smooth. Return to soup pot; simmer 25 minutes. Add allspice and cream; serve hot with crisp crackers or toast points. Serves 7.

Oxtail Soup

3 tablespoons salad oil
1 onion, chopped
1 oxtail, cut in pieces
2 quarts water
2 teaspoons salt
3 whole cloves
½ teaspoon pepper
½ cup carrots, chopped
½ cup celery, chopped
3 tablespoons barley

Preheat oven to 500 degrees. Place oil, onion and oxtail in a Dutch oven. Place on bottom shelf of oven and cook for 20 minutes or until oxtail is browned.

Remove from oven and reduce heat to 300 degrees. Add water, salt, pepper, cloves, carrots, celery and barley. Cover and return to bottom shelf of oven for 2½ hours. Allow to cool. Skim fat from top; remove oxtail from bone and return meat to soup.

Vegetable

DELIGHTS

Vegetable Soup

Barb's potato recipe (see page 121)
Cauliflower (optional)
1 pint corn
1 pint peas
1 pint green beans
1 can chunk beef
   seasoned salt
   Salt and pepper

Cook cauliflower; drain. Add to potato soup with corn, peas, green beans, beef, seasoned salt, salt and pepper. Simmer 15 minutes.

Asparagus Cheese Casserole

2 cups cooked asparagus (fresh, frozen or canned)
3 hard-cooked eggs, sliced
½ cup buttered bread crumbs
1 cup shredded cheddar cheese
3 tablespoons butter
1 tablespoon chopped onion
2 tablespoons flour
1 cup milk
½ teaspoon salt

Melt butter; add onion and cook until tender. Add flour and blend. Add milk and cook until mixture thickens. Finally, add seasoning and cheese, cooking until well-blended. Alternate layers of cooked asparagus and egg slices with sauce in a buttered baking dish. Top with buttered crumbs. Bake in a moderate oven at 350 degrees for 25 minutes, or until crumb topping is browned and sauce bubbles up through the mixture.

Delicious Herbed Eggplant

1 large, firm eggplant, peeled and sliced
⅓ cup light cream
1¼ cups herb-seasoned stuffing mix, divided in half
1 (10¾-ounce) can cream of celery soup, undiluted
1 slightly beaten egg
   Salt to taste
2 tablespoons butter
½ teaspoon oregano

Place eggplant in a 2-quart casserole; cover with plastic wrap. Microwave on HIGH for 7 minutes; drain. While eggplant is cooking, combine cream, egg and ¾ cup stuffing mix, soup, salt and oregano; blend well and stir in drained eggplant. Return mixture to 2-quart casserole.

Combine butter and remaining stuffing mix. Sprinkle over eggplant mixture. Cover with waxed paper. Microwave on HIGH for 7–9 minutes. Let stand, covered, 3–5 minutes. Serves 4.

Corn & Broccoli

4 cans creamed corn
8 eggs, beaten
1½ (1-pound) bags broccoli
   Toasted bread crumbs
   Sour cream
   Chives

Combine corn, eggs and broccoli; top with toasted bread crumbs. Season with sour cream and chives. Bake at 250 degrees for 1½–2 hours.

Vegetable Stuffing

8 cups cubed whole-wheat bread
2 cups diced celery
1½ cups shredded carrots
½ cup chopped parsley
½ cup margarine
1 cup chopped onion
2½ cups sliced mushrooms
1 teaspoon salt
¼ teaspoon pepper
1½ teaspoons ground savory
1 teaspoon ground sage
½ teaspoon nutmeg
1 teaspoon dill weed
1 chicken bouillon cube
½ cup hot water

Combine bread, celery, carrot and parsley; tossing gently to mix. In skillet, melt margarine; sauté onion and mushrooms about 5 minutes, stirring frequently. Stir in seasonings. Dissolve bouillon cube in hot water. Add onion mixture and bouillon to bread mixture in bowl, tossing until well-mixed. Will stuff a 12-pound turkey.

Tomato Oysters

1½ cups tomato juice
1 egg, beaten
½ teaspoon salt
1¼ cups cracker crumbs
½ teaspoon sugar
¼ teaspoon pepper

Mix together tomato juice, egg, salt, cracker crumbs, sugar and pepper. Drop by spoonful in frying pan. Fry in shortening on both sides until brown.

Potatoes Au Gratin

1 medium onion, chopped
2 tablespoons margarine
1 tablespoon flour
1 teaspoon salt
¼ teaspoon pepper
2 cups half-and-half
2 cups shredded cheddar cheese
6 medium potatoes, sliced
¼ cup fine dry bread crumbs

Cook onion in margarine until tender; stir in flour, salt and pepper. Cook over low heat, stirring constantly, until mixture is smooth and bubbly; remove from heat. Stir in half-and-half and 1½ cups cheese. Boil and stir 1 minute.

Place potatoes in ungreased 1½-quart casserole. Pour cheese sauce on potatoes. Bake uncovered until top is brown and bubbly, 1 hour. Combine remaining ½ cup cheese and bread crumbs. Sprinkle with cheese-crumb mixture. Bake an additional 15–30 minutes.

Candied Yams

4 medium-size yams, cooked
¼ cup butter
⅓ cup brown sugar
¼ cup coffee liqueur

Cut yams into serving-size pieces. Melt butter with sugar; add liqueur; cook 1 minute. Add yams; turn until brown on all sides. Cover; reduce heat, cook 15 minutes. Turn 1 more time before serving. Makes 4–6 servings.

Onion Patties

¾ cup flour
2 teaspoons baking powder
1 tablespoon sugar
1 teaspoon salt
1 tablespoon cornmeal
¾ cup milk
2½ cups onion, chopped

Mix together flour, baking powder, sugar, salt and cornmeal; add milk. Batter should be fairly thick. Add onions and mix thoroughly. Drop by spoonfuls into deep fat. Flatten slightly when you turn them.

Savory Stuffing

3 quarts coarse day-old bread crumbs
¾ cup butter
2 cups chopped onions
2 cups chopped celery
1 cup chopped mushrooms
2 cups raisins
1 cup browned, crumbled sausage
¾ cup broth
½ cup chopped pecans
⅓ cup coffee liqueur
¼ cup chopped fresh parsley
2 teaspoons dried thyme, crushed
2 teaspoons grated orange peel
1 teaspoon salt
½ teaspoon dried sage
½ teaspoon pepper

Bake bread crumbs at 350 degrees for 5 minutes; stir; continue baking an additional 5 minutes longer until lightly toasted. Remove from oven; set aside. Melt butter in pan; add onions, celery and mushrooms; sauté lightly.

Remove from heat; add raisins, sausage, broth, pecans, liqueur, parsley, thyme, orange peel, salt, sage and pepper; pour over bread crumbs. Toss to moisten. Stuff turkey. Makes enough for a 12–14 pound turkey.

Squash Strips

1 pound crookneck squash, cut in ¼-inch-thick strips
1 pound zucchini, cut in ¼-inch-thick strips
¼ cup chopped green onions
½ teaspoon dried leaf basil *or* 1½ teaspoons fresh chopped basil
¼ teaspoon dried leaf thyme
Dash white pepper
Pimiento strips
Fresh basil sprig, if desired

Place crookneck squash and zucchini in a 1½-quart microwave-safe casserole. Sprinkle with green onions, basil, thyme and pepper. Cover tightly. Microwave on 100 percent power (HIGH) for 3 minutes. Stir; re-cover. Microwave on 100 percent power (HIGH) for 3–4 minutes more, or until squash is tender. Garnish with pimiento strips and basil sprig, if desired. Serves 8. (46 calories per serving)

Wild Rice Casserole

2 cups raw wild rice
4 cups water
2 teaspoons salt
2 pounds ground beef
1 pound fresh mushrooms, sliced
½ cup chopped celery
1 cup chopped onion
½ cup butter
½ cup sliced water chestnuts
¼ cup chopped black olives
¼ cup soy sauce
2 cups sour cream
2 teaspoons salt
¼ teaspoon pepper
½ cup slivered almonds (reserve a few for garnish)
Parsley sprigs

Cook rice in covered pan with water and 2 teaspoons salt for 45 minutes; drain. Brown beef; set aside. Sauté mushrooms, celery and onion in butter for 5 minutes. Combine soy sauce, sour cream, salt and pepper. Add rice, beef, onion, mushrooms, celery, water chestnuts and olives; add almonds. Bake, uncovered in lightly greased 3-quart casserole at 350 degrees for 1 hour. Garnish with reserved almonds and parsley.

Special Sweet Potatoes

2 (4-ounce) sweet potatoes, peeled and diced
1 tablespoon water
1 (8-ounce) can crushed pineapple packed in unsweetened pineapple juice drained
⅛ teaspoon ground ginger
⅛ teaspoon ground nutmeg
2 teaspoons margarine

In a 1-quart microwave-safe casserole, combine sweet potatoes, water and pineapple. Sprinkle with ginger and nutmeg. Cover tightly. Microwave on 100 percent power (HIGH) for 4 minutes. Stir; re-cover. Microwave on 100 percent power (HIGH) 4–6 minutes more, or until potatoes are tender. Dot with margarine. Serves 4. (158 calories per serving)

Dutch Potatoes

Potatoes, cooked and sliced
Butter
Flour
Salt
Pepper
Milk
Cheese, shredded

Cook potatoes in butter. Sprinkle with flour and add salt and pepper, to taste. When nice and brown, add milk, enough to thicken. Simmer over low heat. When almost done, sprinkle with shredded cheese. Simmer until cheese melts.

Parmesan Corn

4 ears fresh corn
1/4 cup butter *or* margarine
1/4 cup grated Parmesan cheese
1 1/2 teaspoons chopped fresh parsley
1/4 teaspoon dried, whole salad herbs

Remove husks and silks from corn just before cooking. Combine butter and remaining ingredients; stir well. Spread mixture on corn, and place each ear on a piece of waxed paper; roll at an angle and be sure to fold in sides. Arrange corn spoke-fashion on glass plate. Microwave on HIGH for 10–13 minutes.

Stuffed Tomatoes

6 large, firm, ripe tomatoes

Cut off stem end, peel and cut (almost to the base) into 6 wedges. Spread open and stuff with filling (recipe follows) which has been mixed together well and chilled.

Filling

2 cups diced, cooked chicken
1/2 cup diced celery
1 (7-ounce) can mandarin oranges, drained
1/4 cup chopped black olives
2 tablespoons coarsely chopped cashew nuts
1 teaspoon fresh lemon juice
1/2 cup mayonnaise
1/4 cup chutney

Mix all ingredients and chill. Fill tomatoes. Arrange tomatoes on a bed of shredded lettuce. Serves 6.

Two-Potato Bake

1/2 cup unsalted sweet butter
2 large baking potatoes, peeled and sliced (1/4-inch slices)
2 large sweet potatoes, peeled and sliced (1/4-inch slices)
1/2 cup sliced (1/4-inch) green onion
1/4 teaspoon caraway seed
1/4 teaspoon salt
1/8 teaspoon pepper
1/4 cup chopped, fresh parsley

Heat oven to 350 degrees. In 3-quart saucepan cook butter over low heat, stirring occasionally, until light brown in color, about 30 minutes. Add remaining ingredients, except parsley. Stir to coat potatoes. Place in an ungreased 13 x 9-inch baking dish. Cover; bake 40–55 minutes, or until vegetables are tender. Sprinkle with parsley. Makes 6 (1-cup) servings.

Hot Pepper Jelly

2 cups sweet peppers, chopped
1 3-inch jalapeño pepper, chopped
Water
1/2 cup vinegar
1 box pectin
5 cups sugar

Combine peppers and cook until tender. Add water to make 4 cups. Add vinegar, pectin and sugar. Cook until 2 drops form together and sheet off spoon, or until it coats a fork. Pour into jars and seal. Shake the jar several times while cooling to keep fruit and liquid from separating.

Cabbage & Noodles

1 large head cabbage
1 onion, chopped
Salt and pepper, to taste
2–3 handfuls homemade noodles
1 1/2 sticks butter
Garlic powder to taste

Melt butter in skillet; add onion and cabbage chunks. Cook until tender. Cook noodles in boiling water; drain. Place noodles in skillet, add salt, pepper and garlic powder. Cook for 30 minutes over low heat, stirring often.

Scalloped Corn

1 small onion, chopped
1/2 small green pepper, chopped
2 tablespoons margarine
2 tablespoons flour
1 teaspoon salt
1/2 teaspoon paprika
1/4 teaspoon dry mustard
Dash pepper
3/4 cup milk
1 (10-ounce) package frozen corn, cooked and drained
1 egg, slightly beaten
1/3 cup cracker crumbs
1 tablespoon margarine, melted

Sauté onion and green pepper in 2 tablespoons margarine until onion is tender; remove from heat. Stir in flour, salt, paprika, mustard and pepper. Cook over low heat, stirring constantly, until mixture is bubbly; remove from heat.

Gradually stir in milk; heat to boiling, stirring constantly. Boil 1 minute; continue stirring; add corn and egg. Pour into ungreased 1-quart casserole. Mix together crumbs and margarine; sprinkle over corn. Bake, uncovered, at 350 degrees for 30–35 minutes, until bubbly.

Baked Zucchini & Peas

1 (10 1/2-ounce) can mushroom soup
1/2 pound mushrooms, sliced
2 tablespoons butter
5 zucchini, sliced
1 (10 1/2-ounce) package peas, partially defrosted
1 (4-ounce) jar salted pumpkin seeds

Cook mushrooms in butter until lightly browned. Arrange a layer of mushrooms in buttered casserole, then a layer of zucchini. Spread with some of the mushroom soup and add a layer of peas.

Repeat until all vegetables are used, reserving a little of the soup for the top. Spread remaining soup over casserole. Cover and bake at 350 degrees for 30 minutes. Remove casserole from oven and cover thickly with pumpkin seeds. Bake, uncovered, for 15 minutes longer. Serves 8.

French Onion Soup

4 medium onions, sliced
2 tablespoons margarine
1½ cups water
⅛ teaspoon pepper
⅛ teaspoon dried thyme leaves
1 bay leaf
2 cans condensed beef broth
4 slices French bread, toasted
1 cup shredded Swiss cheese
¼ cup grated Parmesan cheese

Cook onions in margarine over low heat until tender, 20–30 minutes. Add water, pepper, thyme, bay leaf and broth; boil; reduce heat. Cover and simmer 15 minutes. Remove bay leaf. In 4 ovenproof bowls, place bread, onions and broth; top with Swiss cheese. Sprinkle with Parmesan cheese.

Place bowls on cookie sheet. Broil until cheese is melted and golden brown, 1–2 minutes.

Red Beet Jelly

4 cups red beet juice
½ cup lemon juice
1 (6-ounce) box raspberry gelatin
1 box Sure-Jell
6 cups sugar

Cook juices, gelatin and Sure-Jell for 3 minutes. Add sugar and boil 5 minutes longer. Place in containers and seal.

Artichokes & Peas

1 (10-ounce) package frozen artichoke hearts
1 (10-ounce) package frozen green peas
¾ cup water
1 teaspoon salt
1 tablespoon margarine, melted
1 tablespoon lemon juice

In saucepan, heat artichoke hearts, peas, water and salt to boiling. Reduce heat; cook until vegetables are tender, 5–8 minutes; drain. To serve, pour margarine and lemon juice over vegetables.

Pearly Carrot Combo

1 cup water
⅔ cup pearl barley
1½ cups milk
5 carrots, grated
¼ teaspoon salt
½ teaspoon honey
¼ teaspoon nutmeg
2 eggs, beaten
2 tablespoons butter *or* margarine, divided
3 tablespoons bread crumbs

In a saucepan bring water to a boil; add pearl barley; simmer until water is absorbed; cool. Mix next 6 ingredients with pearl barley. Grease a 1½-quart casserole with 1 tablespoon butter; sprinkle bottom of casserole with half the bread crumbs. Pour mixture into baking dish; sprinkle top with remaining bread crumbs; dot with remaining butter. Bake at 375 degrees for 40 minutes, until golden and bubbly. Serves 5.

Brussels Sprouts & Chestnuts

1¼ pounds small brussels sprouts, washed, damaged leaves removed
2 cups water
4 tablespoons (½ stick) unsalted butter
1¼ cups all-purpose flour
1 cup chicken broth
1 cup half-and-half
1 cup shredded Swiss cheese
1 (15½-ounce) can chestnuts, drained, rinsed, cut in half
Salt and freshly ground white pepper

Trim stems of sprouts and cut crosses in them to speed cooking. Boil water in a small skillet. Add brussels sprouts. Cover. Reduce heat and cook 6–7 minutes, or until just tender. Drain.

In the meantime, heat butter in medium saucepan. Add flour. Stir until smooth and lightly golden. Gradually whisk in broth and half-and-half, stirring constantly over low heat until thickened and smooth. Add cheese and stir until melted. Add sprouts and chestnuts; cook, stirring until just heated through. Season with salt and pepper and serve hot.

Whipped Potato Casserole

8 medium potatoes, cooked, mashed
8 ounces cream cheese
8 ounces sour cream
Garlic salt to taste
1 tablespoon garlic powder
2 tablespoons butter
1 teaspoon paprika
1 cup grated cheddar cheese

Beat cream cheese and sour cream in with potatoes until light and fluffy. Beat in garlic salt and powder. Place in greased 2-quart casserole. Dot with butter and sprinkle with paprika and cheese. Bake at 350 degrees for 1 hour. Makes 10–12 servings.

Slow-Cooked Potatoes

5 pounds potatoes, peeled, cooked, mashed
1 (8-ounce) package cream cheese
1 stick butter
1 (8-ounce) container sour cream
¾ cup milk
Chopped onion, if desired

Mix together potatoes, cream cheese, butter, sour cream, milk and onion, if desired; cool completely. Place in slow cooker; refrigerate. Heat on low 4–5 hours, stirring occasionally, before serving.

Canned Tomatoes

Tomatoes
1 teaspoon salt

Dip tomatoes in boiling water for 30 seconds. Cool in cold water; drain. Peel and core tomatoes. Remove all spots and green parts. Cut in half or quarter. Pack into jars with 1 teaspoon salt in each jar. Pack tightly so juice comes to within ½-inch of top of jar. Place on lid, screw down band. Process in boiling water bath for 35 minutes for pints and 45 minutes for quarts.

End of the Garden

1 cup sliced cucumbers
1 cup sweet peppers, chopped
1 cup cabbage, chopped
1 cup onions, sliced
1 cup green tomatoes, chopped
1 cup carrots, chopped
1 cup green beans, cut in 1-inch pieces
1 tablespoon celery seed
1 cup celery, chopped
2 tablespoons mustard seed
2 cups vinegar
2 cups sugar
2 tablespoons turmeric

Soak cucumbers, peppers, cabbage, onions and tomatoes in salt water overnight. (Add ½ cup salt to 2 quarts water.) Drain.

Cook carrots and green beans in boiling water until tender; drain water. Mix soaked and cooked vegetables with celery seed, celery, mustard seed, vinegar, sugar and tutmeric; boil 10 minutes. Place in clean jars. Adjust caps. Process in boiling water bath for 5 minutes.

Tangerine Sweet-Potato Bake

2½ pounds cooked sweet potatoes
8 tablespoons butter *or* margarine, melted
6 tablespoons brown sugar, divided
3 tablespoons orange juice
¼ teaspoon salt
½ teaspoon cinnamon
¼ teaspoon allspice
3 tangerines
½ cup chopped pecans *plus* 6 whole pecans for garnish

Whip together sweet potatoes, butter, 3 tablespoons brown sugar, orange juice, salt, cinnamon and allspice. Peel tangerines and section; fold half the fruit and chopped pecans into sweet potato mixture; turn into a 2-quart casserole. Arrange remaining tangerine sections and whole pecans on top; sprinkle with remaining brown sugar. Bake at 375 degrees for 30 minutes. Serves 6.

Holiday Vegetable Trio

6 medium-size potatoes (about 2 pounds)
1 (16-ounce) bag carrots
4 large parsnips (about 1 pound)
⅓ cup hot milk
4 tablespoons (½ stick) butter *or* margarine
1 tablespoon brown sugar
1½ teaspoons salt

In 4-quart saucepan over high heat, heat potatoes and enough water to cover to boiling. Reduce heat to low. Cover and simmer 25–30 minutes until potatoes are fork-tender. Drain. Cool potatoes until easy to handle. Peel. Return potatoes to saucepan.

Meanwhile, peel and cut carrots and parsnips into 1-inch chunks. In 3-quart saucepan over high heat, heat carrots, parsnips and ½ inch water to boiling. Reduce heat to low. Cover and simmer 20–30 minutes until carrots and parsnips are tender. Drain.

In saucepan with potatoes, add carrots, parsnips, milk, butter, brown sugar and salt. With potato masher, mash vegetables until almost smooth. Serves 12.

Broccoli-Rice Casserole

1 package frozen chopped broccoli
1 medium onion, sliced *or* chopped
¼ cup butter
1 cup cooked rice
½ cup milk
1 can cream of mushroom soup
¾ cup sharp cheddar cheese, grated
1 cup buttered croutons

Cook broccoli, onion and butter until tender. Mix together rice, milk, mushroom soup and cheese. Cook over medium heat and combine with broccoli in a casserole dish. Garnish with buttered croutons and grated cheese. Bake, covered, for 30 minutes at 350 degrees. Remove lid and brown 15 minutes more.

Hot Pepper Butter

40 small hot peppers
6 cups sugar
1 tablespoon salt
1 quart yellow mustard
1 quart vinegar
1½ cups flour
1½ cups water

Grind peppers; mix sugar, salt, mustard and vinegar; cook 10–15 minutes. Mix flour and water. Slowly add to pepper mixture. Boil 5 minutes more. Keep stirring and seal while hot. I use only half of the peppers and it's still HOT!

Grandma's Sweet Ketchup

2 quarts ripe tomatoes
1 cup onions, diced
2 medium peppers
1 pint celery, chopped
1 cup apples, chopped
1½ cups vinegar
2 teaspoons mustard seed
½ teaspoon cinnamon
2¾ cups sugar
1 tablespoon salt.

In a large cooker, place tomatoes, onions, peppers, apples, celery, vinegar, mustard seed, cinnamon, sugar and salt. Bring to a boil; cook slowly until color changes. Process in pints in boiling water bath for 30 minutes. Makes the best sloppy joes!

Steury Special

2 quarts potatoes, peeled and diced
   Onion, diced
   Salt
3–4 cups macaroni
   Milk
1 quart tomato juice

Place potatoes, onion and salt in a 6-quart pan. Cover with enough water so potatoes are a little more than covered.

Cook until almost soft; add macaroni and cook until soft. Remove from stove. Add enough milk to cover then add juice. This is delicious with peanut butter spread.

Crisp Braised Celery

1½ large bunches of celery with leaves
2 tablespoons vegetable oil
1 tablespoon butter
½ teaspoon salt
1 teaspoon sugar
¾ teaspoon celery seed
⅓ cup chicken broth

Trim celery, reserving leaves; rinse and cut it diagonally into ⅛-inch-thick slices. (There should be about 8 cups sliced celery.) In a large heavy skillet, heat oil and butter over moderately high heat until fat is hot but not smoking; add celery, salt, sugar and celery seed; sauté celery, stirring, for 1 minute. Add broth and reserved leaves. Bring liquid to a boil; simmer mixture, covered, for 3–5 minutes, or until celery is crisp-tender. Serves 10.

Corncob Jelly

12 bright red corncobs
3 pints water
1 package Sure-Jell
3 cups sugar

Boil broken cobs in 3 pints water for 30 minutes. Remove from heat and strain the liquid. Should have 3 cups; if not, add enough liquid to make 3 cups. Stir in Sure-Jell and bring to rolling boil. Add sugar and boil 2–3 minutes or until jelly stage. The finished product tastes a lot like apple jelly, and has an attractive reddish color.

Pickled Beets

10 quarts red beets
2 pints vinegar
10 cups sugar

Cook beets until soft, about 2–3 hours. Remove from heat. When cool, peel and cut into quarters; put into jars. Make juice with 2 pints vinegar to 4 pints hot water and 10 cups sugar. This is enough juice for 10 quarts. Cold pack ½ hour. With the juice of the cooked red beets I make our favorite jelly! My mother never threw anything away!

Good Pickles

Pickles
Onion
Celery
1 teaspoon turmeric
Pinch alum
4 cups sugar
3 tablespoons salt
4 cups vinegar
2 cups water

Slice pickles in cans; put slice of onion and piece of celery in each can. Add turmeric and alum. Stir together sugar, salt, vinegar and water. Heat until sugar is dissolved; bring just to boiling point. Pour over pickles in jar to ½-inch of top. Process in boiling water bath.

Pickle Relish

1 gallon ground pickles
1 pint ground onions
¼ cup salt
5½ cups sugar
3 teaspoons celery salt
3 teaspoons dry mustard or mustard seed
2 cups vinegar
2 cups water

Combine pickles, onions and salt and let stand for 2 hours; drain. Boil sugar, celery salt, mustard, vinegar and water. Place in cans with pickle mixture and seal in boiling water bath for 10 minutes.

Green Tomato Mince

1 peck green tomatoes, chopped or ground
5 pounds brown sugar
3 pounds raisins
2 tablespoons ground cloves
2 tablespoons cinnamon
2 tablespoons allspice
2 tablespoons salt
1 cup vinegar
6–8 apples, finely chopped

Combine tomatoes, brown sugar and raisins. Cook slowly until tender. Add cloves, cinnamon, allspice, salt and vinegar. Boil about 45 minutes. Add 6–8 finely chopped apples and cook until apples are tender. Pack in hot jars. Seal in boiling water bath for 10 minutes. Makes about 18 pints.

Asparagus Stuffed Eggs

12 hard-boiled eggs
6–8 cooked fresh asparagus spears
1 teaspoon finely minced shallots or scallions or chives
3–4 tablespoons mayonnaise
Salt and pepper, to taste

Cut eggs lengthwise; shave thin strip off bottom of each egg so they do not rock on dish. Cut tips off 6 asparagus spears (½-inch), slice in half lengthwise. Cut off tender part of stalks and purée them in blender or food processor. On a clean dish towel, place purée in corner and twist to extract juice. Purée must be as dry as possible. (Towel will clean up nicely, just rinse and wash.)

Blend purée into yolks with shallot and just enough mayonnaise to soften and smooth. Season with salt and pepper. Fill eggs with yolk mixture; decorate with asparagus tips. Cover and refrigerate until ready to serve.

String Beans in Sauce

3 slices bacon, fried crisp and crumbled, reserve drippings
2 cans string beans
1 teaspoon salt
4 tablespoons bacon drippings
1 large onion, chopped
1½ tablespoons flour
½ teaspoon pepper
1½ teaspoons sugar
1 tablespoon vinegar
½ cup grated cheese

Cook beans in microwave until hot; drain, reserving ¾ cup liquid. Return beans to microwave to keep warm.

In skillet, sauté onion in bacon fat. Stir in flour. Add bean liquid and cook until thickened. Add remaining ingredients, except beans, and cook until cheese melts. Pour sauce over beans and serve hot.

Cauliflower Custard Au Gratin

1 medium-size cauliflower
2 beaten eggs
¼ teaspoon salt
⅛ teaspoon pepper
1 tablespoon butter *or* margarine, melted
1 cup whipping cream
½ cup grated Swiss cheese

Clean cauliflower; cook in boiling water until just tender. Chop cauliflower rather fine; add all remaining ingredients, except cheese. Turn into a buttered baking dish; sprinkle top with Swiss cheese; set in a shallow pan of hot water. Bake at 325 degrees for 45 minutes, or until top is set and golden brown. Serves 4.

Swiss Vegetable Casserole

1 (16-ounce) bag frozen broccoli, carrots and cauliflower combination, thawed and drained
1 (10¾-ounce) can cream of mushroom soup
1 cup shredded Swiss cheese
⅓ cup sour cream
¼ teaspoon black pepper
1 (2.8-ounce) can French-fried onions

Combine vegetables, soup, ½ cup cheese, sour cream, pepper and ½ can onions. Pour into a 1-quart casserole. Bake, covered, at 350 degrees for 30 minutes. Top with remaining cheese and onions. Bake, uncovered, 5 minutes longer.

Barb's Potatoes

4 potatoes, peeled and cubed
2 onions, sliced (dried or salts can be used)
Celery, diced (dried or salts can be used)
Margarine
Salt and pepper, to taste

Put potatoes, onion, celery, margarine, salt and pepper in pan. Cover with wate and cook until potatoes are soft.

Family Favorite

Barb's potato recipe
1 cup macaroni
1 can cream of mushroom soup
1 cup cheese
Salt and pepper, to taste
Milk (optional)

Cook macaroni until soft; drain off water. Combine macaroni with potato recipe; add soup, cheese, salt and pepper. If too thick, add milk. Serve with salad!

Steury Special

Barb's potato recipe
1 cup macaroni
1½ cups milk
1 pint tomato juice
Salt and pepper, to taste

Cook macaroni until soft; drain. Mix in with potato recipe. Add milk, heat, do not boil. Remove from heat and add tomato juice and salt and pepper to taste. This was a soup my mom fixed often when I was a girl. Now I often use it, too. Is delicious with bread and butter and red beet jelly.

Creamed Potatoes

Barb's potato recipe
2 cups milk
Milk
3 tablespoons flour
Cheese (optional)

When potato recipe is soft add 2 cups milk. Mix 3 tablespoons flour with more milk as thickening. Slowly put into potatoes and milk, stirring constantly, until done. If not thick enough add more thickening. This is also delicious by adding cheese, cover to melt!

Sweet Potato Crunch

3 cups sweet potatoes (about 5)
1 teaspoon vanilla
½ cup evaporated milk
1 cup sugar
⅓ cup butter
2 eggs
Sprinkle cinnamon
Topping (recipe follows)

Peel and boil sweet potatoes until softened. Mash potatoes; add remaining ingredients and mix well by hand with spoon or fork. Pour into 8 x 8-inch baking dish that has been well-greased.

Topping

⅓ cup flour
⅓ cup butter
1½ cups chopped pecans *or* walnuts

Combine ingredients well. Place on top of sweet potatoes. Bake in 350-degree oven for 30 minutes.

Corn Relish

10 cups corn on cob
1 cup green pepper, chopped
1 cup sweet red pepper, chopped
1 cup onion, chopped
1 cup celery, chopped
1 tablespoon salt
1½ cups sugar
2½ tablespoons mustard seed
1 teaspoon celery seed
½ teaspoon turmeric
2½ cups white vinegar
2 cups water

Drop ears of corn in boiling water; boil 5 minutes. Dip in cold water. Cut from cob; measure. Combine corn with rest of ingredients and boil for 15 minutes. Pack into jars; adjust caps. Process in boiling water bath canner 15 minutes. Yield: 5–6 pints.

Beans With Apples

2–3 slices bacon, diced
1 cup red beans, cooked until tender, drained *or* 1 (19-ounce) can baked beans
4 cooking apples
2 tablespoons margarine
½ cup brown sugar

Partially fry bacon. Place beans in 1½-quart casserole. Pare, slice and grate apples; sprinkle over top of beans. Dot with margarine and sprinkle with brown sugar. Top with bacon pieces and bake at 350 degrees until done.

Mashed Potato Puffs

1½ cups seasoned mashed potatoes, chilled

3 eggs, beaten to blend

3 generous tablespoons all-purpose flour

2 tablespoons minced onion *or* snipped chives

1 tablespoon baking powder

¾ teaspoon onion powder

¾ teaspoon garlic powder

¾ teaspoon salt

Vegetable oil

Sour cream

Applesauce

Blend all ingredients, except oil, sour cream and applesauce. Heat ½ inch oil in heavy skillet over medium-high heat. Drop batter by tablespoonfuls into oil; cook until crisp and golden brown, about 4 minutes per side. Remove, using slotted spoon, and drain on paper towels. Serve immediately. Pass sour cream and applesauce separately. Serves 6–8.

Corn/Zucchini Scallop

1 (16-ounce) can corn kernels, drained

1 tablespoon flour

2 cups thinly sliced zucchini

½ small onion, minced

3 tablespoons margarine

1 teaspoon salt

1 cup cottage cheese

1 egg, lightly beaten

¾ cup buttered bread crumbs

Mix corn and flour together until kernels are coated. Place 1 cupful on bottom of well-greased 1½-quart casserole. Arrange zucchini slices on top of corn in 1 even layer, then onions. Dot with margarine and sprinkle with salt. Cover with remaining 1 cup corn.

Mix cottage cheese and egg together; pour over corn. Sprinkle with bread crumbs and bake at 350 degrees for 45 minutes. Serves 6.

Double the recipe and this makes a delicious buffet or potluck offering.

Marinated Vegetables

2 pounds carrots *or* 1 pound carrots and 1 head cauliflower

1 can tomato soup, undiluted

1 cup sugar

½ cup salad oil

¾ cup vinegar

1 teaspoon salt

½ teaspoon pepper

¼ teaspoon dill weed, *not* dill seed

1 large onion, sliced into rings

1 large green bell pepper, cut into thin slices

Wash and peel carrots or cauliflower into 1-inch pieces. Cook until tender. Drain and cool. Combine soup, sugar, salad oil, vinegar, salt, pepper and dill weed in saucepan. Bring to boil and stir to dissolve sugar. In a 2-quart casserole, combine cauliflower, carrots, onions and green pepper. Pour hot soup mixture over vegetables. Cover and chill in refrigerator overnight. Serves 8–10.

Lemon Dilled Brussels Sprouts

3 (10-ounce) packages frozen brussels sprouts

1½ cups water

¾ teaspoon salt

¼ cup (½ stick) margarine

½ teaspoon dried dill weed

1 tablespoon lemon juice

1 (8-ounce) can sliced water chestnuts

Combine water and salt in large saucepan; bring to boil. Add sprouts; cover saucepan and return water to boiling. Lower heat and simmer, covered, for about 12–15 minutes or until sprouts are tender. Drain sprouts and return to saucepan.

Meanwhile, melt margarine in small pan. Add dill weed, lemon juice and water chestnuts (drain chestnuts before adding). Set aside. To serve, pour margarine and dill mixture over the sprouts. Toss together until sprouts are well-coated. Serve immediately.

Cabbage & Swiss Cheese Casserole

½ small head cabbage, about 8 ounces

1 tablespoon butter *or* margarine

1 slice onion, chopped

1 tablespoon flour

½ teaspoon salt

⅛ teaspoon paprika

⅔ cup milk

½ teaspoon mustard (Dijon-style, preferably)

¼ teaspoon caraway seed

⅓ cup grated Swiss cheese

Buttered bread crumbs

Paprika

Rinse and core cabbage; cut into 2 wedges. Place a cut side of each wedge on cutting board; thinly slice to shred. Place in small amount of boiling, salted water; cover; cook rapidly (steam actually) until tender, about 5 minutes. Turn into strainer to drain.

Meanwhile preheat oven to 350 degrees and grease a small baking dish. In a medium saucepan melt butter; add onion; sauté until soft. Stir in flour, salt and paprika; cook 1 minute; whisk in milk, mustard and caraway seed.

Bring to boiling; reduce heat; simmer a few minutes. Stir in cabbage and cheese. Turn into prepared dish. Sprinkle with buttered bread crumbs or a dash of paprika for color. Bake until heated through, 15–20 minutes. Serves 2.

Mashed Potatoes, Italian Style

3 cups mashed potatoes

½ cup whipping cream

¼ teaspoon pepper

½ teaspoon salt

½ cup grated Parmesan cheese

Mash potatoes until fluffy without adding butter or milk. Place potatoes in casserole. Whip cream. Add pepper and salt; fold in cheese. Spread over potatoes and bake in a 350-degree oven for about 30 minutes, or until top is browned. Serves 2.

Black Beans Rodriguez

1 pound black beans
1 chopped onion
2 cloves garlic, chopped
1 teaspoon chili powder *or* 1 chili, roasted in oven
1 carrot
3 tablespoons oil
White wine *or* water

Wash beans and soak overnight. Next morning add onion, garlic, celery, chili and cut-up carrot. Cover with water or white wine; simmer until beans are almost tender.

Remove vegetables; add oil or margarine and put in casserole with remaining juices. Add enough water or wine to bring liquid almost to top. Cover and bake at 350 degrees until tender. Add a dollop of sour cream to each serving. Serve with hot corn bread made with jalapeño peppers. Serves 6.

Mexican Beans

2 large cans kidney beans
2 pounds chunk beef, cut into 1½-inch chunks
2 pounds onions, chopped
1 cup diced celery
2 teaspoons chili powder *or* 1 green chili, roasted
2 cloves garlic, minced

Slice and fry chopped onions and garlic. When partially done, add beef and brown well. Place in a large Mexican bean pot with remaining ingredients and bake at 350 degrees for 1½ hours.

Eggplant Mexicana

1 medium (1 pound) eggplant, peeled and cut into cubes
1 (16-ounce) can tomatoes, *or* medium fresh tomatoes, peeled and chopped
1 clove garlic, minced
2 tablespoons chopped onion
¼ teaspoon chili powder
Dash pepper

Combine all ingredients in skillet and simmer gently 15–20 minutes or until eggplant is tender. Serves 6. (30 calories per serving)

Vegetable Medley Turkey Stir-Fry

1 (1¼-pound) package fresh turkey breast slices *or* fresh turkey breast tenderloins
⅓ cup soy sauce *or* lite soy sauce for lower sodium content
1 tablespoon dry sherry
1 clove finely chopped garlic
1 tablespoon cooking oil
2 cups broccoli florets
1 medium red *or* green pepper, cut into ¼ x 1-inch strips
2 cups sliced fresh mushrooms
3 ounces fresh pea pods
4 green onions cut into 1-inch pieces
1 cup bean sprouts
¼ cup chicken broth
1–1½ teaspoons cornstarch

Cut turkey into ½-inch pieces. Mix soy sauce, sherry and garlic. Stir in turkey. Let stand 15 minutes. Heat oil in large non-stick skillet or wok over high heat until hot. Stir-fry turkey in oil until no longer pink. Remove turkey from skillet. Add broccoli and red pepper; stir-fry 2 minutes.

Add mushrooms and pea pods; stir-fry 1 minute. Add green onion and bean sprouts; stir-fry 30 seconds. Mix chicken broth and cornstarch; add to skillet. Stir in turkey. Heat to boiling, stirring constantly; boil and stir until sauce is thickened and clear. Salt and pepper to taste. Serve immediately. Serves 6. (190 calories per serving)

Red-Wine Sauerkraut Provencal

1 (1-pound, 11-ounce) can sauerkraut
1 onion, thinly sliced
½ cup red wine
1 cup beef bouillon *or* consommé
1 cup sour cream
¼ cup caraway seed

Drain sauerkraut; place in saucepan. Add onion, red wine and bouillon; cover; cook slowly for 20 minutes. Place in serving dish; dollop with sour cream; scatter caraway seed over all. Serves 4.

Duchesse Potatoes

3 pounds large boiling potatoes
1½ cups minced scallions with greens, divided
1 cup milk
½ cup plain yogurt
2 large egg yolks
¼ cup (½ stick) unsalted butter, softened
White pepper and salt to taste

In a kettle combine potatoes and enough cold water to cover them by 1 inch. Bring water to boil and simmer potatoes for 30 minutes, or until tender. While potatoes are cooking, in a small saucepan, combine ½ cup scallions and milk. Bring milk to a simmer and simmer mixture for 15 minutes. Drain potatoes.

Return them to kettle and cook, covered, over moderate heat for 5 minutes to evaporate any excess water. Peel potatoes. Mash them coarsely, and in a heated bowl with electric mixer, beat them while still hot with milk mixture, yogurt, egg yolks, butter and remaining cup of scallions, white pepper and salt to taste until smooth.

With a large pastry bag fitted with a 1/2-inch star tip, pipe potatoes decoratively into a buttered 2-quart gratin dish and bake them in a preheated 400-degree oven for 20 minutes. Serves 4–6.

Frozen Stuffed Green Peppers

1½ cups creamy cottage cheese
½ cup Roquefort cheese
5 green peppers
¼ cup cooked diced ham
¼ cup cooked diced chicken
¼ cup finely chopped radishes
¼ cup finely chopped chives
¼ cup finely chopped raw cauliflower
½ cup mayonnaise
French *or* Thousand Island dressing (optional)

Mix all ingredients except green peppers; blend well. Wash and seed green pepper; fill peppers with mixture; place in freezer for 2 hours. Slice each pepper into ½-inch-thick rounds; serve over chilled lettuce. If desired, pour French or Thousand Island dressing over all.

INDEX

INDEX

INDEX